New Religiosity in Contemporary Sweden

New Religiosity in Contemporary Sweden

The Dalarna Study in National and International Context

Liselotte Frisk and Peter Åkerbäck

equinox

SHEFFIELD UK   BRISTOL CT

Published by Equinox Publishing Ltd
UK: Office 415, The Workstation, 15 Paternoster Row, Sheffield S1 2BX
USA: ISD, 70 Enterprise Drive, Bristol, CT 06010

www.equinoxpub.com

First published in Swedish as *Den mediterandedalahästen: Religion pånyaarenor i samtidens Sverige* by Dialogos, Stockholm, 2013.

First published in English by Equinox Publishing Ltd, 2015.
First printing in paperback, 2017.

© Liselotte Frisk and Peter Åkerbäck 2015

British Library Cataloguing-in-Publication Data
A catalogue record for this book is available from the British Library.

ISBN 978 1 78179 117 2 (hardback)
      978 1 78179 616 0 (paperback)

Library of Congress Cataloging-in-Publication Data
Frisk, Liselotte, 1959- author.
[Mediterandedalahästen. English]
New religiosity in contemporary Sweden: the Dalarna study in national and international context / Liselotte Frisk and Peter Åkerbäck.
    pages cm
Includes bibliographical references and index.
ISBN 978-1-78179-117-2 (hb)
1. Sweden—Religion. 2. Cults—Sweden. I. Åkerbäck, Peter, 1967- author.
II. Frisk, Liselotte, 1959- Mediterandedalahästen. Translation of: III. Title.
BL980.S8F74813 2015
200.9487'8—dc23
                        2014044376

Typeset by S.J.I. Services, New Delhi
Printed and bound in Great Britain by Lightning Source UK Ltd., Milton Keynes and Lightning Source Inc., La Vergne, TN

Contents

Acknowledgements

First and foremost, we would like to express our gratitude to the Swedish Research Council for the financing of our project. We would also like to thank all the fantastic people who welcomed us into their homes and their places of work, and who so openly shared their experiences with us. Without you, this project would never have been realized. Our gratitude also goes to everyone in Dalarna who helped us in our work, some even providing us with a roof over our heads as we travelled to and fro throughout the county. We would further like to thank staff at Dalarna University, who skilfully managed the project and assisted us with arrangements for travel and accommodation. We owe thanks as well to the MIA-seminar at Dalarna University, which afforded us the opportunity to discuss any theoretical and methodological problems we may have had and provided us with important critique as the text developed. A big thank you goes to Professor Ingvild Gilhus of the University of Bergen, who assisted us in our final seminar, giving us invaluable critique and advice with regards to our manuscript.

We thank the two foundations, Stiftelsen Längmanska kulturfonden and Stiftelsen Berndt Gustafssons minnesfond, for their generous contributions towards the publication of the original Swedish edition of this book.

Thank you, as well, to our respective families. Liselotte wishes to especially thank Brendan and Susanna: you have been such a great support at all times. Peter would like to thank Ludwig and Anton, who always had great understanding for their dad's work; Lisa for her encouragement, understanding, and support throughout the difficult times; and Kristian Pettersson for the long discussions about the complex issues of methodology and theory. We both thank Kristian for the invaluable advice he gave us on the first version of our manuscript.

Finally, we would like to thank our very patient translator Mandy Bengts, as well as our friend and colleague Jim Lewis, who so kindly edited the final English version of the manuscript.

Chapter 1

The Meditating Dala Horse Project: An Introduction

What characterizes expressions of religion in a fairly secularized and modern European country like Sweden? What kinds of options, practices, and alternatives are available to those who still ponder and search for the answers to life's great questions? Where and in what form do these religious options manifest themselves, and why? These were just a few of the questions we had in 2008, when we began working on our research project, *The Meditating Dala Horse: Globalized Contemporary Religiosity in Local Expression and in New Arenas*. Once in the field, we soon became aware of the wide diversity of phenomena related to religion that are expressed in contemporary society.

In the village of Vikmanshyttan, a Church of Sweden service was held that included a healing technique whose aim was to activate kundalini energy and thus bring about a higher level of consciousness. At a health fair in the small town of Säter, visitors were offered chances to communicate with deceased relatives, to have their fortunes told with tarot cards, to receive a massage, and to sample the health drink noni. In another town, Rättvik, one woman practised automatic writing and, upon reading her text, saw that the words had come to her from the Lords of Lake Siljan, spiritual beings said to belong to the lake, and foresaw the spread of a new spirituality from the area around the lake to the whole of Europe. At our own university in Falun, we learnt from a clairvoyant that there were goblins beside the coffee machine. In Älvdalen, another village in Dalarna, one woman, inspired by various forms of yoga that she had learnt, had developed her own method of yoga practice and teaching. In the town of Falun, we met a woman who had experienced automatic writing, practised yoga, and worked voluntarily in the Church: she held that spirituality is about considering all people to be of equal worth and that we practise spirituality when we meet others with empathy and love.

A life coach in northern Dalarna wanted to help people realize their inner potential, giving them the opportunity to make decisions based on freedom rather than on powerlessness and crisis. Among her clients were a number of local businesses as well as the local town council. At a gym in one of Dalarna's largest towns, BodyBalance[1] was performed in front of a statue of the Laughing Buddha. At a retreat centre in southern Dalarna, we spoke with a man who many believe has achieved enlightenment or an inner state of conscious awakening, of the same kind as the Buddha, Siddhartha Gautama, achieved in the sixth century BCE.

As we can see, the contemporary landscape of the popular religious milieu comprises arenas that exhibit religious elements beyond those of the established churches, and takes many forms of expression: for example, healing, séances, astrology, energy massage, life coaching, and courses of many different kinds. These phenomena, about which we know little beyond the fact they are mobile and prone to rapid change, are the main focus of this book.

A religious landscape is never static; rather, it is in a constant state of flux as a result of different kinds of social change. In recent decades, studies have shown that processes of religious change are ongoing in Sweden as well as in many other European countries (Heelas and Woodhead 2005, Höllinger and Tripold 2012, Botvar and Schmidt [eds.] 2010). Engagement in traditional religious organizations is in constant decline, whereas interest in other activities that are less obviously religious is on the increase (see, for example, Partridge 2004). This process is 'silent' in that it is not associated with any organization in the traditional sense and as such is not immediately visible. Nonetheless, there are social dimensions to consider. Many people take courses that have religious associations; others visit healers and health fairs or take part in physical and mental health activities, aspects of which may be only vaguely religious.

Our research project *The Meditating Dala Horse* received funding from the Swedish Research Council from 2008 to 2011. The aim of the project was to survey and examine the religious landscape of Dalarna, focusing on the popular religious milieu. It was a local study: that is to say, we examined religious expression within a defined geographical area. We chose the county of Dalarna, an area in central Sweden with a population of about 277,000 in 2010.[1]

1 http://www.regiondalarna.se/dalafakta/befolkning/.

The Dala horse, which gave the project its name, is a small wooden horse decorated with characteristic traditional painting. It has been produced in the area since at least the seventeenth century and has long been considered a local symbol. At the world exhibition in New York in 1939, a large Dala horse represented Sweden, and since then, it has become a national symbol. The traditional Dala horse is portrayed in a standing posture. Although it remains a popular handicraft, over the years it has morphed into other forms: it has become the Dala elephant, the Dala camel, the Dala rhinoceros. Yet it was one Dala horse in particular that drew our attention and that served as the inspiration behind the naming of our project. We came across it in the logo of a retreat centre, Baravara outside Rättvik, which depicted the horse in a state of meditation. Both the set-up and design of the retreat centre as well as its logo illustrate the point of intersection between the local and the global, and thus represent the very reality of contemporary cultural and religious expression, which is the focus of this book.

The Dalarna study demonstrates how religion is expressed in a specific part of Sweden, one that is characterized by certain local features (as discussed in chapters 2 to 4), as well as illustrates the processes and features of the contemporary religious milieu that are characterized by a high level of universality. Our experiences in the field, as described above, provide examples of some of these characteristics: individualism, experience orientation, and the current tendency of the individual to combine elements from many different religions and global regions. Further, our interviewees were active in places and arenas that are not traditionally considered religious – for example, health centres and gyms. In these milieus, there are also clear overlaps with therapy, psychology, and medicine. The fundamental questions of the project were as follows: *what* (What do contemporary religious expressions look like? What forms do they take?); *how many* (How many people are involved in the various expressions of contemporary religion?); and *why* (Why is contemporary religion expressed in the manner and form that it is?). It is these questions that, based on our empirical findings, we will discuss in this book.

Rapid change in many different areas is characteristic of modern times. One area that has experienced and continues to experience such change is that of communication and the distribution of information, which impacts the contemporary process of globalization. Modern communications technology (the Internet, social media) is important to this process, having contributed to the accelerating spread of various cultural elements, both religious and non-religious, throughout the world. These globalized elements then change in form upon encounters with local cultures. Our book focuses on one particular area, Dalarna, and the way in which global elements have taken root and undergone change there. One of the central perspectives that we will develop in this book is that of globalization and the manner in which it changes the basic conditions and expressions of a culture (mainly in chapter 8).

'Religion' is a central concept in the project. One of our most significant conclusions is that globalization and other social processes have contributed to changes in religious arenas and expression that have led to the need to reflect on the concept of religion from a number of different perspectives and dimensions. We begin below with a short discussion about problems with the conceptualization of religion and the ways in which we have chosen to delineate and understand it in this study. The problematic field with different frameworks for understanding religion and the way religion is currently expressed will be developed throughout the book in conjunction with presentation of empirical material. The focus of the book is on our empirical findings; however, to understand these, we also present various relevant theoretical approaches and perspectives.

The general aim of our project was to discuss the religious context as a whole and as it exists in the county of Dalarna, but our more specific intention was to focus on certain areas of the religious landscape. After discussing the problem of how to understand religion, we present the ways in which we chose to limit our study and understand those parts of Dalarna's religious context that lie at the forefront of our interest.

The Concept of Religion

The forms of expression which are termed 'religious' or 'religion' vary between cultures. Nevertheless, they are at the same time expressions of, and form part of, a given culture. Therefore, limiting what can and cannot be conceptualized as 'religion', in general terms, has proven difficult. These constructed boundaries not only vary from culture to culture and context to context, but can also change over time. The concept of religion has its origins in Western society and has been characterized by particular Christian forms of expression; in other cultures, there are not always clear equivalents. The shaping of the concept of religion has also been characterized by ethnocentrism, imperialism, and colonialism (see, for example, Asad 1993 or Fitzgerald [ed.] 2007). Robert Orsi (2004: 178–80) stresses the importance of taking a critical view of the concept of religion since it developed within a European context where colonialism was a matter of fact and where aspects of Christianity were unconsciously included in the construction of the cultures of other peoples dominated by Europeans.

The academic study of religion has also been constructed on the basis of various Christian and morally informed values that have limited our perception of what should be defined as religious expression. The field of Religious Studies has developed normative distinctions between different religious behaviours and beliefs. This has led to more or less concealed conceptions of 'real' religion and other expressions that represent its perversions and corruptions. Concepts such as superstition and magic have traditionally served to delimit what is 'genuine' religion, and have generally been studied outside of religious perspectives. A variant of normative distinctions that currently finds expression among a set of cultural interpreters is the notion that, should any form of financial transaction be involved, then the subject is not 'real' religion (see, for example, Rothstein 1997: 305–18). Many Christian churches are financed through taxes, something that is possible for an organization only when it maintains a position of dominance in society. In a number of other cultures, it is considered neither 'bad' nor 'disingenuous' to pay a religious practitioner to perform rituals or ceremonies, hold a healing ceremony, or offer fortune-telling services.

The prominent sociologist Meredith McGuire discusses definitional boundaries concerning religion and other closely related concepts. She argues that the understanding of religion based in the Protestant tradition of what religion *should* be and what the definition should include or exclude does not correspond with what she calls *lived religion*. In everyday life, many people do not distinguish between terms such as magic and religion, sacred and profane, non-official religiosity and official religiosity. These terms can prevent us from achieving a broader understanding of religion as it is lived day-to-day by the common person. McGuire observes that concepts such as 'religion' are socially constructed in different ways in different historical and cultural contexts, and that factors such as social class and political power serve to shape these as a means of privileging certain groups while marginalizing others. In this way, various types of religion are perceived positively and accepted, whereas others are disparaged and perceived as sinful, false, or ridiculous (McGuire 2008: 19, 22). Alongside such terms as superstition and magic, contemporary problematic and pejorative terms for religious phenomena could be, for example, 'sect' or 'New Age', both of which are used for a number of contemporary religious expressions studied in our project. In many social sectors, New Age is regarded as more or less farcical. One reason for this is that expressions of New Age religiosity include phenomena that might fall into stigmatized categories such as fortune-telling, healing, and superstition and, what is more, involve such aspects as the economic transactions so alien to church-related religiosity. A further important fact is that middle-aged women, a marginalized and invisible group within society, tend to dominate New Age religiosity milieus (a pattern we discuss in chapter 3).

Since Christianity and Christian organizations have been the prototypes for what is deemed 'real' religion, it is not surprising that most people as a matter of course perceive what is practised within the Church of Sweden and free churches as being 'religion'. In addition, a number of migrant faiths are often recognized as being religious, though some less obviously so. Yet other forms of cultural expression are frequently perceived as dubious and problematic in terms of whether they should be classified as religion or not. In our project, the cultural fields we examined were characterized by clear overlaps with fields that are perceived as non-religious. An important question for this study was thus how we should set limits for what to include. We sought broader perspectives that would allow for elements of creative experimentation. One view on the concept of religion that meets these criteria has been developed by the anthropologist Benson Saler: we describe his perspective below.

A Multidimensional and Open Interpretation

Benson Saler (2000; 2009) proposes that we approach religion as an unbounded and graded category. By this he means that the concept of religion can be defined in different ways in different contexts, and that clear boundaries between religion and other phenomena need not be constructed. Rather, he uses 'centrality' and 'more or less' as important terms. He argues that religion can be seen as a pool of elements that often cluster together, although they may do so to greater or lesser degrees depending on the context. The different examples under the category popularly termed *religion* need not have a single common feature.

It is thus up to the individual anthropologist or scholar of religion to choose the criteria with which to experiment or on which to base his or her argument in a given context. Abrahamic religions (Judaism, Islam, and Christianity) are connected in complex ways with the development of the Western category 'religion', and ideas about and from them continue to influence how those living or educated in the West use the term. As such, Saler suggests that these religions might be used as a productive starting point, or 'prototype', for understanding the concept 'religion'. He argues that it is better to consciously use such an ethnocentric basis than to be an unconscious victim of it. Yet he also encourages us to selectively borrow non-Western categories and experiment with them to examine and describe cultures where they are not used, just as the category religion is used to examine and describe cultures where there is no word for religion. Saler proposes the term *dharma* as one such example.

Whatever criteria are chosen, the degree of their centrality in different phenomena is crucial. Through reasoned argument, it is possible to establish a number of clear examples of religion and, subsequently, examples that become less clear and more problematic the further we move towards the periphery. In these cases, we should apply discursive arguments of reasoning as a means of deciding if the various examples – in this particular context – are to be included within the concept of religion or not.

According to Saler, there are no clear boundaries as to what should be regarded as religious; it is we who determine the criteria. Elements that some may perceive as religious might be found in different phenomena that many would not be prepared to call religion. Saler argues that by systematically exploring elements that we associate with religion in contexts that may be perceived as less clear examples of religiosity, we can increase the number of ways in which we can study religious elements in different contexts.

Saler's perspective clearly demonstrates the problems that exist with the conventional concept of religion. An important observation is the way in which this concept has been constructed in a Western context. Accordingly, an unbounded concept of religion offers an increased opportunity to construct and creatively focus on what is current and contemporary in contrast to more traditional and conventional concepts. Further, the grading of central tendencies is interesting: rather than constructing boundaries, use a central-peripheral perspective, where the placement of various phenomena on a scale is explored and debated, and may differ depending on context and purpose.

Our Demarcations and Positioning

Saler's perspective highlights a number of issues that we were forced to confront during the course of our project. The cultural fields we studied are often characterized by obvious overlaps with fields that may be considered non-religious – for example, holistic medicine, physical health care, and therapy. The question was where to set limits as to which phenomena to include.

After some consideration, and inspired by Saler, we chose the expressions and practices to include in the study based on two principal criteria: these we call *existential* and *super-empirical assumptions*. One argument for choosing these is that related criteria regularly appear in suggestions for how to define religion. As such, these criteria presumably fit with the prototypical perception of religion in our culture.[2] Nevertheless, we would like to stress that our choice of criteria is not based on defining and limiting what religion as a concept ought to include; rather, we wanted to choose criteria for this specific study that were orientated towards certain types of cultural manifestations. We did not want to set limits, but rather we wanted to establish a context for discussing different phenomena from a central-peripheral perspective. From an experimental and multidimensional perspective, we could just as readily have selected other criteria.

What do we mean by existential and super-empirical assumptions? Illustrative and central prototypical examples could be ideological elements that deal with the meaning of life, life after death, or non-empirical beliefs such as those concerning energy dimensions

2 For an overview of basic religious definitions and theories, see King 1987: 7692–706. One current academic approach is heuristic, using one (or more) classic definition(s) and from that (or those) devising a definition that can be utilized for a specific purpose. Also see Kunin 2003.

in the body or the existence of supernatural beings.[3] In chapter 2, we delineate how we used the criteria as a means of including or excluding various phenomena for the purposes of this study.

Our study was based on a survey of *producers* – that is to say, people and organizations (associations, retreat centres, businesses) that set up and arrange various kinds of religious meetings, sessions, and courses. Our general understanding and interpretation of the various activities offered by these producers determined their inclusion (or non-inclusion, as the case may be) in our study. Professor Siv Ellen Kraft, at the University of Tromsø, describes how our field of interest presents many phenomena that are open to a number of interpretations. She calls these 'hybrid products' – that is to say, an understanding with religious elements is presented as a possibility, which each person can either choose, reject, or ignore. Various forms of understanding are often contained in the same concept, and a potential religious interpretation can lose its meaning for the individual, either completely, partially, or not at all (Kraft 2011: 78). How *consumers* interpret their practice can thus vary.[4]

Our goal was to map the entire religious landscape; however, we wanted to focus on certain specific parts of that landscape, as outlined below.

Religion in Different Arenas: Jonathan Z. Smith's Model

Jonathan Z. Smith, an historian of religion, presents an interesting model for religion. Its focus is spatial categories or *places for religious expression*. His proposal is based on religion in Antiquity and Late Antiquity, from Iran and Mesopotamia in the East to the Mediterranean in the West. However, the general model could also be used for the contemporary religious situation in Sweden.

Smith defines religion as 'manifold techniques, both communal and individual, by which men and women [...] sought to gain access

3 At the periphery of, or outside, our field of interest, we place beliefs the veracity of which it would be possible to prove empirically – for example, that different races have different characteristics. The simple existence of beliefs is not enough to qualify a producer for inclusion in our study; rather, their beliefs must also be super-empirical in nature.

4 Hypothetically, the producers' interpretations can naturally vary. We did not contact each and every producer in the study as a means of determining his or her personal position; rather, our approach was to look at how the phenomenon in question was generally described, for example, on websites.

to, or avoidance of, culturally imagined divine power by culturally patterned means' (2004: 323). He structures the religious landscape into three spatial categories: *here*, which he defines as domestic religion in homes and at burial sites; *there*, which he defines as civic religion and state religion, as practised in temples; and *anywhere*, which he defines as a rich diversity of religious formations that occupy the space between *here* and *there*. Religion *anywhere* includes religious enterprise, religious associations and societies, and magic. Smith argues that one difference between Antiquity and Late Antiquity in terms of Mediterranean religions was that the third component – religion *anywhere* – increased greatly during Late Antiquity, whereas the two others declined. Smith relates this to, among other things, geographical relocation, which caused people to look to social groups other than the family; as well as new theological and political ideals, which were developing during this period in history (2004: 323–32).

Smith further defines religion *here* as that practised in a place not especially sacred, that has family as its focus, and that is passed down orally. According to Smith, religion *there* does not require any particular presentation, since at its root it represents what generally comes to mind when we hear the word religion: that is to say, the dominant deities and their respective mythology and liturgy, as well as the belief that there are people with a specialized ability to distinguish between the sacred and profane, between the pure and unpure. A distance between gods and human beings is postulated.

Religion *anywhere*, on the other hand, does not relate to any particular place and can manifest itself in many forms. Here belong different types of organizations and religious businesses that are not officially acknowledged by powers within society. These offer ways to reach or avoid culturally constructed divine powers that are not encompassed within religion *here* and *there*. Religion *anywhere*, Smith explains, replaced religion *here* in ways that better met the changes that took place during Late Antiquity. In response to a sense of unrest, a new, often urban social space opened up. A number of religious fellowships were first formed as immigrant fellowships, whereas others were formed around holy figures, gods, and goddesses, often characteristic of religion *there* (Smith 2004: 323–34). Religion *anywhere* also involved magic. Yet Smith criticizes the term *magic*, opining that it is better to use other and more precise categories such as divination, healing, and execrative (2004: 218).

Professor Ingvild Saelid Gilhus applied Smith's structure to contemporary religiosity during a seminar in Bergen in November 2010, revising it at the same time by including a fourth aspect: religion *everywhere*. This aspect was to encompass religion in popular culture, visible, for example, in various media: literature, TV, Internet, and advertisements.

Our Demarcations and Positioning

In our study, it is predominantly the religious arena *anywhere* (to use Smith's term) that is in focus. Religion *there*, in the established churches, constitutes more of a background. Neither religion *here* (everyday religion practised at home – to a degree perhaps to be labelled private religiosity) nor religion *everywhere* (the popular aspects of religion in, for example, film or literature) are examined in our project. Smith's reflections on relating the increase in religion *anywhere* to social changes are also interesting within the present context. We discuss contemporary social change and its relation to religious change in chapters 8 and 9.

The religious arenas that form the principal focus of study in this project can thus be found somewhere between church religiosity and private religiosity; can be expressed by businesses, associations, and societies in places other than conventional temples/churches; are characterized by tension with the religious and social mainstream; often come about in response to a sense of unrest resulting from social change; and may focus on, for example, healing and divination. However, no clear division exists between the various types of religious arenas suggested by Smith; rather, the places for social meetings that religion *anywhere* offers the individual may partly serve to inspire him or her to consider private existential questions – and may further, as we shall see in chapter 7, form the basis of inspiration and change for conventional churches.

The Study: Approach, Structure, and Terminology

We began our study with the aim of conducting a comprehensive survey of the religious landscape in Dalarna based on the criteria described above. The project aimed to focus on social contexts (meaning meetings of at least two people) where answers to existential questions or super-empirical beliefs are offered. Of particular interest for the study were activities in places other than the home and the churches, organized by businesses, associations, or societies.

In the mapping process, we found the following to be particularly useful with respect to established religious organizations: Internet catalogues and registers listing parishes and congregations; the Swedish search engine Eniro; and registers provided by many of the larger organizations that had their own information about Dalarna's parishes and congregations. We also used previous mappings and compilations of religion in Sweden.[5] All organizations were contacted by phone or email, and were asked questions about membership numbers and activities in Dalarna. We also conducted a number of interviews with representatives or other individuals who were engaged at some higher level within these organizations.

Yet the focus of this survey was very much on those elements of the religious landscape that are to be found outside the established churches. Our first challenge was to locate these. We commenced by visiting a number of key places that we knew of in the larger towns within the county. There we collected further names and addresses from public notice boards and through direct contacts. We took the help of students at Dalarna University, asking them to investigate all religious activities close to their homes. We also made use of the Internet and existing contacts in the region.

With time (and using the snowball method), we made contact as well with producers who did not advertise their activities by way of the usual channels. Subsequently, we developed a register that contained a great deal of available information about different phenomena. We selected certain activities and attended as many of them as we could, interviewing many key individuals and other people who attracted our attention for different reasons. We also conducted a large number of telephone interviews.

5 See, for example, *Religion i Sverige* (ed. Ingvar Svanberg and David Westerlund), *Det mångreligiösa Sverige* (ed. Daniel Andersson and Åke Sander) and *Från kyrka till wellbeing: Handbok i kyrkokunskap* (ed. Carl Eber Olivestam, Mimmi Eriksson, and Stig Lindholm). Information about the Church of Sweden was kindly provided by Peter Brandberg of the research and analysis centre of the Church of Sweden in emails dated September 22 and 26, 2011. Information about free churches was kindly provided by Öyvind Tholvsen, Programme Leader, Evangeliska Frikyrkans Församlingsprogram, in the form of the text by Öyvind Tholvsen, 'Frikyrkan flyttar. En studie av frikyrkornas utveckling i Sverige 2000-2010', an unpublished study, provided by email, September 22, 2011.

In chapter 2, we present the results of our survey and discuss various perspectives on Dalarna's religious landscape and the problems that arose while the survey was being conducted. We will also discuss to some extent questions of quantity and degree of activity. In chapter 3, we take a closer look at religion *anywhere*, where we mainly examine businesses and phenomena that are entrepreneurial in character. In chapter 4, we compare our study with similar studies in other European countries as a means of gaining perspective on which aspects might be common and what is locally specific to Dalarna. We also discuss terms that some academics use in these contexts, such as New Age and spirituality. In chapter 5, we present some of the new arenas or places where contemporary religion is practised. Chapter 6 discusses one of the phenomena that we studied closely: mindfulness. In chapter 7, we look at encounters between the Church of Sweden and religious currents outside of it, and in chapter 8, we focus our discussion on globalization. In chapter 9, we describe and discuss other social processes that influence contemporary religious expression.

Every study involves a number of limitations and demarcations, and ours is no different. Change over time, for example, is something that we can only comment upon in vague terms. Assumptions about change require two points in time for comparisons to be made, and another study such as ours but conducted at some other point in time is difficult to find. Nevertheless, there is much to be said where similar research exists, and we will comment on this – for example, the development over time of the more established organizations.

One further demarcation in our study is our decision to focus on producers and our understanding of what they describe. We are unable to comment to any great extent on the recipients or consumers of the various methods and practices, or on the way they might describe what they believe in or do.

Initially, we decided not to limit our study by using in a definitive way any of those terms that are often used within our field of research – for example, New Age, spirituality, new spirituality, new religiosity, and holism. We are aware of the problems associated with these, and we are also, to a certain extent, critical of these terms, something we discuss in chapter 4. Our intention was not to allow these terms or their usage to impede our study. Our ambition was to try to adapt the project according to the contexts and situations we met, not vice versa, and to look only at what we had defined and categorized in advance as a certain type of religiosity.

Nonetheless, we still required an umbrella term for the multi-faceted milieus on which our book focuses and which actually comprise many disparate fields that are, furthermore, in a constant state of flux. The area on which our study focuses forms a part of everyday lived religiosity – the part that takes place in social spaces. In terms of content, there are, when seen historically, a number of influences from a variety of different sources. In those sections in the book where we use Smith's model, we will apply his descriptor religion *anywhere* – yet as an everyday descriptor of the contexts that interested us, this term did not quite fit.

After some consideration, and inspired by the British religious studies scholar Steven Sutcliffe, we decided – where an umbrella term is required – to use the term 'popular religious milieus'.[6] Sutcliffe uses the term popular religion in a relational sense and not to describe any particular type of content. He opines that popular religion can both be and not be associated with organizations; it can be practised in a dynamic relationship vis-à-vis hegemonic formations and normative models, as described in elitist 'high-culture' (2006: 298). A classic in the field, written by cultural historian Peter Burke, uses the term 'popular culture' in a similar way. He describes it as being unofficial – as the culture of the non-elite (2009: xiii). Burke stresses that homogeneity does not exist in popular culture; rather, one should use the plural form popular cultures (2009: 7). A number of the other academics we refer to in this chapter proceed from a partly power-oriented perspective, where the part of the religious landscape that interests us here mostly deviates from a hegemonic view of what is 'right' religion (see also Selberg 2011: 10). This view accords with Smith's perspective on religion *anywhere*, which he argues is not officially recognized by social powers. As with all other terms, popular culture and popular religion present a number of challenges (see, for example, Burke 2009 for a discussion of some of these). Our study does not look at these challenges in detail (see, nevertheless, our further discussion about terms in chapter 4).

6 We will use this term in both the singular and plural form so as to allow for variation and to indicate that perspectives can be used to demonstrate both similarities and differences. Whenever we refer to the statements of other people – researchers and interviewees alike – we use the terms that the individuals themselves used in relation to the context in question.

Chapter 2

The Religious Landscape in Dalarna

In this chapter, we will present the general results of our survey of Dalarna's religious landscape, focusing on the popular religious milieu. We will also touch on the problematic issue of quantity – that is to say, how many people are active in the various areas of this landscape, again with respect to the popular religious milieu. We begin with an overview of the county of Dalarna where our study was carried out.

Dalarna: A Profile

The county of Dalarna lies within the province of Dalarna: the county is 30,298 km², about the size of Belgium, and the province is 31,351 km². In 2010, the population of Dalarna stood at 277,047. The two largest towns are Borlänge and Falun, the municipalities of which have populations (in 2010) of 49,251 and 56,044, respectively. The regional university, Dalarna University, was established in 1977 and has about 18,000 registered students. The Falun World Heritage Site, which centres on the copper mine in Falun and the mining industry for which Dalarna is well-known, has been featured on UNESCO's list since 2001.

The natural terrain in Dalarna is extremely variable, the county being among the few in Sweden which include a range of geographical zones. The county has a mountainous region with alpine vegetation, deciduous and coniferous forests, and marshlands. Eight per cent of the county comprises lakes and other bodies of water, 80 per cent of which feed into the important River Dalälven. The area around Lake Siljan, most likely formed as a result of a meteor strike some 360 million years ago, has been a popular recreational destination for many years and is the location of a great number of historical spas.

Tourism and outdoor recreation are extremely important for Dalarna's economy: it is the third most popular region in Sweden, with the tourist industry employing some 5,350 people. To develop the forestry industry in Sweden, changes of ownership of both forested and agricultural land were implemented, starting in the eighteenth century. This, however, was not the case in Dalarna, where such divisions were opposed. Not until 1932 was this change implemented with the enactment of the so-called *Dalalagen* law, which remained in effect until 1984. As a result of this opposition to land division, forests remained untouched for many years, and Dalarna retained many of its old settlement areas and beautiful villages, all of which evoke images of days gone by. There is a strong tradition of handicrafts in the county, such as the nationally recognized *kurbits* painting tradition that is seen on the Dala horse. In just about every large village local handicrafts can be found: including high-quality cloth, embroidery, woodwork, and metalwork (www.lantmateriet.se and http://dalarna.se/det-har-ar-dalarna/).

Ethnologist Göran Rosander highlights the strong sense of cultural identity in Dalarna, and explains how its people have long cherished traditional values. In the area known as Ovansiljan, remnants of medieval times existed well into the 1800s. Throughout history, many Swedish leaders sought support in the Lake Siljan area – Engelbrekt, Sturarna, Gustav Vasa, and Gustav III (Rosander 1994: 58). Rosander opines that history legitimizes Dalarna: age and uniqueness are perceived as cultural indicators. By being consumers of culture, we become part of a social and historical community (1994: 70). In this way, Dalarna has become both an ideal and a symbol of genuine national culture, values, and traditional heritage for many Swedes. This, Rosander states, is one reason for Dalarna's popularity as a tourist and recreational destination (1994: 68–9).

Results of the Survey

Categorization and classification invariably pose problems since in any attempt to provide structure, we create boundaries and categories that might not be apparent on the ground. Depending on the criteria used, one and the same phenomenon can fit within a number of different categories; furthermore, there are always phenomena that for any number of reasons fall between the boundaries we construct.

In chapter 1, we described Smith's model, in which the relevant categories are religion *there*, which he defines as civic religion and religion as practised in temples, and religion *anywhere*, which he defines as a rich diversity of religious formations that lie between *here* and *there*, including religious enterprises, associations, and societies. (As mentioned earlier, religion *here* is not examined in our study.) In tables 1 and 2, we present the contemporary religious landscape in Dalarna based on this underlying model, which, we might add, is not without problematic aspects (discussed in chapter 3).

Table 1. The Religious Landscape

Religion *here*	Religion *there*	Religion *anywhere*
Domestic religion located at home and at burial sites	Civic religion and state religion, as practised in temples	The rich diversity of religious formations that occupy the space between *here* and *there*

Table 2. Religion *There*

Svenska kyrkan (Church of Sweden) and Related Organizations	Free Churches*	Immigrant Religions	Others
• Svenska kyrkan (Church of Sweden) • Dalarnas Fridsförening (Laestadianism, a Swedish revival movement) • Evangeliska Fosterlands-Stiftelsen (A Swedish mission movement within the Church of Sweden) • Evangelisk Luthersk Mission – Bibeltrogna Vänner (An independent Swedish mission movement)	• Adventistsamfundet (Seventh-day Adventist Church) • Baptistsamfundet (Baptist Union of Sweden) • Evangeliska Frikyrkan (Evangelical Free Church in Sweden) • Frälsningsarmén (Salvation Army) • Missionskyrkan (Mission Covenant Church of Sweden) • Nytt Liv (A part of the Word of Faith movement) • Pingstkyrkan† (Pentecostal Church) • Segerbaneret (A part of the Word of Faith movement) • Svenska Metodistkyrkan (The Swedish Methodist Church)	• Dalarnas Thailändska Buddhistförening (The Thai Buddhist Congregation of Dalarna) • Islamiska förbundet (Islamic Association) • Katolska kyrkan (Catholic Church) • Rysk-ortodoxa kyrkan (Russian Orthodox Church)	• Jesu Kristi Kyrka av Sista Dagars Heliga (The Church of Jesus Christ of Latter-Day Saints) • Jehovas vittnen (Jehovah's Witnesses)

* This table shows a traditional division of free churches as was the case until a few years into the twenty-first century. A number of the churches listed here are currently in the process of merging under new names. In addition, there are free congregations that are not directly related to the established free church communities – for example, Fristaden in Falun.

† There is also a Pentecostal congregation in Borlänge, established in 2011, which belongs to the Nigerian movement, Redeemed Christian Church of God (RCCG).

Religion There: *Results*

Obviously representative of religion *there* are the Church of Sweden and the free churches – powerful organizations with Protestant Christian backgrounds. We use a third subcategory for immigrant religions: these religions are, in their countries of origin, the standard for that society and are practised in temple buildings or similar structures. (Muslim groups in Sweden sometimes use buildings other than mosques while awaiting the construction of a mosque.) We interpret Smith's model to mean that established immigrant religions can be placed in the religion *there* category, especially in a pluralistic society. These religions comprise groups with non-Protestant as well as non-Christian backgrounds that arrived in Sweden from other cultures and that mainly attract members who have roots in the culture of origin. After deliberation, we created a fourth subcategory that we simply term 'other', comprising smaller organizations that practise their religion in church-like buildings.

The Church of Sweden and Free Churches

Proportionately, the Church of Sweden has a somewhat larger following in Dalarna than in Sweden as a whole. As with the rest of Sweden, the county has seen a decline in church engagement. In 2000, 90.3 per cent of Dalarna's population were members of the Church of Sweden: this compares with 82.9 per cent on a national scale. In 2010, figures stood at 78.4 and 70.0 per cent respectively. In 2000, 89 per cent of all children in Dalarna had been baptized compared with 73 per cent in Sweden as a whole; in 2010, the figures stood at 62.5 per cent for Dalarna and 53.7 per cent for Sweden. In the year 2000, the average percentage of attendees at church services, not including ceremonies, was 3.7 per cent of members in Dalarna and, in 2010, 3.3 per cent. For Sweden as a whole, figures for these two years were 4.0 and 3.4 per cent. In 2010, there were 102 priests in the Church of Sweden, making 2,139 members per priest, compared to one priest per 2,716 inhabitants in Dalarna (email from Peter Brandberg).

The free churches[1] showed a membership of 1.9 per cent in Dalarna in 2010 (2.0 per cent in 2005) compared with 2.3 per cent for

1 We expand upon the concept of the free church by including within it, for example, Word of Faith congregations, as well as parts of the Lutheran church – such as Laestadian revival movements and Evangeliska Fosterlands-Stiftelsen – which have a concept of membership similar to that of the free churches.

Sweden (2.5 per cent in 2005). Membership numbers in Dalarna are therefore lower than in the nation as a whole, whereas the reverse is true in terms of those people who actively take part in the organization whether they are members or not. In 2005, free churches in Dalarna served 5.0 per cent of the population (4.9 per cent for all Sweden), whereas in 2010 they served 4.6 per cent of the population (4.4 per cent for all Sweden). As with Sweden in general, there were fewer free church congregations in 2010 than there were in 2005 (email from Öyvind Tholvsen). The Mission Covenant Church of Sweden has the largest number of congregations in Dalarna (33), the Pentecostal Church has 22, the Baptist Union of Sweden and the Evangelical Free Church in Sweden have 18 each. The town of Rättvik is home to the Word of Faith Movement congregation Nytt Liv (New Life), which was established in 1995 and which by 2009 had 40 members (interview with Pastor Conny Thimberg). Nytt Liv, as with Segerbaneret (The Banner of Victory) in Leksand, is affiliated with Livets Ord (The Word of Life, the first and perhaps most influential congregation in the Word of Faith Movement in Sweden) in Uppsala. In 2012, Segerbaneret had about 50 adult members (email from Markus Holgersson). Segerbaneret also has a school in Leksand. It was set up in 1991 for children from pre-school to grade 9 (16 years old) (www.banerskolan.se). In the school year 2011/12, Banérskolan had 44 pupils (email from Deputy Headmistress Åsa Högås).

Immigrant Religions

There is one Catholic congregation in Dalarna: Saint Katarina. In modern times, regular Catholic mass began in 1940 in Ludvika, the parish of which at that time belonged to that of the town of Gävle (which is located outside Dalarna). After the Second World War, many immigrants arrived in Dalarna, especially from Poland and Italy, and as a consequence, the number of masses being held increased. In 1950, Saint Katarina became independent from the parish in Gävle and, by 1952, a permanent chapel had been established. A few years later, in 1965, Falun became the parochial centre, leading to the 1973 opening of the Gode Herdens (The Good Shepherd's) Catholic Church in the town. In recent years, the Saint Katarina parish has grown significantly as a result of increasing numbers of immigrants. Currently, there are 725 parishioners from some 30 countries. The Church's website states that the number of Catholics in Dalarna is likely twice that. According to the local priest, each year there are about two or three converts (native Swedes). Most of them have come into contact with Catholicism through the House of St David at Foundation Berget (a retreat centre that we discuss along with other retreat centres in Dalarna in chapters 4 and 6).

Currently, mass is held regularly in the towns of Falun, Hosjö, Borlänge, Ludvika, Hedemora, Rättvik, Mora, and Malung. On average, there are about 125 attendees (some 70 in Falun alone). There is one priest for all of Dalarna. The Bridgettine sisters founded a convent in Hosjö, just outside Falun, in 1968. At present, eight sisters, who also run a guesthouse, live there. All are from non-Swedish backgrounds. In addition, there is one Benedictine sister at the House of St David, where there is also a Catholic chapel that holds mass twice per month. There is a youth centre in the village of Sågmyra, but it belongs to the Stockholm parish and is not particularly active (www.sanktakatarina.se and interview with Priest Raphael Kurian).

In the Russian Orthodox Church, Father Mikael Liljeström holds church services three to five times annually in Dalarna (email and interview with Mikael Liljeström).

In Dalarna, there is only one Buddhist organization that is a member of the Swedish Buddhist Cooperation Council, Dalarnas Thailändska Buddhistförening (Wat Dalarnavaranam, founded in 2003). The monks are from the Thai order Thammayut Nikaya, who receive financial support from Maha-Therasamakom, the highest Sangha authority in Thailand.[2] On July 20, 2005, a centre and temple were officially opened in the village of Ulfshyttan just outside Borlänge. This is home to a number of Thai monks, some whom live here permanently, some temporarily. The Dalarnas Thailändska Buddhistförening has about 200 members. Buddhist ceremonies are held, with attendees being mainly from Thai backgrounds. Courses in meditation (*vipassana*) are also held, which are also attended by Swedes (interview with a representative for Wat Dalarnavaranam, respondent 21).

The Islamic Association in Borlänge was established in 1991. Prior to this, worshippers gathered in an apartment for Friday prayers. After the number of Muslims grew further, the association moved

---

2 Certain information exists about another Thai association in Borlänge; however, we were unable to find any means of contacting them.

to its own premises. At the time of this writing (2011), the organization was seeking a permit to build an Islamic centre (mosque). The association has about 200 paying members, originally from some 10 countries. Among its members are five to 10 converts (native Swedes). The number of Muslims in Dalarna is estimated by leaders in the association to be about 6,000.[3] There are smaller Muslim communities in the towns of Avesta, Ludvika, Falun, Orsa, and Malung. About 150 to 200 people attend Friday prayers in Borlänge. There are two imams in Borlänge and one in each of the other towns, who work on a volunteer basis (interview with Hussein Hamad[4] and email).

Other

Two movements from the 1800s that can readily be placed under Smith's category religion *there* are Jehovah's Witnesses and the Church of Jesus Christ of Latter-Day Saints. Jehovah's Witnesses have nine congregations in Dalarna with a total of about 550 members (email from Folke Hasselmark). These members are very active and on average some two-thirds attend meetings (interview with Olivia Lindholm). The Church of Jesus Christ of Latter-Day Saints (the Mormon Church) has one congregation in Dalarna (Falun), with about 200 members, 60 to 70 of whom are active (respondent 23).

The twentieth-century Hare Krishna movement is not active in Dalarna, despite there being a few individual members resident in the county.

Religion Anywhere· *Initial Considerations, Challenges, and Demarcations*

We begin this section about religion *anywhere,* which constitutes the focus of our study, by discussing some of the problems that pertain to how we conducted the study and that at the same time demonstrate characteristics typical of this milieu. Other elements of the religious

3 There is a large discrepancy between the number of members and the estimated number of Muslims in Dalarna. One explanation for this could be that the immigrant Muslim population may not have the custom of being organized into an association or community to the same extent as other Swedes. This implies then that a significantly larger number of people would call themselves Muslim than those who are involved with the association.

4 Hussein Hamad is in charge of youth activities and projects in the Muslim community in Borlänge.

landscape, as discussed above, serve more as a background for our study, whereas religion *anywhere* is discussed throughout the book.

The Grey Zone between Religious and Secular Arenas

One problem was the result of the somewhat vague boundaries that exist between popular religious arenas and secular ones. As described in the introduction, we chose a producer perspective for this project, aware that many phenomena – to use Siv Ellen Kraft's term – are 'hybrids' open to both secular and religious interpretations. One example of hybridity is yoga. By way of interviews in the field, we came to understand that most yoga instructors, regardless of the type of yoga they teach, include various degrees of existential or super-empirical dimensions in their personal understanding of what yoga is, in contrast to the perceptions of many ordinary practitioners who view it as nothing more than physical exercise.[5] We nevertheless chose to include yoga in our survey. Presently, however, there are a number of different forms of yoga. Some of these more obviously embrace existential dimensions. This will be discussed further in chapter 5.

Massage is yet another complex arena, where we included some forms and excluded others. We excluded those types that the producers described in purely physical terms, such as classic massage. On the other hand, we did include, for example, energy massage (which includes beliefs about energy channels in the body) and the Rosen Method (which includes beliefs that massage can free the mind of restrictive memories). These types of massage were less problematic than, for example, aromatherapy or aroma massage and Thai massage. After some consideration, we included both of these in our survey – aromatherapy since certain oils are felt to have healing qualities (super-empirical dimensions) and Thai massage since it is thought to work with a system of energy channels that exist within the body (also, then, super-empirical dimensions). Here,

---

5 This view is not unique to yoga and can exist in more definitively religious contexts. An arguably good example for comparison is the baptism of children within the Church of Sweden. The fact that in most cases the priest performing the baptism would ascribe existential or super-empirical dimensions to the event need not mean that the parents who have chosen to baptize their child interpret the event in the same way. They may view the baptism of a child as nothing more than a tradition or something done to gratify relatives. It might also simply be seen as a beautiful ceremony in a beautiful setting (Gustafsson 1997: 174).

too, we adopt the perspective of the producer since the consumer is undoubtedly not always aware of such dimensions.

Further examples that fall within the grey zone are relaxation, stress management, positive thinking, personal development, and mental training, all of which can readily be used in completely secular contexts, but which nonetheless often coexist in popular religious contexts, where 'existential' and 'super-empirical' elements are featured. For example, one business in Dalarna advertises hypnosis, mental training, and past-life therapy. Where we have had to consider phenomena with similar keywords, we have made a *contextual assessment* and included them if we judge the broader context to relate to phenomena that are super-empirical and existential in character.

A more recent problem area is mindfulness. It has its origins in Buddhism, yet is currently used by conventional psychologists specializing in cognitive behaviour therapy as well as entrepreneurs with clear orientations towards spirituality or new religiosity. Katarina Plank (2011: 186, 210) distinguishes between Buddhist mindfulness, therapeutic mindfulness, and mindfulness in New Age contexts. Using this classification, we have included mindfulness in our survey wherever this technique is used by independent entrepreneurs. We have not, primarily, included those psychologists and counsellors in Dalarna – of whom, according to our survey, there are many – who use the technique in their practice. Mindfulness in a therapeutic context will be discussed further in chapter 6. Of course, the degree to which different therapists consider mindfulness to connect with existential and super-empirical dimensions may vary. It would have been interesting to examine the extent to which psychologists and counsellors attribute super-empirical and existential dimensions to mindfulness. Dr Jon Kabat-Zinn, the founder of Mindfulness-Based Stress Reduction, was undoubtedly influenced by Buddhist and existential perspectives. This may also be the case with other doctors, psychologists, and counsellors active in the field of therapy in mainstream society. A further point to consider is what bearing this has on their therapeutic methods, and how these are perceived by clients.

A further somewhat new and debated term is coaching, which has found a place in both secular contexts and contexts with existential and super-empirical dimensions. In a recent publication, historian of religion Anne-Christine Hornborg studied this phenomenon in much more detail than we have here (2012a). In our survey, we include coaches whose aims are clearly not purely secular – for example, life coaches and spiritual coaches. Other coaches are excluded. We discuss coaching in greater detail in chapter 5.

Phenomena that we, after consideration, excluded from the survey are, for example, water therapy treatments (such as floatation therapy – intense relaxation in body-temperature salt water) and face and body treatments (using creams, clays, oils, and so forth) that are offered at various spa facilities. A number of initial questions during visits to find out about these forms of therapy indicated that the producers did not ascribe super-empirical or existential dimensions to them. Consequently, we decided that this extensive field was outside the realm of interest for the purposes of our study. Nevertheless, we have included bio-detox treatments that involve placing the client's feet in a special receptacle containing warm water: the receptacle is said to ionize the water and thus detoxify the body. This treatment, according to our assessment, has super-empirical elements, though it arguably is one of the few borderline cases.

Despite our chosen demarcations and considerations, many phenomena still presented challenges in terms of interpretation and classification.

Silent Entrepreneurs

Our aim was to map all religious phenomena in Dalarna based on our chosen criteria and demarcations. Yet it is likely that there are many phenomena that would have met our criteria but that we simply, for different reasons, were unable to locate. One significant reason for this is that some phenomena are not very visible. Our field of interest is characterized by a low level of organization, and much that occurs within this field is neither advertised nor visible in other ways. It was by way of the snowball method that we found, for example, a number of mediums and healers who did no advertising but who nevertheless had a steady stream of regular clients. Most likely, we did not become aware of every one of these; they may exist in relatively larger numbers and several of them may be active in small circles only. We further discovered some groups that had religious dimensions to a certain degree, but that did no advertising whatsoever. These tended to comprise a few practitioners who were previous acquaintances: this was the case, for example, with gatherings within the Saint Germain Foundation, a movement from the 1930s with ties to Theosophy and the I AM tradition, as well as the Japanese movement Sukyo Maikari, which holds small gatherings in the town of Rättvik.

Those producers whose work is commercial in nature were relatively easy to locate, at least in terms of their business names: surprisingly few, however, had websites. It is difficult to determine why this was the case: perhaps the producers were generally more advanced in age, which may have meant that the Internet was not an obvious medium of choice for them. We used the Swedish search engine Eniro and similar websites to search for 'health', 'fitness', and other relevant phrases and words. This resulted in lists of businesses, addresses, and telephone numbers. We telephoned those on the list when it was unclear from our Internet search exactly what product was being offered. A business name such as Lisa's Massage and Health Care, for instance, says little about what the business offers. Despite many attempts, we failed to reach some businesses by phone, and these potential producers have been excluded from the survey, despite the fact that some of them perhaps offered services that would fit within our criteria. In some cases, it was not at all simple to find out what activities the business in question offered. For example, upon questioning which products a company offered, we might receive the answer 'classic massage'. However, after asking whether the business offered reflexology, acupuncture, and healing we might learn that these too were available. We may well have missed a number of relevant producers, since we were unable to compile a comprehensive list of services with every phone call.

Besides using the Internet, advertisements, and notice boards, we also found information by enquiring of each person we met what other activities in the field they knew about. In some cases, this was a useful tactic; however, we were at times surprised as to how little the entrepreneurs we spoke with knew about other practitioners. This may indicate that the field is less homogeneous than is often presumed in some research contexts, or in a few cases it may indicate people's reluctance to give information about those who they may view as competitors. In answer to the question about others offering similar types of therapy, the response was, for instance, 'Yes, I think I've heard of an Yvonne somebody near Rättvik, but I'm not sure what she does or what her last name is.' With vagueness such as this, we were unable to locate every potential producer. There are probably several what we would term *silent entrepreneurs*, but we were able to locate only a few of these.

Below, we describe two examples of *silent entrepreneurs*:

Example 1: Karl (respondent 4)

We heard about Karl as a result of the snowball method. He is referred to with obvious respect by many. Karl does not advertise, nor does he take payment for the telephone guidance he provides. He is not active with any particular religious group.

Born in the late 1930s, Karl lives in a town in Dalarna and describes himself as an existential advisor and mystic. After a number of years working as a doctor, he suffered a crisis in his 50s that was related to workplace bullying. This crisis resulted in a powerful inner experience that caused him to realize a sense of deep meaning in life, while feeling no sense of beginning, ending, or form. Subsequently, he changed the way he worked with patients, discovering that the best means of helping them was often simply to sit and talk to them, bring up existential questions in the conversation, and view the person as a whole being. Karl opines that questions of an existential nature are fundamental to many problems – and if they do not already exist, then they develop through problems. Karl came to work a great deal with pain and he feels that pain sooner or later will always bring with it a sense of existential anguish.

Karl believes that people move on after crises by finding an identity that is disconnected from other people. He further believes that an inner light exists within each individual and that each of us has an absolute value. It is this light and absolute value that we must experience. And to do that, we must move past our obstacles and different forms of pain.

Karl does not have a religious background; however, before his crisis and also later in life, he tried many activities that are, potentially, religious in nature – for example, yoga, meditation, relaxation, and psychosynthesis. In addition, he has been active at the retreat centre Berget as well as within the Missionsförbundet (Mission Covenant Church of Sweden). As a professional, he has led many courses of different kinds, particularly in pain management and group habilitation, as well as, for example, qi-gong. Some of the courses were organized by the Swedish Social Security Agency and the Rheumatism Association, with others were being held at Berget. Karl explains that he has studied most religions in-depth, apart from Islam: 'They need to stop fighting first.' He believes that we must be careful when it comes to 'beliefs'. We see our beliefs as truths to save ourselves from anxieties and fears. It is the experience that is important – the experience of 'being'.

Karl no longer holds courses; however, he says his telephone is always ringing. People facing crises call him for existential guidance. Karl believes that each and every person has a transcendent longing. He calls himself a mystic, describing how he sees himself as a part of a whole – with complete belonging and complete freedom. He argues that there is an incredible spiritual longing in Sweden that religion cannot satisfy. The era of Christianity and other religions is, according to Karl, over – symbols that appeared 2,000 years ago no longer have a place in today's society. Karl is anti-organization and does not like New Age. He finds it confusing and feels it will cause people to seek experiences simply in their search for something new. Karl believes his function is to serve as a catalyst to help people understand themselves.

Example 2: Monica (respondent 5)

As with Karl, we heard about Monica as a result of the snowball method. She does no advertising.

Monica is a middle-aged woman who lives in the town of Borlänge. She grew up in the Pentecostal movement but has never felt the need to go to church, saying that she has her own sense of inner peace. She described to us how she has been able to see spirits and to know things that others do not, ever since she was small. She made no reference to any theological ideologies or courses that she has taken, and we got the sense that she is somewhat self-taught. It also emerged during our interview that she has read a great many books about what she terms spirituality.

Monica provides spiritual counselling – basically advising people to let go of their fears and not look back, just simply to be. She describes the importance of changing our thought patterns. Over the years, she has used a number of resources, such as tarot cards and crystals, which she has learnt about from books. In the late 1990s, she worked full-time as a spiritual counsellor but suffered a breakdown. Since then, she accepts no more than two clients per day – a total, currently, of only about 10 people per month. Besides this, Monica works in home-care services. She says, however, that people phone her every day who she must decline. She has never advertised, yet people still hear about her. Ninety per cent of her clients come back for further consultation – some once a year, others more often. She estimates there to be a total of about 100 people who seek her help every once in a while.

Dalarna or Not

Our aim was to conduct a survey of producers of activities in Dalarna that had religious dimensions where at least two people were present. We soon realized, however, that there were many borderline cases. Some activities were occasional in nature – such as a lecture or course held by an individual who is not based in Dalarna. We have kept such activities as these outside the framework of our survey, choosing to include primarily those producers who live permanently in the county (though we do include some practitioners who live part-time in Stockholm and part-time in Dalarna).

Courses at retreat centres are a further example of a transboundary activity that draws people to the county from other places. However, the retreat centres themselves are permanent within Dalarna, and as such we have included them in our survey. Many practitioners are active at such centres: we attempted to include those who reside in Dalarna, although this information can naturally vary over time. We discuss retreat centres further in chapter 5.

Changeability and Continuity in the Field

Our survey took three years and six months to complete. In those cases where we followed up on some enterprises, we discovered that the arenas we were studying were highly changeable. Over time, entrepreneurs may include new areas of specialization or may drop others. They also move – to, from, and within Dalarna. New businesses and organizations appear; others disappear. At the end of the project period, we phoned every fourth producer to ask for quantitative information.[6] Approximately 10 per cent informed us that they had either closed down or were on temporary sick leave. Nevertheless, all had been active over the previous three years and therefore remained in our register. In some cases when we tried to call, we found the telephone number to be out of service. This may indicate a move; however, it may also be the case that some are now using only a mobile telephone and have not employed a call-forwarding service.

With all this mobility and changeability, our survey was, of course, unable to keep up. Characteristic markers of the field are, in fact, that it is non-static and prone to change.

Even if we sometimes felt that our interviewees appeared to lack clear knowledge about the local market, they nevertheless frequently had some sort of network within the area. Certain organized general networks have been particularly significant, a number of which have existed in Dalarna and were referenced by some of our interviewees. One is the Siljansringens ufogrupp (Lake Siljan UFO Group). The network was established in 1985 and at its peak of popularity had 100 to 200 members who would gather for UFO observation evenings as well as for discussions, not only about UFOs but also about anything supernatural. The network was established as a result of the many claims of unidentified flying object observations around Lake Siljan, dating back to the 1960s. The aim of the group was to prove the existence of UFOs and to have this accepted as fact. The group was also intended to be a point of contact for the general public when it came to questions on the subject.

Over a two-week period in January 1985, there were 200 UFO sightings reported in Dalarna. We met one woman who during this time had been driving her car near a forest one evening when

6 The exact approach and results are described below.

suddenly its engine stopped. She then noticed a light to her left that was so intense that she was unable to look straight at it. There was a smell of burning in her car, and she was unable to close her mouth completely, something she attributes to the amalgam fillings in her teeth. She sensed a feeling in her chest that was like an electric shock. The experience lasted for about 30 minutes, after which the car started again. Once home, the car was found to have no mechanical issues (respondent 1).

Those interviewees who were active in this network maintain that the existence of UFOs proves we are not alone in the universe. They further maintain that UFOs show themselves as a way of warning humanity that they need to improve conditions on Earth for the future. Our interviewees also stated that there is something very special about the Lake Siljan area – said to be located on a heart meridian. They say it is Earth's strong radiation in that area that perhaps prompts UFOs and other phenomena to appear there. Our interviewees point out that light phenomena have been observed close to Siljan from times long past.[7] In the early 1990s, the Siljan UFO group suffered from bad publicity, and some of the members began to move in different directions, doing their own thing, which resulted in the decline of the group. However, many members still maintain contact with one another and, despite the fact that the group is not currently active, it has significantly influenced the current religious situation in Dalarna.

---

7 Many other interviewees (including some not part of the UFO network) also referred to the special historical significance of Lake Siljan. Yet a visit to the archives (Dialekt-och folkminnesarkivet) in Uppsala (March 30, 2012) could not confirm this. As with many other lakes, there are records of the so-called *sjörån* in Lake Siljan – a mystical mermaid-like creature, believed to inhabit the bottom of the lake where she tends cattle and other livestock. The *sjörån* was said to be a harbinger of storms and to be responsible for drownings and other such accidents. There is one tale of the Old Man from Rättvik, who while out on Lake Siljan in his boat was caught by a storm. Fearing he would not survive, he promised to present the Church with a sack of peas if only he could make it to shore alive. The storm subsided when he was close enough to shore to know that he would live. At once, he retracted his promise, only to feel the rise of the storm once more and be thrown back into the depths of the lake. Another story went that tossing a coin into the lake could produce a wind that would set a boat on course. As is the case with other lakes, there are also stories about church bells lying at the bottom of Lake Siljan (Record 12142, Dialekt-och folkminnesarkivet, Uppsala). These, however, could not be related to contemporary beliefs about Lake Siljan.

Another example of a former network is Hälsoringen (The Health Circle), a collective of health and fitness entrepreneurs in Rättvik that maintained an active website between 2004 and 2007. Under the heading Alternative Medicine, it advertised, among other things, acupressure, skin-care products, the mapping of the Earth's energy grid system using a divining rod of some sort, kinesiology, and cupping. Other topics were Nutrition and Health; Body Treatments; Spiritual Health; Stress Management; and Retreat Centres and Courses. In 2007, this network was also hit by bad publicity and over time became inactive.

These networks are but two examples; there are many others that have been active in Dalarna and that offered a variety of activities. However, we do not wish to detail the history of networks in the county; rather, we simply wish to explain that some networks have existed from time to time and have been meaningful for developments in the field as a whole. They have also served an important social function for those involved, as different life-orientation views were confirmed and shared.

Religion Anywhere: *Results*

Within the category religion *anywhere,* we distinguish between associations and societies on the one hand, and businesses and business-like set-ups on the other. In the latter category, we have also included individuals who are not entrepreneurs in the legal sense, but who run similar set-ups, commercial or otherwise. In total, we found 443 producers for inclusion in these categories who offered a total of 737 activities. Of these, 12 were associations or societies; the others were businesses or business-like set-ups. Sometimes, however, the difference was difficult to determine. Associations and societies often have active individuals working within them (voluntarily or paid) in a business-like manner. The question is whether to categorize the people or the associations as the actual producer. This is also a problem with retreat centres.

Associations and Societies

In Dalarna, there are currently two active societies that date back to the eighteenth century: Freemasons and Druids. The Swedish Order of Freemasons has one Craft Lodge, Saint Johannes Lodge Gustaf Wasa, in Dalarna, four fraternal societies, and 331 members (email from Jan Lindman, Chancellor, Provincial Lodge in the County of Värmland). The Swedish Order of Freemasons has Christian foundations, and, according to its website, membership involves personal growth in the form of increased humility, tolerance, and compassion through words and deeds, and reaching an inner maturity through teachings as conveyed by the order's rituals and symbols. In addition, funds are donated to medical research and other such social causes (www.frimurarorden.se). During a telephone interview with one representative (respondent 2), we learnt that a freemason should be of Christian faith even though he need not be a regular churchgoer; he should also accept and represent the democratic and humanitarian values that characterize Western society, and try to be a good human being and contribute actively to the betterment of society. The representative also felt that Freemasonry is not to be regarded as religious. In Falun, meetings are held each week, with 30 to 40 members in attendance.

The Swedish Druid Order has a lodge in Avesta which was founded in 1971 and belongs to the International Grand Lodge of Druidism. The order works towards the spiritual and cultural development of its brothers and does not concern itself with religious or political issues. Its aim is to promote self-knowledge and understanding in its brothers for their fellow human beings. As with the Freemasons, the order is for men only; has a number of secret rituals; and is a charitable organization. According to its webpage, the Druid Order has nothing to do with the ancient Celts and their druids; rather, the order bases itself on the romanticized image of ancient druids from eighteenth-century England, with its exciting myths and legends about Celts and druids (www.druidorden.org). The lodge in Avesta has some 40 members. The representative we talked with by phone (respondent 3) preferred to use the term *world view* rather than religion. Nevertheless, the order believes in a supreme power, and, according to the representative, members strive to become better human beings, serving as examples through good deeds and good thoughts, while being forgiving of, helpful towards, and supportive of their fellow human beings. Members may also belong to a religious organization. Charity is important to the order; for example, it currently donates money to prostate cancer research.

The two orders, both of which allow male members only, appear similar in many ways. Most likely, members have the option of incorporating or not incorporating religious meaning into their involvement. Striving to be a good person and working with charities may or may not be based on a religious orientation. Thus both orders can be regarded as hybrids, to once again refer to Siv Ellen Kraft.

Spiritualistic organizations with ties to movements from the 1800s exist in Dalarna today. Contemporary spiritualism in Dalarna comprises a number of independent spiritualistic associations and mediums who operate independently, often as businesses. There is no national organization, and both the associations and the private mediums are often influenced by other sources – for example, healing, tarot, or personal growth. We found six associations that had spiritualistic and parapsychological activities in various locations throughout Dalarna.[8] The ones that provided us with numbers had between 80 and 130 members each. A few others may operate as associations, though they are strongly affiliated with a specific individual, which is why we categorize them as businesses or business-like set-ups.

Anthroposophical activities are represented by Annaskolan, a Waldorf school in the village of Dormsjö in southern Dalarna; Dormsjöskolan, which educates disabled children and which, especially in its early days, was inspired by Anthroposophy; and by one congregation belonging to the Anthroposophically-inspired Christian Community (Kristensamfundet). In 2010, Annaskolan had 48 pupils aged 7 to 16. One of the teachers is a priest trained in the Christian Community. Ten to 20 people normally attend church services that are held once a month. Once a week, nine pupils from grades 7 and 8 (about half of all pupils in these grades; in the age-group 14 to 15) take part in studies as preparation for their confirmation in the Christian Community.[9]

---

8 Late in the project, we found two further groups of so-called 'ghost-hunters' in Dalarna who are interested in the paranormal and, in particular, in houses that are believed to be haunted. These groups are not organized and comprise but a couple of individuals each. Nonetheless, they are visible by way of their blogs.

9 When nothing else is given in this section of text or the one below, information derives from a study trip made to the school on October 11, 2010. The description of Anthroposophy and the Waldorf education system has been read and approved by the headmistress Elisabeth Norman, who was also one of our interviewees. The analysis was written at a later date.

Example: Annaskolan[10]

Annaskolan is a good example of a phenomenon positioned at the interface between the religious and the secular. Located in the village of Dormsjö in southern Dalarna, it demonstrates how the Waldorf education system has established itself beyond urban limits. Anthroposophy and the closely related Waldorf education system are of interest when it comes to the question of whether to classify a phenomenon as religious or secular, and as such is discussed more fully here since it is a prime example of this classificatory problem.

Annaskolan was founded in 1987[11] as a school for children whose parents worked in the local Dormsjöskolan, a school for disabled children that was founded in 1958 and that is based on Anthroposophical principles (Stridell 2008: 5–17, 105). The number of pupils has decreased in recent years. In the academic year 2001/02, there were 86 pupils (Stridell 2008: 105); in 2011, figures indicated that pupil numbers were half that. This fall in numbers is a concern for the school: there must be at least 75, preferably 100, pupils for it to be economically viable. Annaskolan is an independent school; as with other independent schools in Sweden, it receives funding from the state. Waldorf schools are considered to be an alternative education system rather than a religious one.

The Waldorf education system is based on Rudolf Steiner's idea that the human being develops through three seven-year stages during childhood and early youth. The guiding principles are three functions or processes within the human being – i.e. *will, feeling,* and *thought* – which are perceived as working in different ways at different developmental levels. For the pre-school child, will or physical activity is the dominant function; between the ages of 7 and 14, feeling dominates; and from 14 to 21, thought becomes the dominant function (Carlbaum 2008: 10). Creativity and art are very important in Waldorf schools (Liebendörfer 2008: 3), and particular colours and natural materials are preferred in the classrooms (Bjerström 2008: 4). The school's ambition is for pupils to have the same teacher from their early to late school years.[12] Steiner maintains that children between the ages of seven and 14 need to view the teacher as an absolute authority, since they need to learn the difference between right and wrong from a person they both hold dear and respect (1995b: 44–5).

Steiner states that Anthroposophy is a spiritual science (1995b: 33) that helps us see that our deeds on Earth have both a cosmic and universal spiritual meaning (1995a: 27), and also helps us see into the spiritual world where we lived prior to birth (1995b: 36). Consequently, Anthroposophy qualifies as a religion in terms of the definition we utilize in this book. Spiritual science can, according to Steiner, be applied to different practical

10 This section of text is a shortened version of Liselotte Frisk's article 'The Anthroposophical Movement and the Waldorf Educational System' (Frisk 2012a).

11 There was, however, a pre-school dating from 1981 (Stridell 2008: 105).

12 http://waldorf.se/?option=com_content&view=article&id=13&Itemid=16.

activities – for example, education – and the Waldorf education system is based on Anthroposophical understanding of the human being (1995a: 28–30). Steiner further states that a good Waldorf teacher is one who has been moulded by spiritual knowledge (1995b: 51). Despite Waldorf education being based in Anthroposophy, Steiner states that there is no need to incorporate Anthroposophical convictions within Waldorf schools. The schools not should be ideological, sectarian, or denominational (Steiner 1995c: 99).

A visit to Annaskolan demonstrated how this alternative educational approach and world view work in practice. Annaskolan is set up as a foundation and engages 10 part-time teachers. Three of them have completed their Waldorf teacher training, and all but one have at least some form of teacher training. A number of the teachers have an Anthroposophical background though not terming themselves Anthroposophists.

Only a few of the pupils live in the nearby village of Dormsjö or the town of Hedemora. Many must travel a long way each day to reach the school – a few as many as 70 km one way. Some families with children at Annaskolan moved from other parts of Sweden to be close to the school. Annaskolan appears not to be so much a local alternative as an alternative chosen by interested parents, regardless of place of residence.

Waldorf education is thus understood to be a practical application of the spiritual science of Anthroposophy; however, it is stressed that Anthroposophy is merely the inspiration behind the educational methodology and should not itself be taught in Waldorf schools. Determining the exact degree to which Anthroposophy is present in Waldorf schools is complicated, but can be discussed from a number of different angles. Both Anthroposophy and the Waldorf educational system are hybrids, referring once again to Siv Ellen Kraft: both can be religious or non-religious in content depending on the individual and the individual's background. The Waldorf practice of teaching intellectual subjects in the morning, aesthetics in the middle of the day, and handicrafts in the afternoon is based on Anthroposophical ideology, but having handicrafts in the afternoon does not by itself make the education Anthroposophical in the absence of ideological explanations and interpretations. If Anthroposophical ideology is not presented to the children, then their practical experiences from Waldorf are not associated with Anthroposophy. However, if the children are exposed to Anthroposophical ideology – for example, in the home – the case may be different. The practical aspects of the Waldorf education system are not in themselves, therefore, either

Anthroposophical or religious, but can be both if they are filled with such content.

The teacher has a crucial role within the Waldorf education system, and most Waldorf teachers have some sort of Anthroposophical background. Potentially this fact might influence pupils, especially if they have the same teacher over several years, an ideal that is part of the school's philosophy. A long-term relationship with other adults besides parents – especially adults who see themselves as the pupils' role models and authority figures – has, of course, the potential to influence children and young adults. Many parents of children at Annaskolan are themselves Anthroposophists, and as many as 50 per cent of the children who are of age attend the Christian Community's confirmation classes. The assumption here, however, is that it is the religious affiliation of the parents that has the most bearing on the dedication of the child.

There are, however, aspects of Waldorf education that are more obviously religious, such as some songs and morning speeches, where the word 'God' is used. This is not a central feature of the actual education, but nonetheless something that is notable.

Among other associations in Dalarna are Siljans Måsar (The Gulls of Lake Siljan, an association we discuss in detail in chapter 8) and a small group, that in 2009 had four members belonging to the Saint Germain Foundation, who meet in Falun each week. Another small group that is affiliated with the new Japanese religion Sukyo Maikari holds meetings on an irregular basis in Rättvik.

The Church of Scientology, and Pagan[13] and Satanic[14] groups, have no established organization in Dalarna. This is also the case with Theosophy.

Businesses and Business-like Set-ups

Of the 443 producers we studied, 431 were businesses or business-like in nature. They varied considerably – from being one-person enterprises to large businesses, from retreat centres to people working on a volunteer basis with healing, courses, or counselling.

---

13 Late in the project, we heard about meetings in pubs that were organized for anybody interested in Wicca and similar subjects. These meetings took place once a month in Borlänge throughout the duration of our project. We were unable to reach the coordinator.

14 We met a few Satanists, but no organization exists.

The content of these is presented and discussed in more detail in the next chapter in conjunction with a proposal for categorization.[15] We use eight categories: Holistic Massage Techniques; Complementary Western Healing Methods; Eastern Body-Mind Techniques; Eastern Healing Methods; Holistic Psychotherapies; Mediums, Shamans, and Spiritual Beings; Astrology and Other Divination Techniques; and Clearance (harmonization of the surroundings). Characteristic of this section of the religious landscape is, among other things, the way in which the activities are carried out in sessions, courses, and other types of group meetings, such as lectures.

Before we proceed with our discussion of these, we first look at the number of consumers – that is to say, how many people use these types of services.

People Using Popular Religious Services

Besides mapping the number of producers, one of our aims was to make a quantitative estimate of the number of active consumers of popular religion in Dalarna. This, however, is a complex question, with many areas of uncertainty. What, first of all, is meant by 'active'? An investigation carried out by Liselotte Frisk indicated that 85 per cent of those 'active' in the popular religious milieu take courses or attend lectures no more than once or twice each year (Frisk 2000: 76). Another study from 2008 showed that about 30 per cent of a representative segment of Sweden's population answered yes to a question regarding whether they had tried any of 10 listed complementary medical methods such as healing, homeopathy, reflexology, and acupressure (questionnaire funded by the Swedish newspaper *Dagen* in 2008). This means that a fair number of people have experiences of popular religion, even though their involvement is infrequent, perhaps maintained by way of individual practice at home, reading literature,[16] or discussions with like-minded individuals – types of involvement that are not featured in our study.

For this project, we did not examine activities at home, looking only at activities in social milieus in the presence of a producer. So

15 Some of the associations and societies are included in the analysis (see chapter 3).

16 There are many commercial successes in the popular religious milieu: one example is *The Secret* by Rhonda Byrne (2007), which has sold 120,000 copies in Sweden (source: the publishing houses Ica and Energica).

that the figure could be compared with engagement in the Church of Sweden, we decided to focus on the number of people per week present at such social meetings related to the popular religious milieu. Heelas and Woodhead conducted a similar study in Kendal, Great Britain, in the years 2000–2: we discuss the Kendal Project in chapter 4. They sought to attend as many meetings related to the popular religious milieu as they could so that they themselves could count the number of attendees. They complemented this study with questionnaires asking attendees about the frequency of their attendance at similar events (Heelas and Woodhead 2005).

Dalarna is too large for the first method, and questionnaires were not included in our project plan. Instead, we decided, as already noted, to telephone every fourth producer in the register that we had compiled and ask about weekly client numbers.[17] In this way, we contacted 93 producers. Of these, three did not want to answer the question, and seven were eliminated from the quantitative investigation since their answers did not refer to weekly participation and were instead of the type 'x number of members', 'x number of registrants', 'x number in the address list'. We thus had 83 respondents. In total, these respondents reported 1,260 participants per week in Dalarna If those producers we did not telephone had a similar number of participants, we could estimate at least 6,200 participants in the popular religious milieu in Dalarna each week. Naturally, the question arises as to how many took part in more than one activity. Heelas and Woodhead discuss this problem, concluding that about 75 per cent is the correct figure if double visits are excluded. They also, however, exclude those clients (from respondents to a questionnaire) who did not feel their participation

---

17 During the course of our project, we conducted a total of 56 interviews. Interviewees were selected based on a number of criteria: some were chosen because they had been active in historical networks (that are no longer active) that we found to be of interest; others because they represented examples of 'silent participation'; others because their activities were close to being secular and mainstream; and others because we wanted to interview people who offered various types of activities. On most occasions, we asked interviewees for a quantitative estimation of clients each week. Their estimations – in total 42 – are also included in the figures above. We did not select interviewees based on whether they represented activities with many participants; therefore, we believe that our numbers are representative. Our method was to telephone every fourth producer on our list. If a figure was already available for that producer, we telephoned the next fourth producer. If nobody answered, we called the very next producer, and so on.

to be in any way 'spiritual' (Heelas and Woodhead 2005: 25, 139–41). If we presume that participants in Dalarna can be viewed similarly, then we arrive at a figure of 4,410 participants per week. However, our sense is that this figure is at the low end. If we calculate in terms of 60 per cent of the population (166,000 people aged 20 to 64),[18] 2.7 per cent of the population are active in the popular religious milieu every week. If calculated in terms of the entire population, the figure drops to 1.6 per cent.

If we look at an average week's Sunday church service (Church of Sweden) in Dalarna, attendance is about 8,100 people.[19] The number of producers in the popular religious milieu is four times the number of priests in the Church of Sweden in Dalarna. However, it should also be mentioned that in the Church of Sweden there are other positions besides that of priest – for example, youth leaders and deacons. Furthermore, the majority of producers in the popular religious milieu work part-time; some regard their work in this area as a hobby.

If we compare the popular religious milieu with the Church of Sweden, we can determine that significantly more people attend Church of Sweden services each week than those who take part in popular religious activities. Nevertheless, the number of people participating in popular religious activities is more than half the number active within the Church of Sweden. Considering the great historical significance of the Church of Sweden, its position in the public domain, and its relatively large financial resources, the popular religious milieu is actually comparatively extensive.

It is also worth noting that participants in the popular religious milieu in most cases pay between 100 and 600 Swedish kronor per activity, which may well be an issue for many. The Church of Sweden receives its financing through taxes. How active an individual is within the Church has no bearing on the amount of taxes paid. A church service is 'free'. If the situation were to be reversed, we could not rule out the probability that the profile of participation and involvement might be different.

18 A methodology employed by Professor Franz Höllinger in an Austrian study (Höllinger and Tripold 2012). We discuss this study further in chapter 4.

19 Heelas and Woodhead, in their questionnaires to participants in meetings in the popular religious milieu, asked whether participants viewed their visit as having spiritual significance. It may be the case that not everyone who visits the Church of Sweden feels that their visit has spiritual significance.

Chapter 3

Religion *Anywhere*: Structure and Content

In this chapter, the focus of our discussion will be on the most prominent aspect of religion *anywhere*, namely businesses and phenomena with entrepreneurial structures. We will propose a classificatory schema for this facet of popular religion (which includes certain associations and societies), followed by a discussion of content. In addition, we look at a different typology, one developed by the sociologists of religion Ronald Stark and William Sims Bainbridge during the 1980s. We will use this as a platform for discussing some of the problems evident in Smith's model when we apply it to diverse areas within the popular religious milieu. Lastly, we discuss the question of gender, focusing on the question of why 80 per cent of the producers in our study are women.

Categorization of Religion **Anywhere**

As noted earlier, elements within the popular religious milieu can vary over time, and we wanted to bring some sort of order to – and comprehension of – how popular religion is currently being expressed. Our survey gradually broadened our understanding of this field of study, and we were eventually able to distinguish different themes that came to serve as the basis of our eight categories identified in chapter 2. The themes were developed partly on the basis of main orientation and partly on the basis of historical origin.[1] For many reasons, categorization and classification always present challenges, which was the case also with our study.[2]

---

1 We constructed the categories in consultation with colleagues at the University of Graz, Austria, since they were conducting a similar study at the same time. This opened up opportunities for comparison. We examine their study in the next chapter.

2 There are many ways to categorize the phenomena described here. See, for example, a discussion in Ahlin 2007: 35–7 on different approaches to categorization.

Three groups – Freemasons, Druids, and Anthroposophists – did not fit neatly into any of our categories, and were thus set aside. (We will discuss them later in the chapter.) Beyond these three groups, there were 440 producers and 737 activities included in the survey. The structures that dominate the landscape of the popular religious milieu are businesses and business-like set-ups. Besides Freemasons, Druids, and Anthroposophists, there were additionally 9 associations or societies in the material, but these fit into the constructed categories.

Many producers offer a diverse range of activities. On average, each producer offers 1.7 activities. There were some who offered only one activity, whereas others offered as many as 9 or 10. It became apparent from interviews with producers that, over the years, their interest in different techniques varied, and that they had subsequently changed or added to their repertoire.

The following list details the number of producers who offer activities within each category. Several of the producers offer activities in more than one category and subcategory.

1. *Holistic Massage Techniques* – massage 75 (of which the most popular are Thai massage 8; energy massage 7; healing massage 7; aroma massage 6; and Chinese tuina massage 6); reflexology 44; acupressure 38 (including ear acupressure 2); Rosen Therapy 17; shiatsu 12; and Bowen Therapy 6. Total: 155 producers (35.2 per cent of producers).

Holistic massage techniques, or body therapeutic methods, constitute the largest group. It is clear that the well-being of the body is perceived as important in this milieu. The most popular practices are reflexology and acupressure (pressure point methods with Western and Chinese origins respectively) followed by Rosen Therapy, a Western technique based on the belief that chronic muscle pain can result from repressed feelings, followed by shiatsu (Japanese origin) and different kinds of massage, such as Thai massage.

2. *Complementary Western Healing Methods* – for example, healing 68 (including White Time Healing 6; crystal healing 5; reconnective healing 4; and spiritual healing 4); dance 13 (freedom dance 6; sacred dance 6; sacred circle dance 1); homeopathy 12; kinesiology 8; Bach Flower Therapy 6; and Craniosacral Therapy 6. Total: 141 producers (32 per cent of producers).

There are almost as many complementary healing methods in our survey as there are massage techniques in the first category. These

complementary healing methods have a partly Western esoteric/
occult background, and are nowadays often studied as part of the
esoteric tradition (see, for example, Hammer 1999 or Bogdan 2007).
A number of producers also offer just 'healing', without specifying
exactly which healing methods are used and where they originate.
Some have likely developed from creative thinking, with influence
from one or more specific methods. Alongside these, homeopathy
is relatively popular, as is kinesiology. Kinesiology supposedly
measures muscle strength and balance in the body, and is said to
treat imbalances and energy blocks through massage and nutritional
advice. The most popular healing method is White Time Healing, a
method associated with higher spiritual beings and angels.

3. *Eastern Body-Mind Techniques* – for example, yoga 69 (several
unspecified forms, but also kundalini yoga 6; ashtanga yoga 6;
Iyengar yoga 4; and power yoga 4); meditation 24; mindfulness 17;
and Vedic Art 11. Total: 127 producers (28.9 per cent of producers).

Many producers use Eastern techniques that involve both body
and mind. Yoga is often practised in groups, meaning that each
producer (yoga instructor) has contact with several consumers
during each class, which is most often not the case with, for example,
a healer. These techniques can therefore reach more consumers at
one time than can healing techniques. Yoga is the most popular
technique in this category with close to 75 per cent of producers.
Next comes meditation. In terms of mindfulness, which falls in
third place, we do not include conventional therapists. Lastly,
Vedic Art was developed by the artist Curt Källman (1938–2010)
in 1987. Källman came into contact with Maharishi Mahesh Yogi
through Transcendental Meditation. The Maharishi taught him 17
Vedic spiritual principles for art and creativity. In brief, Vedic Art
can be described as a form of art instruction that is based on those
principles (http://vedicart.com/). From a historical perspective,
Vedic Art is interesting since it demonstrates links to Maharishi
Mahesh Yogi and Transcendental Meditation, and the way in which
new religious movements can influence and inspire new cultural
developments.

4. *Eastern Healing Methods* – for example, acupuncture 52; reiki 43;
diksha 13; traditional Chinese medicine 7; and Ayurveda 4. Total:
116 producers (26.4 per cent of producers).

This category comprises healing methods that originate in the
East. The most popular of these is acupuncture (the acupuncture

used by the established health-care system in recent years for the purpose of pain relief is not included in this survey). One reason for the popularity of acupuncture in Dalarna is likely due to there being a school for traditional Chinese medicine in Falun which trains people in the technique. Reiki, a Japanese healing technique which is said to transfer universal energy, is also popular. Originating in India, diksha is a form of healing using touch.

5. *Holistic Psychotherapies* – for example, coaching/life-coaching/ existential guidance 24; personal growth 13; relaxation 11; stress therapy 10; and hypnosis 7. Total: 84 producers (19.1 per cent of producers).

A number of the producers employ methods of Western origin that are more therapeutic than healing in character and more psychological as well. Often, there is some kind of connection with the Human Potential Movement, a movement from 1960s' USA, which had its roots in humanistic psychology and vague associations with religion. Here, coaching, personal growth, and stress management are the most popular methods.

6. *Mediums, Shamans, and Spiritual Beings* – for example, mediums 24; shamans 13; channelling 7; medium counselling 7; spiritualism 7; contact with angels 7; séances 5; and animal communication 5. Total: 71 producers (16.1 per cent of producers).

Producers in this category offer different types of communication with spiritual beings and animals. In particular, we found a number of spiritual activities such as communication with the dead, shamanism, channelling, and animal communication. Also included are, for example, contacts with UFOs, angels, elves, brownies, and fairies (these phenomena account for 2.7 per cent of producers and 1.6 per cent of activities). We found a few activities that made reference to the last three kinds of beings, which in other contexts are often categorized as belonging to folklore. Contact with angels, however, has its origins in various religious traditions (Gilhus 2012).

7. *Astrology and Other Divination Techniques* – for example, tarot 21 and astrology 7. Total: 29 producers (6.6 per cent of producers).

Of the divination techniques offered, the most common form was tarot, which is nowadays most often used for personal growth rather than for fortune-telling purposes.

8. *Clearance (harmonization of the surroundings)* – for example, Feng Shui 8; clearance 3; and dowsing rod 3. Total: 14 producers (3.2 per cent of producers).

This category was not common, being offered by a little more than 3 per cent of the producers. Yet there may be greater interest than is otherwise evident. Svenska Slagruteförbundet (The Swedish Dowsing Society) has its own association in Dalarna, Slagruteföreningen Dalarutan, which, according to its website, has 13 members. Two of these members are included in our survey; the others, as far as we can tell, are not producers, or else they are active in other parts of Sweden.

Reflections on the Results

Below, we present a few topics and discuss them in terms of our system of categories and the survey results.

Healing

A common descriptor for a number of the above categories is *healing*. In this context, healing refers to the use of different methods, often with a focus on the body, to bring about links between the various dimensions of an individual as a way of attaining an ideal state of being. Many other studies indicate that healing is a key term in the popular religious milieu. In a study that examined the frequency of use of different terms in two issues of the magazine *Energivågen*, for the purpose of discovering which elements were central to the 'New Age', healing clearly dominated (Frisk 1997). Such terms as *health* and *body* also ranked high, being closely related to the term *healing.*

Other studies – such as, for example, the study conducted by sociologist of religion Lena Löwendahl in 2002 – demonstrate that in the popular religious milieu, *health* is often perceived as being a normal and primordial condition that comes about when all dimensions of a human being are in balance. When this balance is upset, the result is ill-health (Löwendahl 2002: 212). However, the term *health* is associated not only with physical health or absence of illness, but also with personal growth, happiness, a sense of meaningfulness, peace of mind, harmony, spirituality, love of the self, and divinity (Löwendahl 2002: 188). The causes of sickness, according to Löwendahl, are described as being mainly of the mind – thoughts, feelings, and past experiences – or of the spirit – energies and especially events from previous lives. Lifestyle-related causes are also described, such as poor eating habits (Löwendahl 2002: 212). Healing incorporates psychological factors – the healing of inner problems and traumatic experiences – as well as physical factors, since improved physical health is one step towards becoming a whole individual. There is also a dimension of healing that involves the individual getting to know him- or herself and growing as a person (Löwendahl 2002: 190).

Another sociologist of religion, Meredith McGuire points out that the notion of religion and medicine belonging to two different spheres is a recent one – at the most 200 years old (2008: 119). She describes how both faith and health are social constructs, and how religion and medicine have undergone parallel processes in which powerful interest groups have historically fought for control of definitions and demarcations. After the Reformation, religion had control over the spiritual sphere only, whereas the treatment of the body was relegated to the profane realm. Elements that were excluded from the sphere of religion often survived in popular religion, thus outside or in the margins of 'real' religion. Typical areas of focus were material concerns, such as health, security, and success. McGuire describes how these areas are fundamental within the contemporary New Age context. Currently, the modern Western notion that we can control both our bodies and our feelings leads us to entertain great expectations in terms of improving our health and well-being (McGuire 2008: 129–36).

Different Origins and Cross-influences

The milieus described in this study developed from an admixture of different sources. First, the field is distinguished by what in recent years has come to be labelled as Western Esotericism – that is to say, Western and Eastern ideas deeply rooted in traditions outside of Christianity. Included here are, for example, the nineteenth-century movements Theosophy and Spiritualism, both of which have greatly influenced popular religion, as well as homeopathy and other healing methods, such as Bach Flower Therapy. Second, non-Western religions and cultures have been influential, especially Eastern religions. Included here are Eastern medical traditions such as Ayurveda and acupuncture. Finally, there is a strong psychological and therapeutic component that has its roots in various schools of psychology, though principally in that of the Human Potential Movement.

These various trends have often interacted in varying degrees, which consequently makes them sometimes difficult to distinguish.

Terms like 'Western' and 'Eastern' are themselves challenging. Contact between the two hemispheres has a long history, and cultural elements have migrated and assimilated. After centuries of such contact, it is difficult to maintain any strict division between Eastern and Western cultures. Despite this, we felt that the division still had explanatory value (we discuss this further in a later section).

Divination

Our study included a category for divination or fortune-telling. We were surprised to find that only 6.6 per cent of producers were active in this area; we had presumed the percentage would be higher. The popular religious milieu, however, is in a constant state of flux. One hypothesis is that certain activities are more age-related and become either more or less popular depending on the age group that finds them interesting. A study carried out by the newspaper *Dagen* by way of an online questionnaire in July 2008 shows, for example, that astrology, healing, séances, and channelling are significantly more popular among people in their late 50s and early 60s than among younger age groups; yoga and tarot, meanwhile, are significantly more popular with those under 30. This suggests that, as new generations come of age, yoga is on the way 'in', whereas astrology is on the way 'out'. Tarot – more popular among younger generations – was included in our divination category, yet it seldom featured. One explanation for this might be that tarot reading is mostly practised by young people in private groups and therefore belongs to the areas of silent practice that our study barely touches.

Stark and Bainbridge's Model of Classification

There are many classification models for popular religion or for parts of it (for some of these, see Frisk 1993). Many can broaden our perspective and afford us new perceptions. Though Stark and Bainbridge's theory of religion was formulated in the 1980s, parts of it are arguably still relevant for our study. Their theory is complex; here we examine only those parts directly applicable to our discussion. The two aspects we are interested in are: (1) the relationship of religious phenomena to the mainstream socio-cultural environment, and (2) the degree of organization, and what that means for the level of engagement expected from individuals.

Stark and Bainbridge define religion as a system of general compensators – the promise of rewards that will be received, for example, in heaven after death – that are based on supernatural assumptions. Further, they distinguish between *church*, which is a conventional religious organization; *sect*, which is a deviant religious organization, yet one that has traditional beliefs and practices; and *cult*, which is a deviant religious organization that has new beliefs and new expressions.[3] Sects form as a result of a schism in an existing organization. Cults represent either a cultural innovation or a cultural import. Another way of describing religious deviance is, according to Stark and Bainbridge, that it exists in tension with the mainstream sociocultural environment. A church is a religious group that generally accepts and is in harmony with its social environment; a sect, on the other hand, rejects certain important aspects of the surrounding culture (Stark and Bainbridge 1996: 124–7). Cults may have a low or high degree of tension with their sociocultural environment, depending on the structure of their organization.

Stark and Bainbridge classify cults into three categories based on the degree to which they are an organized group. The least organized, *Audience Cults*, are not formal organizations, and participants are best viewed as consumers (of lectures, magazines, or books). *Client Cults* are more organized and are built around relationships between therapist and patient or consultant and client. The rewards promised by client cults are more specific in nature: for example, curing an illness. Only *Cult Movements*, the third category, promise general rewards that are more traditionally religious in nature (Stark and Bainbridge 1985: 26–30). They are also characterized by a higher state of tension with the sociocultural environment than the other two categories (1985: 36).

Relation to the Sociocultural Environment

The primary criterion in Stark and Bainbridge's model is the degree of tension with the surrounding sociocultural environment, and appears directed to at least two areas: one, traditional religion (*church*) and two, *society* in other senses. Our interpretation is that a cult (with imported or innovative features) is in a state of high

3 This classification of religious organizations differs from those of many other sociologists of religion. See, for example, McGuire 2002.

tension with traditional religion, yet can exist at various levels of tension with the rest of society. The first sub-criterion relates to the distinction between Western and Eastern cultures, though elements can also originate from yet other cultures (or can be *innovative*). In a society where culture and religion are homogeneous, a criterion focused on a state of tension with the sociocultural environment might be useful. However, problems arise with more pluralistic and heterogeneous cultures, as well as the degree to which communication between different cultural orientations exist with a society. This criterion was thus more useful during the 1980s when Stark and Bainbridge formulated their model than it is today.

To now pick up on our non-exact classification of phenomena as 'Western' or 'Eastern': Yoga, for example, can be regarded as an 'import' from India; however, over the last few decades, various American forms of yoga have been developed. The empirical material from our project demonstrates that, currently, there are even local, Swedish forms of yoga. Producers often mix different elements in such a way as to make it difficult to maintain distinctions. Examples of such processes are provided in chapter 7, where the Church of Sweden's relation to the popular religious milieu is discussed. There are traditionally Christian arenas that currently reveal traits of cultural import or innovation.

The other sub-criterion in Stark and Bainbridge's model, namely the degree of tension with society, can be problematized on the basis of our study. Tension with society can be understood in several ways (see, for example, Frisk 1993). Many of the phenomena included in our study were generally understood to be significantly more deviant and odd in the 1980s when Stark and Bainbridge presented their model than they appear today, in our pluralistic, multicultural society. Based on the data gathered for our project, we can see that many of these formerly exotic phenomena are now part of the mainstream. Nevertheless, it is simply the nature of popular religion that it exists in a state of relative tension – more or less – with more powerful groups within society. We discuss this ambiguity further in chapter 6.

Degree of Organization

The second criterion in Stark and Bainbridge's model, the degree of organization, may have a higher level of applicability in our contemporary milieu. Most of the phenomena we placed in the category religion *anywhere* had a low degree of organization and, to use Stark and Bainbridge's terminology, featured particularly Client Cults, as well as Audience Cults. One question is whether the three groups – Freemasons, Druids, and Anthroposophists (all of which we could not categorize within our structure) – could be placed in Stark and Bainbridge's third category, Cult Movements. Arguably, however, only Anthroposophy has a type of membership that demands high levels of engagement.

The empirical material from our project also shows that phenomena requiring a low level of engagement enjoy much greater popularity than those that require a higher level of engagement. We thus surmise that a low level of engagement is an important feature of contemporary popular religious activity.

Gender: A Discussion

Around 80 per cent of the producers in our study were women. There are many other studies of popular religiosity where this ratio of men to women is also apparent (see, for example, Frisk 2000; Woodhead 2007: 115; Willander 2008: 251; Ahlin 2007: 57; Heelas and Woodhead 2005: 94). Meredith McGuire observes that religious rituals and practices socialize men and women into behaviours and feelings that are seen as socially appropriate for the two sexes. The official religions – in particular Judaism, Christianity, and Islam – broadly legitimize patriarchal hierarchy. While official religions have represented the options and interests of the privileged, dominant, and comparatively well-educated social classes – as well as men, colonial powers, and dominant ethnic groups – the non-official religions (as McGuire terms them, exemplified by folk healing, magic, possession, and non-sanctioned religious movements) have been marginalized and suppressed. These spheres have also traditionally been female domains. Many of the new religious movements that emerged during the late 1800s reinterpreted the role of women, granting them positions of leadership and ritually expressing their experiences and needs. Women featured strongly in such movements as Spiritualism, Christian Science and New Thought, both as leaders and as members. These movements focused on, among other things, healing, emotional problems, and relationships with the living and dead. This made them attractive to women who were seeking alternative gender identities during a time of social change (McGuire 2008: 159–69).

McGuire observes that women have the important cultural role that she labels *relational*, both towards other people as well as towards the sacred (however this might be understood), where their tasks are to help other people, and to care and to heal (2008: 154–5). The domain we studied for our project is clearly a continuation of the traditional cultural role of women, including the traditional female healing culture; at the same time it offers women possibilities for a more powerful religious identity. The popular religious milieu affords women a space for religious expression and religious identity in line with the relational orientation which women are socialized to adopt within our culture.

Another expert in the sociology of religion, Linda Woodhead proposes that the need of women to create new social spaces – which are not generally available for them within traditional religions – is one of the most important factors behind the development of modern new religiosity. Woodhead also stresses the tendency of women to prefer a more relational and less hierarchal understanding of the sacred and to place particular value on group settings (2002: 339–40). Sociologist Susan Palmer argues that new religious movements offer women more choice to adopt different roles – including gender roles and sex roles – than does secular society (1994). Ciara O'Connor, writing on women's choices in Ireland, describes new spiritual and holistic movements as a valuable space within which women can express themselves, and proposes that spirituality can be a language of the oppressed (2011: 224). In her study, Lena Löwendahl found that New Age functions as a free zone where women can seek new roles without having to affirm traditional ones; in addition, she states that it also enables men to discover new male roles (2002: 319–25). Löwendahl further found that what is traditionally perceived as female – such as intuition and feelings – are often valued more highly in New Age milieus (2002: 78).

At the same time as popular religiosity ties in with traditionally female roles, it also offers roles that are new and more powerful. Rather than the traditional self-sacrificing role of the woman, the popular religious milieu affords women opportunities in the area of self-development, even if that milieu is disparaged by segments of mainstream society (see, for example, Hornborg 2012a). Linda

Woodhead describes how holistic spirituality is a safe place for the individual to confront feelings of worthlessness and low self-confidence, which in turn relates to the role of women in mainstream society. In the holistic milieu, women can develop a new, stronger identity that surpasses conventional roles. Woodhead states that many holistic practices relate to fundamental identity constructions and can lead to increased self-confidence, self-worth, and greater social activity. According to her, the role of producer in the popular religious milieu can be fulfilling for women as traditional caregivers, and also solves conflicts associated with female identity, since it brings with it the opportunity for professional independence (Woodhead 2007: 121–3).

Besides its focus on relationships and the self, popular religiosity brings with it a strong focus on the body as a place of spirituality and healing. O'Connor (2011: 233) states that in mainstream society, the female body is, instead, objectified. Löwendahl found in her study that more women than men talk about their bodies and, further, that they talk about them in more physical terms. When men talk about their bodies, they focus to a greater extent on abstract – for example, mental and spiritual – dimensions (Löwendahl 2002: 322).

Many of the reflections above regarding the imbalance in gender representation in the popular religious milieu were supported by the findings in our project. We conclude this chapter with the following vignette of Berit, a woman we met in the town of Rättvik. Berit's story is not unique: we heard many such stories from other women we spoke to as part of our project.

Example: Berit (respondent 6)

We met Berit for the first time during a meeting with Siljans Måsar (The Gulls of Siljan, see chapter 8). She had been involved with the group for some time, but by this point had set up her own organization. It became clear from what Berit said that her involvement had given her strength, identity, and purpose. Her story serves as a good example of how such a context offers a sense of empowerment to those people who in other contexts tend to be marginalized and invisible, as is often the case in, for example, the workforce.

Berit was born in 1935 and describes herself as a seeker who has always believed in God but not in the Church. After illnesses and crises that lasted many years, she decided, after being told that she was terminally ill at age

52, that she would become healthy again with the help of different tools and techniques drawn from the popular religious milieu. She did indeed regain her health. Of particular importance to Berit was Findhorn's Game of Transformation, the aim of which is, in Berit's words, to help the player find him- or herself and become the person he or she was destined to be. The player begins the game with a purpose – for example, to be healthy – and discovers what is hindering or helping one to achieve that goal. She believes that sickness is simply repressed power.

Berit also took one year of studies in Anthroposophy. A friend told her that she had dreamt about Berit and learnt Berit had a great task during the time of transition.[4] Shortly afterwards, Berit heard a voice telling her to 'follow me'. She believes that the voice may have belonged to her inner-self. According to Berit, we all have God within us and are all equal. She explains how she had previously lived within a structure of obedience, where she always obeyed others. Nowadays she obeys herself. She believes this is a pattern for many: that people live as others want them to and that it is time we all lived our own lives.

In 2001, she, along with four other women, established a non-profit association in a village in Dalarna. They shared a house and devoted their time to such alternative health practices as qi-gong and living foods. With time, the association developed into a business, but then the women went their separate ways.

Over the years, Berit developed an esoteric model, which also contains its own economic system: it is based on a social and world-order model, which aims to release the inner potential within each of us and has us become what we should be, while seeing the intrinsic and equal value of both ourselves and others. Berit's business is currently registered as an economic association. It operates from its own premises and has 10 paying members. Plans exist for developing the premises further into a place for health and personal growth.

Berit believes that her movement receives spiritual guidance from such figures as Archangel Gabriel. Central to the movement are six women who have different roles. Berit's role is to come up with ideas. One of the women worked at Stiftsgården in Rättvik. All six are pensioners and are no longer responsible for children or family, something Berit feels is an advantage. Previously, they were all active in areas associated with female roles – birth and nutrition – and they all grew from these experiences. Life experience has shown them both positives and negatives. Now, Berit believes, it is time to flourish and break free. Women must be honest and direct, and stand up for themselves and be who they truly are.

4 The expression 'time of transition' refers to the widely shared notion that the world is on the cusp of a new age. The year 2012 is often cited as significant.

Chapter 4

Comparing Dalarna with Other Areas

In this chapter, we will look at local mapping studies similar to ours that were conducted in other parts of Europe. We will discuss whether, how, and why Dalarna differs from other places, while also considering similarities. The studies on which we will focus here were conducted in Kendal in Great Britain; Klagenfurt and Leoben in Austria; Enköping in Sweden; and Århus in Denmark.[1] The studies were organized differently and are to different degrees comparable to ours. First we look at the studies individually; then we compare them with our study. The exception is the Austrian study, which is so similar to our own that it seems only natural to discuss results from our study in tandem with results from Austria.

The different studies raise general questions about how to define and demarcate an area of research and how to approach the challenges posed by terms such as *New Age*, *spiritual*, and *sacred*. We will discuss these related issues in the final section of this chapter.

The Kendal Study, Great Britain

The earliest and most important study, one that is often referenced and used as a prototype by other researchers, is the local study of Kendal, England. The study was conducted by Paul Heelas and Linda Woodhead between the years 2000 and 2002. Their aim was to test the assumption that a spiritual revolution is currently taking place, resulting in a certain type of religiosity – one they term 'spiritual' – becoming increasingly more common at the expense of more traditional religiosity. They based this assumption on studies that indicated a decline in Christianity as well as studies that showed

---

1 There are other studies from, for example, Åbo, Finland (Martikainen 2004); Bergen, Norway (Mikaelsson 2000); and Mikulov and Česká Lípa, Czechoslovakia (Lužný, Nešpor et al. 2008). However, these had a different focus from ours and are only partially comparable, which is why we do not use them here.

a growth in the numbers of those who preferred to call themselves 'spiritual' as opposed to religious.

Heelas and Woodhead begin by distinguishing between two fundamentally different social attitudes, which they call *life-as* and *subjective-life*. They use life-as to denote a basic attitude oriented towards living through exterior roles and duties according to external expectations, while subjective-life means living life through subjective experiences and listening to one's own unique needs and desires. Life-as is oriented towards the established order and tradition, being part of a community, in which the priority is placed on obeying external authorities and thus living a life in which the individual 'I' is rendered less important. Subjective-life, on the other hand, implies an orientation in which states of mind, memories, feelings, bodily experiences, dreams, and the inner conscience are given greater value and meaning. The individual is granted a unique significance and thus also authority, and life is about becoming who we authentically are, based on our inner experience of ourselves (Heelas and Woodhead 2005: 2–4). These two attitudes correspond with contrasting religious orientations: life-as stresses, according to Heelas and Woodhead, a transcendent authority to which the individual must conform, whereas subjective-life stresses an inner authority and a sacralization[2] of the unique 'I' (2005: 6). Religion sacralizes life-as, whereas spirituality sacralizes subjective-life (2005: 5). Heelas and Woodhead focus on the 'sacred', maintaining that there are two different ways of relating to what is regarded as sacred, religion and spirituality representing two distinct approaches.

Heelas and Woodhead opine that in the West a fundamental cultural shift is underway, from life-as to subjective-life, which is affecting culture as well as religion, at all levels (2005: 2). They discuss the cause of this shift in terms of the so-called 'subjectivization thesis', meaning that contemporary culture as a whole is undergoing a 'massive subjective turn'[3] (2005: 2). It is, therefore,

2 Heelas and Woodhead use the word *sacralization* (2005: 6).

3 We will discuss this in more detail in chapter 9, since our thesis is also that one of the most crucial reasons behind the changes in contemporary religion is subjectivization in broad cultural terms. That said, other parts of Heelas and Woodhead's thesis might well be criticized – in particular, the methodology used for the longitudinal study as well as the evaluative word choice in the description of life-as and subjective-life.

only logical that forms of religion which represent living according to external principles are in decline. Heelas and Woodhead contend that many churches and congregations fall into this category. In contrast, forms of religion which represent living according to the deepest sacred dimensions of the human being's innermost self – forms stressing inner authority and the sacralization of the unique 'I' – are presumably on the rise. These forms would thus include (to use Heelas and Woodhead's terms) the spiritual expressions that are known as body-mind, new spirituality, and New Age, as well as alternative or holistic spirituality. The spiritual revolution will, according to them, have taken place when holistic spirituality (subjective-life) is quantitatively larger than congregational religion (life-as) (2005: 7).

Heelas and Woodhead also problematize the extent to which life-as can be related to the congregational domain and subjective-life to the holistic milieu. They argue, however, that they can demonstrate by way of their questionnaires that life-as dominates the congregational domain whereas subjective-life dominates the holistic milieu, even if there are different categories of congrega-tions with different orientations (2005: 13–23).

Heelas and Woodhead's goal was to discover whether the spiritual revolution had actually taken place and they chose the community of Kendal for their study. Kendal had a population of 27,610 in 1999. As we did in our Dalarna study, they focused on what they termed the 'heartlands' of religious and spiritual life, namely those places which were said to have (in their terms) sacred significance (2005: 36–7). These places were divided into congregational and holistic spheres (2005: 8). In terms of the holistic milieu, some 100 producers (groups and sessions) were found in Kendal, all having a self-under-standing that their activities were spiritually meaningful (2005: 24). From the questionnaires completed by holistic producers, Heelas and Woodhead found that the majority believed in a life force. Only 7 per cent from the holistic milieu compared with 60 per cent from the congregational domain felt that spirituality meant obeying the will of God (2005: 25). Heelas and Woodhead concluded that the subjective turn of modern culture was much more evident in the holistic milieu than in the congregational domain. However, there was the issue of what they referred to as a spectrum, meaning the congregational organizations fell into different categories. In addition, of those questioned from the congregational domain, 4 to 6 per cent were also active in the holistic milieu.

Nevertheless, Heelas and Woodhead opine that these two worlds are for the most part distinct, the borders between the two not having disintegrated to any significant degree (2005: 31–2). They refer to a number of studies which indicate that there has been a degree of subjectivization in many parts of the congregational domain as well, but assert that it is not profound enough to completely support the claim of a spiritual revolution in that domain (2005: 67). A certain type of congregation has, however, experienced substantial growth over the last few years – the one characterized by what Heelas and Woodhead term the 'experiential difference'. These are congregations that believe there to be a difference between the divine and the human, but also believe in the ability of the divine to take the form of the holy spirit and thus be experienced subjectively by individual members (Heelas and Woodhead 2005: 17, 75).

In terms of the congregational domain, Heelas and Woodhead (and their team) attended church services so that they could count the number of attendees on an average Sunday. By questioning each attendee, they were able to avoid double counts. They found that 7.9 per cent of Kendal's population attended church services on the particular Sunday in question (2005: 34–5). In terms of the holistic milieu, they decided to count participants over a typical week as there are no particularly significant days in this milieu. They further decided not to include activities at, for example, schools, while also counting only those producers who felt their activities to be sacred and who related to the spirituality of subjective-life. Since there were two large holistic centres just outside Kendal, Heelas and Woodhead further decided to include Kendal's immediate environs: this meant that the total number of people included in the study of the holistic milieu rose to 37,150. They scanned advertisements for relevant activities, and also used the snowball sampling method. They interviewed more or less all the producers to investigate whether they felt their activities had spiritual dimensions (including producers who used closely related terms such as chi, energy, and vibrations), and whether the activities were felt to be related to subjective-life. They took part in all group activities, noting the number of participants. In addition, those producers who met with one person at a time were interviewed to find out how many clients they met each week or month. Based on this method, an estimated number of participants was arrived at.

A questionnaire was distributed both to church congregants and to participants in the holistic milieu. The one used in the holistic milieu asked respondents about the activities they had taken part in over the prior week. In this way, Heelas and Woodhead were able to determine how many took part in more than one activity. Participants were also asked whether they felt these activities had a spiritual dimension. The questionnaire was used to investigate the popularity of activities as well. The most popular activities in Kendal proved to be yoga, aromatherapy, massage (non-specific), homeopathy, reflexology and the Alexander Technique, in that order (Heelas and Woodhead 2005: 156–7).

It was found that 95 producers offered activities that generated 840 participants in the holistic milieu over the course of one week. After checking for double participation, the figure came to 600 participants per week, equal to 1.6 per cent of the population (Heelas and Woodhead 2005: 36–40). Fifty-five per cent of participants (0.9 per cent of the population) felt the activities had a spiritual dimension. Heelas and Woodhead used the higher figure (1.6 per cent) when they compared it with the congregational domain (7.9 per cent), given that what participants in the congregational domain felt about church services in terms of spirituality was unknown (2005: 46–7).

Heelas and Woodhead then made a longitudinal estimation. But because they lacked trustworthy figures for the holistic milieu, their method was unreliable. They used interviews as well as old brochures and telephone directories as their material (2005: 42–3). They concluded that, in 2001, five times more people were involved in the congregational domain than in the holistic milieu: in other words, the spiritual revolution had not yet taken place. They also concluded, however, that the holistic milieu was growing, whereas the congregational domain was in decline; if this trend continued, the holistic milieu would, in quantitative terms, surpass the congregational domain within 30 years. So, Heelas and Woodward maintain, there is a significant and visible change on the landscape of the sacred that in time may lead to the spiritual revolution (2005: 45). In addition, it is also apparent that the type of congregational organization which – despite being characterized by life-as – tends to be open and permissive to individual and subjective religious experience is more successful than congregations that do not encourage this form of religious expression (2005: 75).

David Voas and Steve Bruce (2007) are critical of Heelas and Woodhead's study. They contend, for example, that many of the activities Heelas and Woodhead include – such as yoga and massage – are not necessarily spiritual. They also criticize the study's selection criteria and methodology. For example, they argue that participants who answered the question about whether or not the activity had a spiritual dimension were not representative. In particular, though many of the activities can certainly be said to involve supernatural forces, most have relatively little to do with the 'sacred'. Voas and Bruce contend that much of what Heelas and Woodhead describe as spirituality ought instead to be described as pseudoscience (for instance, the belief that energy circulates in the body). They further assert that when Heelas and Woodhead describe spirituality in their questionnaire, it has, for the most part, nothing to do with either the supernatural or the sacred: instead, it seems to be a code-word for well-being. Eastern medicine, for example, may be holistic, but it need not be spiritual. For the most part, spirituality means love, being a good person, or living life to the full. Voas and Bruce thus contend that Heelas and Woodhead distanced the sacred from the concept of spirituality. Further, they contend that what is described is actually part of an ongoing secularization process, not the replacement of religion with spirituality. Furthermore, there is no indication that the holistic milieu will expand in the future, since it is mostly middle-aged or older women who are active within it (Voas and Bruce 2007: 46–57). Heelas responds to the criticism in an article where, in brief, he uses the same argument as Lars Ahlin (see below): beliefs associated with people who say they have a spiritual orientation show that they in fact do have a spiritual orientation; they believe, for example, in God (Heelas 2007: 65).

In another article, Steven Sutcliffe criticizes Heelas and Woodhead's study, presenting a number of points of contention. One of them is the lack of definition of the term spirituality; another is the question of how typical Kendal is on a national scale (Sutcliffe 2006: 307–9).

The way in which the Kendal study was conducted differs from ours in a number of ways. For example, there were, relatively speaking, many more producers in Kendal than in Dalarna, yet the number of consumers was almost equal. Either there are more producers in Kendal who tend to work part-time, or Dalarna has more group activities.

The Study in Austria

Inspired by the Kendal study, the Austrian study, headed by Professor of Sociology Franz Höllinger of the University of Graz, is the most similar to our own study in terms of structure and method. Like ours, the Austrian study is a relatively recent one, conducted in 2008–9, and is presented in the book *Ganzheitliches Leben: Das holistische Milieu zwischen neuer Spiritualität und postmoderner Wellness-Kultur* (Höllinger and Tripold 2012). The research group surveyed what they termed holistic producers in the town of Klagenfurt (92,000 inhabitants) and in the district of Leoben (64,000 inhabitants, including the district's main town of Leoben, population 25,000). The producers were located via the Internet as well as by snowball sampling. The key word in the Austrian study was 'holistic'. In cases where it was unclear whether the activity was holistic or not, the researchers looked for the use of terms such as spiritual, body-mind-spirit, universal life energy, energy flow, sources of inner power, awareness, and personal growth (2012: 105–7). The list of producers came to include 345 individuals, two-thirds of whom offered more than one holistic method (2012: 108). This is very close to the corresponding figure for Dalarna.

This means that Höllinger's group found 2.2 producers per 1,000 inhabitants, which is about 50 per cent more than in Dalarna. Of the 345 producers, 122 were interviewed by telephone. Out of these, 23 participated in a structured interview. Further, parts of a questionnaire that had been distributed to a representative segment of the Austrian population were distributed to 207 people active in the holistic milieu. A total of 13 of these were interviewed (Höllinger and Tripold 2012: 14–15). The Austrian study was, therefore, more extensive than ours and to a certain extent related to other sorts of questions.

In Austria, the researchers used similar categories to ours. One difference was that they placed kinesiology in its own category called Healing Techniques of Diverse Origin.[4]

---

4 Here they refer to the Taoist influence in terms of meridian and energy teachings in kinesiology (Höllinger and Tripold 2012: 109).

The proportions in each category are quite similar in both countries, though there are also differences (see table 3). In Austria, more holistic Western healing techniques are offered than are offered in Sweden if one includes kinesiology. However, kinesiology accounts for a great deal of the difference and seems to be significantly more common in Austria. In Sweden, there are more Eastern body-mind techniques and more producers who offer shamanic and spiritualistic techniques.

Table 3. Comparison of the number of different techniques in Klagenfurt/Leoben* and Dalarna (as percentages of total numbers)

	Klagenfurt/Leoben	Dalarna
Holistic Massage Techniques	22.7	21.0
Holistic Western Healing Methods	29.1	19.1
Eastern Body-Mind Techniques	11.2	17.2
Eastern Healing Methods	18.3	15.7
Holistic Psychotherapies	10.1	11.4
Mediums, Shamans, Spiritual Beings	3.0	9.6
Astrology, Divination	4.8	3.9
Clearance	3.2	1.9

*These figures are from Höllinger and Tripold 2012: 109.

Certain differences exist between the exact numbers of specific techniques in the two countries. On the one hand, there are methods that are not available in one of the countries – or that are at least very uncommon in one country and significantly more common in the other. Vedic Art is found in Dalarna, but not in Austria (which may not be so surprising, given its Swedish origins). In Dalarna, we did not come across *Klangschalenmassage*, a form of massage that is relatively popular in Austria (18 therapists in the study offer this). Reflexology is more common in Dalarna than it is in Austria (44 therapists offer it in Dalarna compared with 16 in Austria), whereas shiatsu is more common in Austria (26 therapists offer it in Austria compared with 12 in Dalarna). Acupressure is also less common in Austria than in Dalarna. One reason for Eastern body-mind techniques being significantly more common in Dalarna than in Austria is yoga, which is offered by 69 producers in Dalarna compared with only 30 in the Austrian study.

Under 'Holistic Western Healing Methods', most producers in Dalarna state that they offer 'healing' without being more specific (34 cases). In Austria, Bach Flower Therapy (26 cases) and homeopathy (25 compared with 12 in Dalarna) are most common. Among methods of holistic psychotherapy in Dalarna, coaching/ life-coaching/existential counselling tops the list (24 cases), followed by personal development (14) and stress therapy (10). Austria has, instead, Family Constellation Work[5] (10) and Neuro-Linguistic Programming (9), two methods that are all but non-existent in Dalarna. There is no mention of life-coaching in the Austrian study (Höllinger and Tripold 2012: 109).

In quantitative terms, the calculation is that 3.8 per cent of the population aged 20 to 65 are active once a week in the town of Klagenfurt, whereas the figure is 2.6 per cent in the district of Leoben, which is more rural (these figures are corrected for double participation) (Höllinger and Tripold 2012: 113).

The Enköping Study, Sweden

Another important study relevant to our project is the one conducted in Enköping in 2004 and presented in *Guds närmaste stad? En studie om religionernas betydelse i ett svenskt samhälle i början av 2000-talet* (Ahlstrand and Gunner [eds.] 2008). The aim of this study was to understand the significance of religion in a Swedish municipality in the early 2000s (Ahlstrand et al. 2008: 10). The Enköping study was also inspired by the Kendal study, though its focus was somewhat different and it did not claim to be a comprehensive inventory of the religious landscape. The municipality of Enköping has a population of just over 38,000. As in Kendal, a questionnaire was sent to randomly selected residents. Out of 1,956 people, 1,045 (53 per cent) responded. This questionnaire was then complemented with another one intended to examine the connection between religion, spirituality, and health: this was sent to 93 'health-promoting entrepreneurs', 52 of whom responded (Ahlstrand et al. 2008: 10). Based also on these questionnaires, a number of interviews were conducted.

Below, we will examine parts of the Enköping study we found relevant to our study. Of the 10 articles included in the Enköping study report, there are two we consider to be the most relevant:

5 Family Constellation is a form of therapy developed by the German psycho-therapist Bert Hellinger.

(1) Erika Willander's study of holistic or alternative spirituality and holistic healing treatments, and (2) Brian Palmer's study of spirituality in everyday life.

Erika Willander's study looked at people who run health-promotion businesses in Enköping with a focus on what they regard as spiritual and on how their view of spirituality accords with Heelas and Woodhead's subjective-life spirituality (Willander 2008: 242). Willander conducted a survey of alternative health businesses (including businesses built around tarot and astrology), since they seem to have a close connection with 'the personal life-experience spirituality' that she translates as subjective-life (2008: 244). However, Willander avoids defining the term *spiritual*, and her interpretation of Heelas and Woodhead's definition is problematic.

The Enköping study made use of the business register from Statistics Sweden (subheadings Alternative Medicine and Other Services; under Other Services, an assessment was made as to which businesses would be relevant for the study). The research group also used names of leaders of study circles listed under the heading Body and Soul. These data were then complemented by information from the local *Yellow Pages*, websites, and advertisements. Ahlstrand et al. found 89 businesses and four study circles, to each of which a questionnaire was sent. Fifty-two responses (56 per cent) were received (Willander 2008: 250–1). Holistic healing activities were defined as health-promoting activities conducted by practitioners other than academically-trained medical doctors. It was not presumed that everyone selected for the study regarded themselves as spiritual or had a New Age connection; rather, this was what would be investigated (2008: 276). The study focused on health; spiritual activities that had no connection with health were not examined (though tarot and astrology were included as the research team thought they were related to subjective-life spirituality, despite not being defined as alternative medicine). Five producers in the health branch were interviewed (2008: 250–2).

In Enköping, massage made up almost one-third of the health-promotion sector. A few producers offered other activities (one to three each), of which a number were in the area of exercise and bodybuilding (2008: 256–7). The number of producers was, however, too small for any more general conclusions to be drawn.

In their response to the questionnaire, just over 30 per cent of the health-promoting entrepreneurs stated that they regarded themselves as spiritual (Willander 2008: 267) and 70.2 per cent that their activities included spiritual aspects to a greater or lesser extent (mostly lesser). Willander writes that all of the activities that were felt to be spiritual in nature were to a high or very high extent based on some form of physical touch involving massage (this seemed to be the case with about eight responses). Since the body in traditional Christian spirituality plays a subordinate role (body and spirit even being regarded as opposites), Willander states that what is perceived as spiritual within the health industry may not necessarily be perceived as such by churches (2008: 270–2). Spirituality was also discussed with the five interviewees from the health branch. Willander discusses how the term was related to relaxation and recovery in the interviews (2008: 262–3) and believes that it is the relaxing effect of massage that is labelled spiritual (2008: 272). She therefore concludes that the interviewees' experiences of spirituality were associated with being 'relaxed and touched' (2008: 272–3).

In chapter 10, Brian Palmer describes the way in which 23 interviewees selected from general survey respondents perceive spirituality. His interpretation is that they perceive spirituality as involving a break from the stresses of life, a moment of escape from a world of constant stress, a chance to feel whole and alive, and to connect with something greater. Their stories often contain one or more of the following elements: a removed place (often in nature); detachment from time; a protected sphere in which one is free to be alone (with no expectations from others); passiveness and reception (no sense of responsibility). Palmer questions whether these should be considered spiritual or something else – for example, relaxation, rest, or entertainment. Further, he notes that if people value having time to themselves, this can have consequences for church service attendance since church services may be perceived to be something you have to find time for in a tight schedule (Palmer 2008: 278–90).

There are many differences between the ways in which the Enköping study and our Dalarna study were conducted. This makes it difficult to make comparisons at any level. Nevertheless, the Enköping study is interesting since its focus borders and at times overlaps with ours.

Religious Diversity in Århus, Denmark

As part of the project entitled *Det Danske Pluralismeprojekt* (which began at Århus University in 2001), a study was conducted in 2004 of the religious and spiritual market in the municipality of Århus, which at that time had a population of 290,000 (Fibiger 2004: 8). A description of all religious groups that had an address in Århus was published in the book *Religiøs mangfoldighet: En kortlægning af religion og spiritualitet i Århus* (Fibiger 2004). Those groups who did not want to be included were removed from the study: for example, mention is made of (esoteric) lodges that declined inclusion. The end result is a book in which some 75 different groups are described. These are divided into the following categories, mainly based on the major religions, which each has its own chapter in the book: Christianity (Den Danska folkkyrkan, Christian Free Churches, Religious Groups with Christian Foundations); Islam; Other Groups from the Middle East; Hinduism; Buddhism; New Spiritual and Religious Groups; and Alternative Treatment and Spirituality. Yoga comes under the chapter on Hinduism, where various yoga groups are described.[6] Under New Religious Groups, there are, for example, Anthroposophy, a Druid order, a witches' lodge, Martinus, Scientology, Theosophy, and Satanism.

In the final chapter, the relationship between the term spirituality and alternative treatment is discussed (Ahlin 2004). Lars Ahlin, author of this final chapter, builds on the results from his study published in *Krop, sind – eller ånd? Alternative behandlere og spiritualitet i Danmark* (2007). Ahlin, who has conducted studies in Sweden as well as Denmark, defines alternative treatments as those outside the established health system, stating that about 50 per cent of all Danes at some point in time have been recipients of them (2007: 7). The Danish research group had intended to investigate the New Age milieu, but chose instead to focus on alternative treatments, since they felt these were linked with New Age spirituality in a way that would make it difficult to demarcate the two. They sent a questionnaire to producers of alternative treatments. Their intention was to investigate the producers' position on spirituality as well as to find out what significance producers attributed to their practices. The

---

6 Yoga is included in a list of alternative practices just before the chapter about alternative therapists; however, it is not mentioned directly in this chapter, nor is there any discussion as to the kind of activities chosen in the survey.

idea was that alternative treatments might be perceived as channels for the spreading of spirituality to what amounted to a significant proportion of the population. The research group assumed it would be difficult to determine the level of spirituality simply from the producers' advertisements, as certain types of activities, such as astrology, past-life regression, and clairvoyance, according to Ahlin, have an explicit relation to the spiritual, whereas other techniques, such as massage, acupuncture, and reflexology, can, but need not, be spiritually related (2007: 10–11).

A questionnaire was sent to the 385 producers who had been located by way of publicly accessible sources such as websites, telephone directories, and newspaper advertisements (Ahlin 2007: 14). The aim of the questionnaire was to study whether religiosity and spirituality played any part whatsoever in the treatments they offered. Responses were received from 170 producers (44 per cent). The most popular methods were, in the following order: reflexology, healing, massage, Craniosacral Therapy, and acupuncture/ acupressure (Ahlin 2004: 477). Almost a third of producers stated that they offered only one technique, whereas the others each offered, on average, three (Ahlin 2007: 31). Responses indicated that these alternative treatment producers viewed themselves as being broadly religious or spiritual. For one question, where respondents had the option of ticking more than one descriptor for themselves, answers were as follows (the first figure being the percentage of alternative producers who ticked that option, the second being the percentage of respondents from the general Swedish population):

Christian	65/40
Religious	50/15
Spiritual Seeker	68/21
Has Attained Spiritual Clarity	47/not an option
No To All Of These	4/47

Ahlin notes that a great many producers ticked several options. This, he states, may indicate that they did not fully identify with any one of the descriptors. Some 20 per cent ticked all options, while another 20 per cent ticked all but one. Respondents seemed not to see any great contradiction in being Christian/religious and being spiritual (Ahlin 2007: 66–7). In addition, beliefs were noted that at times are associated with New Age: for example, 43 per cent of producers believed in reincarnation compared with 9 per cent of Danes in general (2007: 71); many more of the producers believed that our astrological signs influence our lives, and that the dead can communicate with the living (2007: 73). They also had many more spiritual experiences than the general Danish public (2007: 86). In terms of treatments, about 20 per cent of Danes felt that spirituality was extremely significant; 20 per cent that it was very significant; 26 per cent that it was somewhat significant; 20 per cent that it was barely significant; and 15 per cent that it was not significant. Thirty-five per cent of the producers believed that spirituality was an indispensable part of their treatment, while another 23 per cent believed that it was very significant for their treatment (2007: 89–90).

Ahlin writes that the term 'spirituality' was not defined; rather, respondents were allowed to use their own understanding of the term. He notes, however, that we can indirectly obtain a picture of what the producers felt to be spiritual by dividing them into three groups based on how important they felt spirituality to be in the treatment(s) they offered and by studying which beliefs and forms of expression were the most and least common in each group. The result was that the producers Ahlin characterized as being spiritual to a much greater extent felt that one answer about belief in a god was insufficient; they believed in a higher power or energy and an omnipresent god (though the non-spiritual were overrepresented when it came to seeing God within the human being); believed themselves to know what happens after death; believed in reincarnation; believed that our astrological signs determine our personalities; believed that there are paranormal phenomena; used terms such as channelling, chakra, aura, and karma; and believed that energy is important for treatments (even about one-third of those who were non-spiritual stated that energy has meaning for treatments, despite not attaching any importance to spirituality; so energy can clearly have both spiritual and non-spiritual purport) (2007: 91–103).

The Danish study differs greatly in structure and organization from ours, so it is difficult to make any direct comparisons.

What, If Anything, Is Special about Dalarna?

The four studies referred to above were conducted in different ways, had different aims, and were presented with different challenges. Combined, these naturally affected the final results. (Some of the challenges related to the definition and use of terms, as discussed in the subsections below.) Many studies focus, for example, on holistic or alternative therapies and health promoters outside the conventional health sector. A decisive difference between the studies is whether any attempt was made prior to the study to determine which of these had religious dimensions and which did not. Our study is directly comparable to the Austrian study, as it was conducted in a similar way; and partly comparable to the British study, even though the selection criteria differed.

Quantitatively, the Austrian study – the approach of which was very similar to that of ours – indicated that there were almost 40 per cent more producers per 1,000 inhabitants compared with Dalarna (2.2 compared with 1.6 in Dalarna). In Kendal, 2.6 producers were found per 1,000 inhabitants; here, however, only those who considered their activities to be spiritual and to relate to subjective-life were counted. One reason for the differences might be the emphasis on yoga in Dalarna. Yoga is practised in groups, and the number of producers relative to consumers is therefore smaller than when producers interact with one client at a time. In Århus, 1.3 producers per 1,000 inhabitants were found; there, however, only holistic therapists were included. The selection criteria in the Danish study are unclear. Yoga appears to have been included with the Hindu groups, and movements such as Anthroposophy and Martinus with new religions. The aim of the portion of the Danish study on which we focused in the above discussion was to study holistic producers outside the established health sector and their relation to spirituality. It is possible that classic massage, for example, was included; however, this remains unclear from the information. In Enköping, this was clearly the case, as the focus was on health-promoting businesses; yet here yoga is included, as well as astrology and the tarot. In Enköping, 2.5 health businesses were found per 1,000 inhabitants.

Only the Austrian and British studies calculated weekly participant numbers in the same manner as we did. Both the rural district in Austria and Kendal showed the same percentage as Dalarna, whereas the town Klagenfurt showed a significantly higher percentage. If we follow the Austrian practice of calculating in terms of population aged between 20 and 65 (about 60 per cent) and the Kendal practice of removing 30 per cent for double participation, the result is that 2.6 to 2.7 per cent of the adult population in

Dalarna, Kendal, and Leoben are involved in holistic activities each week, whereas the percentage for the town of Klagenfurt is 3.8.

Therefore, Austria's higher figures can be explained by the fact that a large town (Klagenfurt, 96,000 inhabitants) is included. It is evident from the data that Klagenfurt has significantly more producers and consumers in relation to the population than the rural district. This holds true for Dalarna as well, where there are two urban centres: Borlänge and Falun (though both are considerably smaller than Klagenfurt, with populations of 49,000 and 56,000 respectively), where the number of producers per inhabitant is higher than in the rural areas. In Dalarna, we also surveyed the more organized religious groups. Compared with Århus, which has a similar population size to Dalarna but only one large town, Dalarna has significantly fewer religious groups. For example, the Church of Scientology, Hare Krishna, Wicca, Theosophy, and Satanism all had an organized presence in Århus, but not in Dalarna.

It could be argued that lower numbers of producers and consumers in the popular religious milieu in Dalarna compared with Austria and Great Britain are to be expected. First, Sweden is situated on the fringes of Europe and somewhat on the periphery of global trends (especially true of Dalarna, a rural county); second, its position in terms of most religious indicators in the World Values Survey is lower than that of Austria and Great Britain. In addition, Sweden is generally thought of as being a much more secularized country.[7] Nevertheless, the low figures for Christian activity do not appear to correlate with low figures for the popular religious milieu, even if the interest in certain types of content can be affected by the low level of religiosity (see below).

Certain local differences become apparent when we look at the level of various kinds of holistic activity found in the individual studies. Once again, the Austrian study is most comparable to our study. Dalarna features more yoga, coaching, personal development, and spiritualism, whereas Austria features more Western healing techniques. Cultural differences might be a significant factor here. Austria has historically had a stronger tradition of esotericism than Sweden, and this may still be an influential factor. The wider interest in spiritualism in Sweden likely correlates with popular television

7 Among the indicators were belief in God, belief in life after death, and attendance at church services (http://www.worldvaluessurvey.orgwvs.jsp).

shows in recent years that deal with spiritualistic issues. There are no corresponding programmes on Austrian television. Yoga, which is more common in Sweden, is an activity that can readily be interpreted as purely secular for those so inclined, just as is the case with coaching and personal development, which may explain the higher figures. Apart from this, local differences may simply be the result of chance – that is to say, they could be a function of the producers who have chosen to establish themselves in the area.

How representative is Dalarna in the context of Sweden? Can we draw general conclusions for Sweden from our Dalarna results? As previously mentioned, Dalarna is a mostly rural county. We would most likely have found more producers, techniques, religious groups, and consumers in larger cities like Stockholm, Gothenburg, and Malmö. Nevertheless, what is interesting is that we found the popular religious milieu active in Dalarna too. This leads us to believe that the popular religious milieu is also very much active in other rural areas throughout Sweden. As such, our project allows us to draw the general conclusion that the popular religious milieu does not exist solely in large urban centres, but is most likely alive at the grassroots level in all of Sweden.

Nevertheless, there are factors that point to a possible overrepresentation of the popular religious milieu in Dalarna compared with the rest of Sweden. Dalarna is one of the country's key tourist and cultural centres. Its natural surroundings, along with the preservation of much of its old folk culture, have made it attractive for recreation and tourism ever since the 1800s (Rosander 1994: 70). This is particularly evident from the seven retreat centres related to the popular religious milieu that are based in Dalarna and that attract participants from all over Sweden. The close proximity to Stockholm (about three hours by train) also means Dalarna is well-placed as a holiday destination and as a location for retreats. During our interviews, we met many producers who had relocated to Dalarna from other parts of Sweden and who, for various reasons, felt Dalarna to be an attractive place both to live and to work. One important reason for their establishing themselves in Dalarna was the cost of living, which is much lower compared with, for example, the Stockholm area. A number of them were returning to Dalarna after having lived and worked elsewhere: they had family connections in the county and had decided to return at this later stage in their lives. In addition, when there is an area where large

numbers of people live who have an interest in popular religiosity
– for example, in the area around the retreat centre in Stjärnsund,
which is also close to Annaskolan – it becomes more attractive for
others with similar interests to move there.

The image of Dalarna as special has thus most likely influenced
the establishment of a number of activities in the county. We
continue this discussion in chapter 8, in which we examine Dalarna
from both a local and a global perspective.

Terms Used: A Discussion

The differences between the studies referred to here clearly
demonstrate the problems involved with selection, definitions, and
delimitations regarding the popular religious milieu as discussed in
this book. All of the studies are interested in examining phenomena
that can be perceived as religious. However, different methods
were chosen to determine what should be understood as religious
phenomena, and which religious phenomena should be included in
the study in question.

The Term Spirituality

Some studies – Kendal, Enköping, Århus – chose to focus on the term
spiritual and examined the extent to which the producers questioned
would term themselves spiritual or regard their activities as having
a spiritual dimension. It is interesting to note that not one of the
studies initially defines what is meant by 'spiritual'; rather, they all
rely upon the respondents' own understanding of the term. Nor do
Voas and Bruce, in their criticism of Heelas and Woodhead's study,
define what they mean by spirituality, although it is apparent that
they consider spirituality to involve supernatural powers and
furthermore to relate to 'the sacred' – a term that again they neither
define nor discuss.

In Enköping, the research group followed up their questionnaire with five interviews, in which they asked interviewees how
they might define 'spiritual'. The answers given can be assessed as
unclear, unfocused, and difficult to interpret. Willander's interpretation is that spirituality is understood by many to be something
involving relaxation and the sense of being physically touched. She
questions whether spirituality in the health sector is really the same
as spirituality in the context of organized religion. Palmer too, in the

same book, discusses how spirituality is regarded by the average individual as a 'break from the stresses of life', and wonders whether spirituality is the appropriate term for this. Although the evaluation that spirituality is an ambiguous term may be correct,[8] we would like to question Willander's interpretation of the interviewees' responses. Just because an individual experiences something he or she may label spiritual at times of relaxation does not necessarily mean that spirituality and relaxation are *one and the same*.

According to the Enköping study, about three of every 10 health entrepreneurs regard themselves as spiritual, and about seven of every 10 believe their methods to be spiritual in some degree (most said a low degree). Here the results are really worth pondering. What does the respondent mean when he or she answers that a method is spiritual 'to a low degree'?

From the Danish questionnaire, we can conclude that holistic producers regard themselves as being both religious and spiritual to a much higher degree than do others. Furthermore, they ticked a great many more options regarding the question about religious or spiritual self-identity than did others: one-fifth ticked all alternatives and another fifth all but one. Ahlin's observation that this may indicate that the answers did not quite fit their views is well worth noting.

In other studies, too, it is clear that there are a number of overlaps between self-definitions of spiritual and religious identities. A Swedish Internet-based study from 2008, in which the respondent had to choose only one answer, is presented in table 4.

Table 4. Self-Identification as Religious/Spiritual (percentages)*

	Everyone	Men	Women
I see myself as being religious	5.6	5	6
I see myself as being spiritual	21.5	16	27
I see myself as being both religious and spiritual	10.9	11	11
I see myself as being neither religious nor spiritual	62	69	55

*This questionnaire was financed by the newspaper *Dagen*. There were 927 respondents, who constituted a representative sample of the population of Sweden. They were selected from a pool of about 200,000 people who had expressed a willingness to take part in online questionnaire studies.

8 Ahlin writes that the term *spirituality* has always been used in Christian contexts, but that it has become more widespread over the last two decades and, as such, has changed in meaning so that often it is not understood as profound

The researchers who conducted the Enköping study gave a question to a representative sample of Enköping residents in which respondents could indicate the degree to which they considered themselves believers, spiritual, religious, seekers, or doubters. From the answers, the researchers were able to conclude that many indicated they were more than one of these to some degree, even though the most frequent response was 'not at all'. Based on this study, Bromander concludes that a larger proportion of people in Enköping would call themselves Christian (to a greater or lesser extent) than those who would call themselves religious or spiritual (2008: 70–1).[9] By means of statistical analysis of the questionnaire responses, Bromander also demonstrates that the terms *believers*, *spiritual*, and *religious* belonged together, whereas *seekers* and *doubters* belonged together (the same individuals tending to identify with more than one term within each group). From this, Bromander concludes that people in Enköping equate being religious with being spiritual (2008: 71). With our study in mind, however, we find this conclusion to be overly categorical. The Internet study above further demonstrates that overlaps exist between the terms, which is sufficient to argue that in one way they do belong together; however, there are other indicators which demonstrate that for many individuals, they have different significances (we develop this point below).

In his questionnaire for producers in Århus, Ahlin does not ask respondents how they would define spirituality; however, he maintains that a picture is formed of what spirituality means to producers when we examine the most common beliefs and expressions related to those who thought spirituality important in

---

religiosity but rather as the opposite of religion (Ahlin 2007: 12). Spirituality has been discussed in the twenty-first century by many scholars of religion. Spirituality is generally understood to be a more personal and individual concept than religion (King 2001: 4–9, Roof et al. 1995: 247–2, Barker 2004, Hanegraaff 2005), being more about the individual than the divine (King 2001: 5–9, Barker 2004), syncretistic and pluralistic (Roof et al. 1995: 247–52, Barker 2004), anti-hierarchical (Roof et al. 1995: 247–52, Barker 2004), and this-worldly (Barker 2004). Robert Orsi notes that in the growing discourse on spirituality, the term is coming to represent the opposite of 'bad religion' (Orsi 2004: 188).

9 Naturally, the question is whether the relatively high figures shown for 'Christian' (16.9 per cent completely, 11.2 per cent to a great extent, 31.2 per cent somewhat) were influenced by context: the alternatives (which could also be ticked off according to a scale) were Muslim, Jew, Buddhist, Hindu, and atheist.

their treatments. He presents a pattern demonstrating that certain beliefs are more common among these producers: for example, a belief in reincarnation and in paranormal phenomena; and a belief in a god or a higher power or energy. The question remains, however, whether this does in fact *mean* spirituality to the interviewee or whether there is just some sort of a link.

Spirituality is a key term for Heelas and Woodhead. They also use the term *sacred* – as do Voas and Bruce, without any definition or discussion – and describe the 'sacred landscape' as comprising two parts: the religious or congregational; and the spiritual or holistic. Religion sacralizes life-as, a transcendent authority to which the individual must conform, whereas spirituality sacralizes subjective-life, the inner unique authority. Heelas and Woodhead also find that holistic producers who consider their work to be to a large extent spiritual express a certain type of belief – for example, belief in God as a life force. However, they did not ask producers what they thought the term *spiritual* meant.

Two smaller studies that were part of the larger 'Meditating Dala Horse' project provide us with further information about what is understood to be spirituality in Dalarna.[10] One of these consisted of 10 interviews with various religious actors in Dalarna: among other questions, interviewees were asked about their definition of the terms *spirituality* and *religion*; the way these two relate to each other; and the way in which they felt spirituality was expressed in everyday life.[11] The second study consisted of a questionnaire that was distributed to one of the groups surveyed, a yoga group (evening class) with 18 participants. They were asked if they perceived themselves as being religious and/or spiritual; in addition, there

---

10 These studies are discussed in detail in the article 'Spirituality and Everyday Life in Sweden' (Frisk 2012c). There was also an eleventh interview with a pastor of a free church in the town of Rättvik: this interview was included in the article but not in this book.

11 One interview was a group interview with four women who had taken part in a channelling workshop, while the other nine interviews were individual. One interviewee was a Church of Sweden priest; the other eight interviewees were active in the popular religious milieu: two members of a UFO association; one a healer; one a yoga instructor; one a yoga instructor, coach, and trance-medium; one a member in the St Germain Foundation; one a shaman and witch; and one a trance-medium. An interesting fact is that three of these individuals were also actively engaged in the Church of Sweden. The interviewees were not chosen because they represented any particular activity; rather, they were random case studies.

were open-ended questions about their definitions of the terms *spirituality* and *religion* and about the differences and similarities between the two. The questionnaire demonstrated that significantly more participants in the yoga group perceived themselves as being spiritual than those in a representative random sample of Swedes, and that significantly fewer perceived themselves as being neither religious nor spiritual. Of the 18 individuals, nine regarded themselves as spiritual, four as both religious and spiritual, one as religious, and three as neither religious nor spiritual.

The interview material revealed that the term *spirituality* can be used in many ways. Most respondents seemed to understand spirituality and religion as somewhat overlapping, whereas the overriding understanding in the yoga group was that religion and spirituality are opposites. The Church of Sweden priest was (unsurprisingly) more positive towards religion than most other respondents, stressing that religion and spirituality complement each other. He stated that spirituality relates to personal inner experience, whereas religion means the structured, contemplated, and discussed experience of God. The spiritual experience is thus primary and religion secondary. Yet both are, according to the priest, essential. He further stated that church services are a natural arena for the primary spiritual experience.

Several other interviewees felt that spirituality can manifest itself in a religious context and that the essence of religion is constructive and spirituality-based. Nevertheless, many spoke about religion in primarily negative terms. Some said that religion can lead to war, that it puts God into a box, that it has a strange and complicated organization, and that it represents power struggles, laws, rules, and hierarchies. Others stated that religion had once been good but that its development over time had been negative. In the yoga group, there were many answers that, apart from relating religion to judgemental attitudes, power struggles, and rigid rules, also related it to groups and doctrines. Two interviewees, and almost all respondents from the yoga group, talked about religion as contrasting with spirituality. One respondent said, for example, that religion means bowing to something beyond oneself, whereas spirituality means seeing the divine within oneself. Another respondent felt that religion is based on fear, whereas spirituality is based on love. Two (female) respondents from the yoga group stated that religion is an expression of male authority. In total, 13 respondents from the yoga group answered the open-ended question about the similarities and differences between religion and spirituality. Only one of these provided an example of a similarity: all of the others described only differences. One of the interviewees talked about spirituality as a continuation of religion for the person who is looking for spiritual growth. He compared religion to primary school and spirituality to university – in this way indirectly indicating the inferior position of religion relative to spirituality.

Spirituality was defined in both groups as follows: inner experience (emphasized by many); something especially personal and individual; the divine within the human being; contact with one's own essence or higher self; and intuition. Yoga practitioners in particular were particularly clear about spirituality being something extremely personal for each individual.

There were many answers to the question about how spirituality is expressed in everyday life. Some from the interview group – in which there were several people active in the popular religious milieu as well as within the Church – stated that spirituality can be expressed in the Church. This sort of answer was absent from the yoga group. Many respondents from the yoga group wrote that spirituality is expressed through yoga, meditation, and healing. Individuals in both groups felt that spirituality can be expressed through a state of presence; through being in touch with one's higher self or listening to one's heart; by way of creative activities such as music and art; or by being alone with nature. In both groups, several people responded that spirituality can be expressed through helping others, by seeing the equal value of others and acting accordingly, and by meeting others with empathy and love. Thus, there also seemed to be ethical aspects to their perceptions of spirituality. In the interview group, there were also some respondents who felt that taking a hot bath or stroking their cat was a spiritual act – that is to say, activities that are generally perceived as being secular or at least this-worldly. Yet this does not indicate that a hot bath or stroking a cat would *always* be perceived as a spiritual act. Spirituality here also seems to be linked to some sort of inner attitude or special experience.

In sum, spirituality seems to have quite different meanings for different individuals. Yet a number of answers appear frequently, especially those that associate spirituality with an inner, personal experience. The relation between spirituality and religion is also perceived in different ways. Quite often, spirituality is constructed in contrast to religion, where spirituality represents positive aspects and religion negative aspects. There is a sense that spirituality can be expressed in different ways, partly in such activities as yoga, meditation, healing, prayer, and church services, but also in quite simply 'being' or 'listening to one's heart', as well as in completely worldly activities such as being in natural surroundings, taking a walk, or bathing. As such, spirituality seems to have the potential to embrace many different aspects of human existence, especially those related to identity, focus, attitude, experience, feelings, and ethics (Frisk 2012c).

Criticism of the Term Spirituality

We made an interesting observation over the course of our Dalarna study: seldom did our interviewees spontaneously choose to use the terms *spiritual* or *religious*.[12] When we questioned our 10 interviewees about their understanding of the term *spiritual*, we often had to begin by first asking whether they used the term at all, since they had not done so up to that point in the interview. We often received undecided answers along the lines of, Yes, I do at times/ on occasion/not often. On the other hand, interviewees recognized the term *spirituality* passively, and were able to relate to it when they heard it used. This is reminiscent of a similar situation when one of us in the years 1994 and 1995 conducted two different studies of what at that time was described as New Age. One of the studies involved a questionnaire that included a question about belief in God: 97 per cent responded that they believed in God (Frisk 2000; 64). The second study examined the terms that were used in this milieu, and found that the term *God* was seldom used (Frisk 1998: 168–70). *God*, in other words, was a term that was recognized at a passive level and related to when heard, but was not a term used or talked about spontaneously. Just as with the term *God*, the term *spirituality* is part of the Western and Christian construction of the concept of religion, and is perhaps not the best to use – with

---

12 Interestingly, Höllinger and Tripold make the same observation. They note that some of their interviewees do not use the terms *religiosity* or *spirituality*, talking instead about, for example, energy work, awareness training, or personal growth. Yet when asked directly, they replied that they regarded themselves as being spiritual (2012: 272).

the empirical data from Dalarna in mind – as a primary means of understanding such milieus.[13]

A further reflection is that the term *spirituality* may be even more difficult to use in Sweden than in other countries. First, the term *spiritual* (*andlig*) in Swedish is to a certain extent associated with Christianity, which can have negative connotations for some people. In Norwegian and Danish, the term 'spirituell' is used instead, and this has a slightly different nuance. This term cannot be used in Swedish since it has another meaning (even if it should be noted that the standard definition – that of being quick-witted, funny, or entertaining – of the word is changing due to Anglicization). The second reason is that Sweden is one of the most secularized countries in Europe. Based on our empirical data from Dalarna, one of our conclusions is that many people do not seem to divide their existence according to terms such as religious-secular, spiritual-secular, or sacred-profane. The use of such terms is inherited from a traditionally Christian understanding of existence that is becoming increasingly dated.

This line of analysis also accords well with an understanding of religion as being part of a cultural construction that really cannot be differentiated from other cultural phenomena in any definitive or meaningful way. Based on our interviews in Dalarna, we would maintain that there are many people who do not (spontaneously) use either the term *spiritual* or the term *religious*. Nor do they in their inner understanding distinguish between life spheres as being *religious* or *secular* in ways that conform to external constructions. Instead, they talk in terms of a life orientation that involves 'being more true to oneself', 'learning to listen to one's inner voice', and 'finding harmony and balance', or of there being a plan and purpose for every individual:

> the internal ability we all have to control our own lives, to guide our own lives. But also to accept and forgive everything that happens, things that we cannot change. Accept, not like, but accept [...] to feel safe in our understanding that we all have a plan [...] That the plan is there and if we simply trust ourselves to let life happen, it will be as is intended and it will come out right (respondent 7).

13 For a description of the increasingly strong dualism between religious and secular spheres within Christianity, see, for example, Knott 2005: 64–5.

The *Expression* New Age

Just as the term *spiritual* is used to separate phenomena with some kind of religious significance from secular phenomena within holistic therapies, the term *New Age* is sometimes used to identify tendencies within the popular religious milieu with relatively low levels of engagement central to the studies discussed above. Lars Ahlin, for example, views New Age as a phenomenon in late modernity that comprises a new type of spirituality, which cannot be placed in a conventional list of organized religious formations. The reason producers of alternative treatments were included in the Danish study was the supposition that overlaps existed between these and New Age practices (Ahlin 2007: 125). Heelas and Woodhead opine that New Age is the former term for holistic spirituality (2005: x).

Opinion is divided as to how New Age orientations should be defined and classified. New Age has been categorized as 'religion' (Hanegraaff 2005), 'a religion' (Hammer 1997), 'a movement' (Heelas 1996), and 'many movements' (York 2005). Some have compared New Age to a buffet from which everybody can choose (Frisk 1997). Yet what is on the buffet table – what is New Age or what is not – remains the question. A number of researchers maintain that there is a certain coherence in terms of beliefs and structures in the New Age milieu which legitimizes using a common term for them (see Hanegraaff 1996: 514). Others focus on certain orientations that they believe characterize New Age tendencies. Suggestions for the latter have been healing (Frisk 1997; York 2005: 29), self-spirituality (Heelas 1996), or the literal meaning of the term: a new age (Melton 1988: 35–6). Regardless of how the term is defined, it gives rise to further discussion and further challenges.

Criticism of *the Expression* New Age

The term *New Age* has been criticized for a number of different reasons, among them that its meaning – a new age characterized by peace and harmony – is but one ideological element out of many. Furthermore, in more recent decades, the expectation of a coming new age has diminished in importance in comparison with other, more individualized elements. Despite the public attention given to the Maya calendar and the year 2012,[14] there were surprisingly

14 For a detailed description of the Mayan calendar and beliefs about the year 2012, see Restall and Solari 2011.

few interviewees who emphasized or even demonstrated interest in such millenarian expectations in our empirical material from Dalarna. In addition, the expression *New Age* has taken on pejorative connotations from which many people involved in the activities associated with the term want to distance themselves.[15] New Age has thus become an etic concept, infrequently used by practitioners. It is perceived as being rather outlandish and thus something with which people do not want to be associated. Throughout the project, it was clear that the term was not at all useful in our attempts to make contacts – which was reason enough to use it with great care.

Critique of the expression *New Age* has accelerated in recent times. Many researchers question whether New Age is a real, identifiable phenomenon, and maintain that it is nothing more than a construction created by researchers and the media (York 2005: 17). Steven Sutcliffe criticizes the term *New Age* as essentialist and far too homogenized. He maintains that it is impossible to distinguish a specific New Age movement. Instead, he is interested in focusing on how the concept is and has been used by different groups (Sutcliffe 2006: 295–6). He also wants to redirect the focus 'from substantive attributes to functional acts' (2006: 299).

The Expression Holistic Milieu

Heelas and Woodhead (2005) as well as Heelas (2008) use the expression *holistic milieu*. The term is neither demarcated nor defined precisely, but is used to distinguish between two different approaches and religious milieus. Heelas and Woodhead divide the activities they judge to be concerned with the 'sacred' into two categories: the congregational domain, which is more visible, and the holistic milieu, which is less visible. Heelas builds on this, stating that the holistic milieu has a specific focus on uniting the different parts of the human being – mind, body, and soul – into a whole (2008: 34). Many of our interviewees stressed a life orientation towards holistic understanding, in which the body and mind are perceived as integral parts of the human being in both outer and inner life, with family and career, yet still allow for a space to pause and experience serenity. Heelas further stresses the significance of healing in the holistic milieu (2008: 34).

---

15 This can also partly be the case with the term *religion* and possibly also *spirituality*.

The expression *holistic milieu* might be useful, since it focuses on a number of important themes in the contemporary popular religious milieu. A further point is that it avoids the dichotomy between the religious and the secular that we criticize above. Yet as a means of demarcation, the term is questionable, as the themes associated with it are important even in some parts of the congregational domain. One advantage of the expression is, however, that it might be familiar to the practitioners themselves.

Other Terms

A further term that in recent times has been used to demarcate a certain field in the contemporary milieu is *Western Esotericism* (Bogdan 2007, Stuckrad 2005). We would, however, maintain that Western Esotericism should be seen as a historical ideological current with specific features. Western Esotericism has influenced the contemporary milieu, yet it is far from being the only or even a dominating ideological trend, so there is no point using it in this context (see Frisk 2013).[16] Sutcliffe criticizes the terms *esoteric*, *occult*, and even *new* because he maintains that these exoticize a form of religious expression that is in actual fact quite ordinary and everyday in post-Protestant cultures. He sees this field not as marginal but rather as central to religious expression, stating that its marginalization can be compared with, for example, the marginalization of men's religion in gender studies (2006: 301–2).

Torunn Selberg, a Professor of Cultural Studies, distinguishes between the terms *folklore* and *new religiosity*, but groups both under the umbrella term 'folk religion'. By this she means that it is a departure from hegemonic religion and above all – as with Burke and the popular culture we discussed in chapter 1 – that folk culture has no definitive content; rather, it is relational, a product of a game about cultural hegemony. Folk religion means religious expressions that throughout time have deviated from the hegemonic view of what is considered 'right' religion. Selberg associates folklore with the past and new religiosity with the present (2011: 10). Her terms could be useful, but in this book we have chosen to avoid *new religiosity*, since the word *new* is simply too problematic: many elements in the domain we are studying have a long history and

16 Yet the term *Western Esotericism* has an important function in the right place: that is to say, to demarcate a specific tradition of ideas.

are thus not especially new. Further, we found the term 'popular religion' more applicable than folk religion or folklore, since – while the links to traditional folklore certainly might be featured – as a rule, they are vague and infrequent.

Discussion

We have questioned a number of common terms used for the milieu examined in our study. A number of them are products of a Western and Christian construction of the concept of religion that are not completely applicable in this domain; their use may therefore solidify and clarify evaluative interpretations of reality based on Western cultural or religious (for example Christian) preconceptions. Also, we have noted that terms such as *spiritual* and *sacred* are used uncritically by some religious scholars with little or no discussion as to potential problems and ambiguities. Distinctions and terms that were established in the Christian tradition have today lost any meaningful function in contexts outside Christianity. Furthermore, many terms focus on certain types of content which can also characterize other milieus. Yet another issue is the ongoing changes taking place within milieus. With all this in mind, we prefer, where an umbrella term is required, to use the term *popular religiosity* in a relational way in accordance with Steven Sutcliffe. Nevertheless, we would still advocate testing many different terms in an experimental and multidimensional way. The construction, definition, and classification of terms are constructive and legitimate working methods that are required for understanding and interpreting reality, and that can be applied depending on one's purpose and context.

One of our conclusions is that the boundaries between what were once regarded as different kinds of religious milieus are becoming less evident. Perhaps there is no longer much purpose in trying to distinguish between these terms or in trying to determine their level of religiosity. A first step for the future could be instead to conduct transboundary and more thematically-based research. Themes such as healing, holism, inner potential, divination, charisma, and relation to ancestors could be used without needing either to utilize the notion of religion or to construct religious milieus.

Chapter 5

Contemporary Religious Arenas: Spaces for Retreat, Health, and Coaching

In this chapter, we shall examine more closely the physical places and locations where the phenomena of contemporary religious expression occur. In chapter 1, we made reference to Jonathan Z. Smith's spatial categories for religious expression: religion *here* (domestic religion in homes and at burial sites), religion *there* (civic religion and state religion, as practised in temple-like buildings), and religion *anywhere*, which includes the forms of religious expression that are the focus of our study. This form of religiosity is expressed in places outside the home and church, and it is to these contemporary religious arenas that we now turn.

The term *space* or *place* can incorporate a number of dimensions. The British Professor of Religious Studies Kim Knott wrote a book about the localization of religion in the secularized Western world which talks about space as being physical, mental (conceived), and social (2005: 127). Physical places are purely geographic; however, when significance and meaning are added, they also become mental or imagined places (Massey and Jess 1995a: 2–3), or social constructions of place (Huigen and Meijering 2005: 21). The *identity* of a place is constructed by people (Knott 2005: 127–8). Social spaces arise from relations between people – social networks that relate to the physical places where they occur. Closely related to both imagined place and social space is our contemporary virtual space. Websites create and convey conceptions and expectations about places, and Facebook groups associated with different religious groups or places serve as virtual dimensions of social space.

Here we will focus on three types of institutions, each common in Dalarna, which feature activities with varying degrees of religious elements: retreat centres, health and coaching institutes, and health fairs. Health institutes in particular exist in many forms. We will also examine virtual places or websites, these being windows used for informational and promotional purposes – a clear aspect of imagined and constructed places.

Retreat centres, health fairs, and health institutes of various kinds are central to the popular religious milieus on which this book focuses. It is here that the most dedicated teachers, healers, and instructors can be found – those we call producers. Here we find purely spatial locations that have been created for specific forms of practice and experience. In particular, retreat centres are central places where the individual can gain inspiration for his or her personal world view, form networks, and find social support for his or her practice and identity. People today employ many cultural resources, including religious resources afforded them by official religion and tradition, which they selectively draw on, change, and share (McGuire 2008: 66). In particular, retreat centres – though also health establishments and health fairs – may be regarded as central resources for forming world views and identities. People construct their religious worlds in the process of interaction with others. An individual's religion derives from shared views and experiences, learned practices, borrowed images, and shared insights (McGuire 2008: 12–13). All new religious arenas – retreat centres, health and coaching institutes, health fairs – form central places where this can happen.

In contrast to churches and chapels, which are built in forms that make them recognizable as sacred places, most buildings where religion *anywhere* is practised are secular, at least from their exterior appearance. Normally, there is nothing to distinguish them from other buildings, yet certain exceptions do exist. The architecture of a number of buildings belonging to Foundation Berget outside Rättvik is, for example, reminiscent of that of a convent. The main building is austere with straight lines, white walls, and large windows. At the bottom of the building are sleeping quarters for participants that somewhat resemble sleeping quarters in a monastery. The small inner courtyard creates a meditative mood, with plants and the rippling water from a small pond. However, there are also buildings that are more traditional in design. The location is close to the forest and nature, which provides a sense of tranquillity and seclusion.

It is mainly inside the buildings that we find features of creative design and symbols that designate the places' significance for specific activities and experiences. However, it is foremost the activities in these places that transform them into something more than simple everyday venues for secular activity (Knott 2005: 61). What follows here is a closer look at some such places in Dalarna.

Retreat Centres

In our survey in 2008–11, we found seven retreat centres in Dalarna[1] that offer activities which to some extent are related to the popular religious milieu. The level of activity at each centre varied. Some held a few courses during the summer; others held courses year-round. Most had limited space (no more than 20 to 30 people at any given time). A couple of the centres had been more active in previous years but now offered fewer courses. In addition to representatives from these seven centres, we interviewed at least three people who were (separately) planning to open retreat centres in Dalarna; however, at the time of writing (March 2012), no information could be found on the Internet about any new retreat centre in the county. Their plans, it would seem, had not been realized.

It must be made clear from the outset that the seven retreat centres specialized in very different areas. Three of them – Baravara, Uniomystica, and Oshofors – have ties to the Osho movement.[2] The level of connection, however, varied, and some of the retreat centres also found varying degrees of inspiration in other sources. One of the other four retreat centres, Solsökehem, is mainly oriented towards Martinus[3] and the Alexander Technique,[4]

1 The retreat centre Baravara, Vikarbyn (www.baravara.se), Shanti Kristian's retreat centre, Gravendal (www.uniomystica.se), Fridhem retreat centre, Stjärnsund (http://frid.nu/), Foundation Berget, Rättvik (www.berget.se), Solsökehem, Ludvika (www.solsokehem.se), Oshofors, Olofsfors (www.oshofors.nu), and Levagården, Älvdalen (www.livshalsa.se). Foundation Berget is further discussed in chapter 7 and Shanti Kristian's retreat centre in chapter 8.

2 The Osho movement was established by the charismatic Indian guru Chandra Mohan Jain, better known as Rajneesh and later Osho (1931–90), who emphasized that human beings become programmed by their environment during their upbringing. Through meditation and different forms of therapy, he intended his disciples to become deprogrammed and free. See Frisk 2007: 126–75.

3 Martinus Cosmology is based on the ideas of the Danish mystic Martinus Thomsen (1890–1981). His life's work is entitled *Det tredje testamentet (The Third Testament)*, since it was thought to complete the Old and New Testaments. The cosmology is a form of evolutionary doctrine concerning both the micro and the macro cosmos. It has connections with both esoteric and theosophical ideas. See Johansson 2004: 335–6.

4 The Alexander Technique was developed by the Australian actor Frederick Matthias Alexander (1869–1955). The purpose of his technique is to find ways back

whereas yet another, Berget, has a predominantly ecumenical Christian orientation. Levagården specializes in yoga and the Oneness movement,[5] and Fridhem, one of the oldest retreat centres[6] in Dalarna, draws its main inspiration from the Findhorn spiritual community in Scotland. Otherwise, though, its profile is relatively ecumenical. It offers various activities that have a place within the popular religious milieu. In addition, it offers courses in certain creative activities, such as painting and drawing. One interviewee noted that the retreat centre aims to be a 'kaleidoscope' (respondent 8). In 2012, for example, Fridhem offered mindfulness, Tantra, Zen, tai chi, liberating dance, and yoga. So, despite the fact that we place these retreat centres under the same heading, and although we describe and discuss a number of similarities below, we would like to stress that great differences exist between them in terms of their orientation and the courses they offer. Their activities could be categorized under most of the eight headings that we used in chapter 3 to classify producers.

Ashworth and Graham (2005: 16) note that the naming of places is about much more than simply facilitating recognition and communication. Naming is also about constructing and expressing meaning and feeling for a place, about relaying its desirable characteristics and, possibly, also relating it to history and linking it to the past. The naming of a place is fundamental to its identity and distinguishes it from its surroundings (Huigen and Meijering 2005: 21). Many of the names given to the retreat centres – Baravara, Fridhem, Berget, Solsökehem, Levagården – carry meanings and associations, and relate exclusively to the activities that take place there and to the atmosphere they aim to create. A place name is chosen that serves the name-giver's purpose, with a view to what the place *ought* to be (Huigen and Meijering 2005: 22–3). Two of the

---

to natural body movement patterns, to improve and ease our physical movements, and to relieve the body from tension. See Schönström 2006: 76–7.

5 The founders of the Oneness movement were Sri Bhagavan (born Vijay Kumar in 1949) and his wife Sri Amma. The movement began in the Indian state of Andhra Pradesh in the early 1990s and since then has attracted many followers throughout the world who practise its central teaching by giving others diksha, a form of spiritual initiation achieved through touching other people's heads as a way of awakening humanity to a higher level of consciousness.

See www.onenessuniversity.org.

6 The House of St David at Berget opened in 1962 and The House of Meditation opened in 1972: see its homepage. Fridhem opened in 1984.

names of retreat centres in Dalarna contain the word *hem* (home), which has particular connotations. Huigen and Meijering note that when we can identify with a place, we then feel 'at home' there (2005: 21). None of the names of the retreat centres refer to a nearby place name, except for Oshofors, where the name Olofsfors has been simply modified by changing 'Olofs' to 'Osho'. Perhaps this change is symbolic of a wish to distance the retreat centre from the local place name; however, it might also simply be a play on words. In addition, it suggests a wish to create something new and to give the retreat centre an identity that is not associated with the local place and history.

A structural similarity between the retreat centres – part of what makes them retreat centres – is that all have overnight facilities for visitors and take payment from course participants. A number of the retreat centres also have permanent residents. On occasion, the websites publish invitations for guests to become part of the community on a long- or short-term basis, and not always in conjunction with any course offering. Sometimes people with a close relationship to a particular retreat centre buy houses in the vicinity, which has resulted in a kind of delocalized community. For example, in the area around the Fridhem retreat centre, there is a community of some 20 people who are actively involved in the centre's activities to a greater or lesser extent. The courses at the centres can be anywhere from two days to longer, and most are thematically based. Sometimes, teachers and course instructors are external to the organization; sometimes, courses are conducted by people living permanently at the retreat centres. Participants are mostly from other parts of the country – some even from other countries. We did not conduct a study of the total number of participants per annum at the retreat centres since most participants are not from Dalarna and therefore ought not be included in the quantitative calculation we presented in chapter 2. However, by way of example, we may mention that Baravara in Vikarbyn outside the town of Rättvik has about 1,000 course participants each year (email from Maria, March 6, 2012). Baravara and Berget are probably the largest retreat centres in Dalarna.

Retreat centres are the most intensive social venues for the expression of popular religion. Their aim is for participants to leave behind for a brief period of time their everyday existence, their relationships, and the factors that mark their identities, and to step into a world where temporary close relationships and social networks are formed. At a retreat centre, a lifestyle and daily activities are consciously and carefully constructed by the organizers. Time spent at a retreat centre is presented as being a break from everyday life and as a time for distance, inspiration, and change. Levagården's website talks about, for example, 'leaving your baggage behind and charging your batteries'. Similar wording can be found on the websites of the other retreat centres. On Baravara's website, we read the following text:

> We have given much thought to the creation of a milieu where it is enough just to be, to experience with all our senses. The food we offer is vegetarian, organically produced, and prepared with love. Outside, one of Sweden's most beautiful natural settings lies before your eyes, with Lake Siljan in the background.

Here we see a clear awareness of how to create a milieu for specific purposes. Reference is also made to the natural beauty of Dalarna. There are many photographs on the websites of each retreat centre. Often these are of stunning natural surroundings and rustic red-painted houses, while others are clearly symbolically charged. One beautiful picture of doors standing ajar on Baravara's website brings to mind Japanese Shinto shrine gates. Foundation Berget shows a meditative picture of an empty, snow-covered bench. Levagården's homepage presents a statue of Buddha against a natural backdrop in Dalarna. Many homepages show details of old cultural buildings and objects set against statues of Buddha and light meditation rooms with creative architecture, often with open timber-beamed ceilings. Global, in particular Eastern, influences combined with inspiration from Dalarna are apparent – a case, then, of Eastern exoticism plus strong local connection.

Fridhem's homepage contains descriptions and pictures of their organic garden. Similar to Findhorn, cultivation is an important feature of the Fridhem retreat centre. Pictures on the homepages together convey a sense of quiet, beauty, and tranquillity. Aesthetics appear to play an important role.

The general impression is that a key purpose of the retreat centres is to provide *experiences*. Previously, research in the field of Religious Studies was cognitively focused on people's beliefs. Nowadays, there is more focus on the subjective experiences of the individual and the creative expressions of religion at the individual level (McGuire 2008: 12–13). Woodhead and Riis (2012) state, for example, that the visceral aspects of religion deserve a significantly larger focus, as do architecture, symbols, and religious objects. The human body is also often essential (and neglected in research) within contemporary religious expression (McGuire 2008: 17). A general impression from the homepages of the retreat centres is that activities there frequently involve the body and at times also physical closeness to other course participants. On many homepages – for example, those of Oshofors, Baravara, and Fridhem – dance is listed as an activity. At the Fridhem retreat centre, most meetings begin with an energy circle where participants join hands (respondent 8). On many of the homepages of retreat centres are pictures of large rooms with mattresses or seating mats on the floor. Yoga (physical movements of the body) and diksha (healing through touch) are two activities offered at many of the retreat centres – despite other dissimilarities. These activities may be filled with alternative significance, or be empty of all ideological content.

Financial arrangements at the retreat centres cannot always be discerned from the websites: there are both trusts and private businesses. Course prices range from about 1,000 to just over 2,000 Swedish kronor (about 110 to 220 euros) per day, including food and accommodation (but may also be lower or higher). Compared with the typical cost of a conference venue for business, association, or academic events, these prices appear reasonable. Here, though, we touch on a particularly sensitive subject. Payment for religious activity is something often criticized in Sweden. Some believe that interest in profit is the foremost driving force behind the selling of courses (Hornborg 2012a: 184, 206). By and large, though, a monetary system is commonly used in our society that involves the exchange of money for products and services. In all such transactions, the value of what is being exchanged is determined by the vendor and the purchaser. Just as with other purchases, a number of consumers may afterwards feel that the product did not meet their expectations.

Health and Coaching Institutes

There are many types of activities with elements that can be interpreted as popular religious, which are practised in independent premises in Dalarna. What is characteristic of these places is that the individual visits them for either courses – group activities – or private sessions or treatments. The individual does not stay the night, as is the case at a retreat centre, but goes there perhaps as regularly as once a week. These activities could, in Stark and Bainbridge's terms (1996), be called 'client cults', which are characterized both by meetings with a teacher or therapist, either alone or in a group, as well as by a low level of engagement on the part of the individual. Time spent at such premises is relatively short, and the sense of closeness within the group is significantly less than at the retreat centres. Despite this, these health and coaching institutes are still quite significant for shaping visitors' world views, identities, and interpretations of life.

Operating from their own premises, these institutions use interior design and symbols to express the activities they offer. In the Yogahuset (The House of Yoga) in Falun, for example, where several yoga instructors share space and hold different kinds of yoga courses, we can find Buddha figures used in the decor. At the School for Traditional Chinese Medicine[7] (also in Falun), where the specialization is acupuncture but where other treatments such as Chinese *tui na* massage are also offered, the entrance is decorated with a Chinese lucky coin. There are many pictures on the homepages – the Yogahuset has mainly pictures of various yoga positions but also includes images of the beautiful venue, this one too with ceiling beams – while the School for Traditional Chinese Medicine contains the yin and yang symbol along with pictures of Chinese temples and pagodas. Such symbolic objects and images as these are important in the creation of an ambience and a basis for clients' experiences, thought patterns, and expectations.

In this section our discussion focuses on places that promote and market activities specializing in *health*. This covers a great many (though not all) of those activities that we surveyed in our project. As early as chapter 2, we noted that the term *health* can nowadays be interpreted in many ways, not all of them relating to purely physical health or absence of sickness. Rather, health can also be associated with harmony, peace of mind, personal growth, purpose, and divinity (Löwendahl 2002: 188). Many of these dimensions can

---

7 Nowadays the school is called TCM-centre Sweden AB; its name when we were conducting our project was Skolan för traditionell kinesisk medicin (School for Traditional Chinese Medicine).

readily – or not at all – relate to something that many would term *religion*. This divergence results in a large spectrum of activities, where overlaps with potentially religious dimensions vary greatly and where there are also different degrees of proximity to the social mainstream. In chapter 8, we present a case study of an institution in a relatively small community in Dalarna where different activities coexist.

Here, we will look especially at places that are close to the social mainstream but that also offer activities that relate to our project. Under the first heading, we focus on more physically-oriented activities for health, such as gyms, exercise centres, health clinics, spas, and health resorts. Under the second heading, we discuss phenomena that are more psychological in nature, namely coaching or life coaching. However, it is not always easy to distinguish between these two kinds of phenomena.

Gyms and Exercise Centres, Spas, and Health Resorts

There are numerous gyms and exercise centres in Dalarna. The gym chains that have established themselves in the county are as follows: Må bättre and Friskis och Svettis (each at six locations); Nautilus (Actic) and T.O.K.A. (Sports as Culture) (each at five locations); Class Gym (at two locations); and Sats (at one location). In addition to these, we found 12 independent gyms and a number of mainly municipal sports halls, where people could rent premises for a host of different activities. This amounts to a total of 37 gyms in different places, although most were located in and around the larger urban centres. It was not the aim of the project to examine or survey small private gyms or company gyms in Dalarna; however, after a review of the five largest gym chains[8] in Sweden, which clearly showed that they all offered different forms of yoga, we decided that the project should examine whether this was also the situation in Dalarna. As it turned out, initial visits to local gyms and websites demonstrated that the trend existed here as well. Of the 37 gyms, 24 held activities that were of interest in terms of our project, in particular yoga. For example, one gym in Falun had 18 yoga classes per week, employing four instructors. We also found reiki healing,

---

8 These were Sats, Fitness 24 Seven, World Class, Nautilus, and Friskis och Svettis.

kinesiology, mental training, coaching, and stress management (the latter, of course, can be totally secular in content).

The websites of the various gyms show certain elements of originality in terms of both design and presentation. Descriptions of the range of activities are quite detailed; in addition, a visitor can often see pictures of the trainers and other employees, and read a bit about what they do. Personal service is the focus, which is perhaps not strange considering the types of services offered. The gyms also show great uniformity in the way they present themselves. The websites are actually quite striking in their similarity, with numerous pictures primarily of exercise equipment set up in large, lighted halls that give a modern and well-organized impression. Further, there are pictures of people working out on the various apparatuses, as well as pictures of group activities. Though performing physically taxing activities, participants look unusually happy and at ease.

Visits to the gyms further revealed their remarkable similarities. Clearly, they all follow the same model for their look. Almost every gym has a foyer with a reception desk and table and chairs to relax in, mirrored exercise rooms with an array of equipment, and large halls where group activities are conducted. The focus of the gyms is naturally physical exercise: fitness is central. Nutritional and health advice is often provided as well.

Besides the gyms, there are exercise centres that do not call themselves gyms. For example, in a town in Dalarna, one particular exercise centre, for women only, offers (according to its website) fitness training and body building, stretching, weight-loss management, and lifestyle management, as well as salsa dancing, aerobics, and classic massage. We phoned the centre and further learnt that it also offers reiki healing, something that was not noted on the website. Two hundred women are registered members of this exercise centre.

At a number of the gyms and exercise centres, we thus came across activities that might be relevant to our project. We decided to look more closely at the yoga offered by the gyms, since yoga is a system deeply rooted in a life philosophy traditionally associated with religion. As with mindfulness, yoga seems to have shifted from the sphere of Eastern religion to a secular Western sphere. By way of its presence in gyms, it has also become part of the social mainstream.

Yoga has a long history, from its beginnings in India several thousands of years ago to its popularization in Western society in the mid-1900s. An interesting development is Westernized yoga forms, mainly in the USA, beginning in the late twentieth century. One example of this is power yoga, which developed from ashtanga yoga.[9] Power yoga is considered to be a simpler form, where the focus is on the physical activity itself rather than on the other dimensions of yoga. Classes consist of warm-ups, breathing exercises, positions, and relaxation (Schönström 2006: 165). Power yoga is described as being an energetic, sweaty, and physical form of yoga, where the aim is for the individual to experience his or her maximum level of strength, sense of freedom. and vitality. Harmony and balance are also important keywords (www.poweryoganu.nl). Of the various forms of American yoga, power yoga is the one most prevalent in Sweden. Other American forms, which are often a blend of different Indian forms of yoga (Cook 2012), are not found nearly as readily in Sweden, at least not in Dalarna. A 'Swedish' form of yoga that can be found in Dalarna is Tomas Frankell's *livsyoga* (Life Yoga). Also available in the county is the more local *minanda* yoga (My Spirit Yoga), developed at a retreat centre in northern Dalarna. There is a clear tendency to merge the various yoga styles according to individual preference. This may be – but does not have to be – a sign of a certain degree of secularization.

There are also exercise forms that merge Eastern and Western techniques that are occasionally practised in gyms: for example, BodyBalance. This exercise form combines movements from yoga, tai chi, and Pilates.[10] It is said to build not only physical strength but also the ability to manage stress and tension. Over time, it is also thought to improve concentration, mental presence, corporal control, and balance (www.lesmills.com/global/bodybalance/bodybalance-group-fitness-class.aspx). Another combined exercise form is T-Flow. As with BodyBalance, different movements from tai chi, Pilates, and yoga are incorporated into T-Flow, which is said to develop the meditative part of the brain, while being both

9 Ashtanga yoga is a very physical form of yoga that involves synchronizing breathing with postures. It was developed by Sri K. Pattabhi Jois (1915–2009) from hatha yoga. See Schönström 2006: 164.

10 Pilates is an exercise form said to strengthen both body and mind. It focuses on presence and conscious breathing. It is practised to improve coordination, posture, and flexibility. It is also used for rehabilitation purposes. See Schönström 2006: 234.

relaxing and energizing (respondent 9). A further form of exercise is chi-ball, which is a combination of tai chi, qi-gong, yoga, Pilates, Feldenkrais,[11] relaxation, and meditation to music (www.chiball.com). BodyBalance, T-Flow, and chi-ball are all available at gyms in Dalarna, and all three have features that make them relevant for our project. During one telephone interview, a BodyBalance and chi-ball instructor stated that these exercises could have spiritual aspects, but this was dependent on the individual (respondent 10).

We interviewed by telephone eight yoga instructors who worked at different gyms throughout Dalarna. Three of them taught at gyms as well as in their own yoga studios. All eight saw a close relationship between yoga at a gym and traditional yoga; however, they stressed that yoga has nothing to do with religion. They agreed that there was a connection between yoga and spirituality and thought this was important, but it was also noted that the practice of yoga in a gym brings with it certain restrictions. The interviewees all said that yoga in a gym can never be as profound as it is in a yoga studio. It was important for the three interviewees who taught in yoga studios to note that yoga has two forms: one that they themselves practised outside the gym and another they taught at the gym. The other five who taught at gyms had also received their yoga-instructor training there, and practised yoga less frequently in other venues. For this group, the spiritual dimensions of yoga were not as clear. None volunteered to remark about any sort of link between yoga and religion or spirituality, a fact worth noting. This question was, however, of interest in terms of our project, which is why the interviewees were asked whether they had any thoughts about the long history of yoga as a religious or spiritual technique. For the five gym yoga instructors, yoga was important for providing one with the opportunity for 'moving into him- or herself', finding quiet, and focusing on the self. They were aware of yoga's connection with spirituality, but they did not state this in the same way as the other three. They felt that although yoga can quite clearly have spiritual dimensions, they did not focus on these at the gym. A few expressed a certain scepticism about the idea that yoga was somehow spiritual.

11 Feldenkrais was developed by Moshe Feldenkrais in the 1940s and is used to improve coordination and to increase physical awareness. Posture and movement patterns are considered to reflect the nervous system. The goal is to be able to move the body freely and without effort. See Schönström 2006: 78–80.

The restrictions that come with practising yoga at a gym are, according to the interviewees, numerous, but two stand out. First, the tempo at the gym is high. Each yoga class has a time slot, which means quickly moving on to the yoga exercises themselves. Second, the yoga instructors stated that there is little time to develop the theoretical basis of yoga at a gym. In addition to the time issue, interviewees also felt that deeper discussions about yoga could easily be misunderstood. Yoga at a gym should not be conceived of as being mystical or secretive, rather, it should be simple and easy. The gym is not a place to explain 'chakras and the like' – that is for the yoga studio to do. It is important to adapt yoga in the gym setting so that participants understand and are not frightened off. Despite acknowledging these differences and the lack of depth in the context of the gym, all respondents maintained that it was yoga they were practising and that they performed all of the exercises, breathing, and meditation in a correct manner, despite some exercises being done rather quickly and with less depth.

Though gyms are less tranquil than the venues otherwise associated with yoga, many of the instructors explain that they do attempt to create a more stress-free atmosphere. The lights are dimmed, and some instructors light candles. Perhaps these elements are what link gym yoga with more traditional yoga. In the room used for yoga at one of the gyms we visited, there was a statue of the Laughing Buddha. Prior to the BodyBalance class (held in the same room), scented oil was used to create an atmosphere of peace and tranquillity.

Gym yoga, therefore, exists precisely at the point of division between the religious and the secular, and exemplifies the difficulty with drawing lines of demarcation. Yoga can have religious significance depending on the instructor and the client. Then again, it can be just as readily non-religious. By offering an experience that is corporeal and by using such expressions as *look inside oneself*, yoga builds a foundation for deeper understanding and interpretation, which may contribute to meaning and purpose for the individual.

Spas

Another phenomenon that might be pertinent to our project is the spa in its various forms. However, gaining an overview of spas proved to be difficult. A search on www.visitdalarna.se generated an initial 562 hits, which seemed rather extensive. However, this number included duplicate entries, meaning that it was less extensive than it originally appeared. One problem was finding a simple way of determining what was in fact a full spa and what was just a minor feature of some other kind of establishment. An extra facility in the form of a spa is currently quite common at hotels, conference centres, and adventure/nature resorts. At 35 locations, however, we found spa facilities that initially seemed to contain more than simply a swimming and sauna area. After contacting most of them, we were able to establish that there was little related to the project's main purpose since their activities did not contain any world-view elements. Often, the spa facility was described as a place for clients to relax and experience a feeling of well-being. There was no suggestion of existential or super-empirical dimensions.

Four of the larger spas offered a relatively wide choice of treatments, and we gave these a closer examination. The aim of a spa is to promote the well-being of its clients. Well-being, however, can take many forms and can be tied to many different forms of treatment; still, there were many similarities in what individual spas offered. The most widespread treatment was massage. Then came different facial treatments, salon-type treatments (including make-up), pedicures and manicures, different kinds of baths, body scrubs, and similar services. Most of these treatments did not include dimensions that would be of interest to our project, and were therefore excluded.

Frequently, classic massage or relaxation massage was offered; however, other forms were also offered, such as Chinese massage, hot stone massage, aroma massage, tactile massage, and partner massage. Chinese massage and aroma massage were included in our survey, since we assessed that they could have super-empirical dimensions (see chapter 2). In the telephone conversations we had with the various spas, however, those questioned most often felt massage to be nothing more than physical and corporeal. Many were surprised to receive a telephone call from a historian of religion and could see no connection with their facility. It was therefore necessary to describe our project and explain that we were looking for expressions of world view, religion, and spirituality in an open-minded manner and with the purpose of discussing the problems with the use of these terms. At best, some of our informants were able to say that the relaxation they offered could perhaps be perceived as a form of spirituality if one so chose.

However, our interviewees at the spas were either managers or held administrative positions. It proved difficult to speak with people who actually provided the treatments, as they were not permanent employees, working on an as-needed basis. In addition, spa staff were reluctant to release their names and telephone numbers. The results may have been different if we had spoken directly to the producers themselves.

Health Resorts

The increasing popularity of spa facilities has been at the cost of the health resorts (*hälsohem*) that were so popular in Sweden during the 1970s and '80s. The health resort Masesgården in Dalarna is one of the last still operating in Sweden.[12] It opened in 1976, when there were some 25 health resorts in the country. What distinguishes a health resort from a spa facility is that the focus is on health rather than pleasure. Health resorts do not offer three-course dinners with wine; instead, they offer a strict vegetarian, alcohol-free, and caffeine-free diet. Food, exercise, and mental health are keywords. The philosophy of Masesgården is based in the views of the well-known Swedish vegetarian health movement's pioneering figure, Are Waerland. These views on the relationship between nutrition and health still characterize Masesgården.[13] The emphasis is not just on vegetarianism, but also on the importance of vitamins, minerals, and fibre for good nutrition, as well as reducing consumption of sugar, salt, white flour, and saturated fat. Alongside this, the importance of physical activity is stressed.

Masesgården was established by Christer Persson, who is no longer the owner but who nonetheless remains active at the facility and manages the course programme. Masesgården is located in the village of Grytnäs outside the town of Leksand and comprises a number of buildings with a dining room, indoor swimming pool, gym hall, and sleeping quarters. It receives a great number of visitors and its facilities can accommodate up to 50 guests in any

12 The following information is derived from a telephone interview with a repre-sentative from Masesgården (respondent 11).

13 Are Waerland (born 1876) was one of the health movement's foremost figures in Sweden between the mid-1930s until the time of his death in 1955. His importance for the health movement in Sweden is described in, for example, Färnlöf et al. 2007: 16–20.

given week. Over the last few years, there has been an 80 per cent occupancy rate.

Visitors to the facility come from all walks of life and situations, from cancer patients who come as part of their rehabilitation to company managers who need to de-stress. Most stay for one week. During that week, a programme is arranged with about 30 activity hours including exercise sessions, lectures, yoga, meditation, and so forth. Visitors organize their individualized programmes in consultation with the facility. Programmes can include a health examination using EIS (Electro Interstitial Scan), which is described as a scanning of the body's various energies using electrodes to measure the flow of electric currents between cells. In addition, such health indicators as oxidative stress, pH values, blood lipids, body mass index, hormones, cholesterol, and inflammation are measured.[14] These are then analysed, after which an individualized treatment programme is drawn up. A conventional doctor is also available to help with these examinations.

The various methods of massage offered at Masesgården demonstrate great similarities between Masesgården and spas. Here, for example, visitors can get classic massage, tactile massage, and hot stone massage, as well as acupressure massage, tuina massage, aroma massage, and raindrop therapy (essential oils are worked into the skin, which are supposed to reduce bacteria and viruses). Treatments are also similar to those found at spas: facial treatments, manicures and pedicures, steam baths, body scrubs, detox treatments, make up, and ear candling.[15]

There are a great number and variety of courses. For example, there are courses in qi-gong, mindfulness, and raw food, and courses with names such as Yoga Weekend, Find Your Own Meditation, Mental Training, Therapeutic Yoga and Ayurveda, Yoga Makes Room for the Soul, Yoga as a Life Path, and Soft Yoga, to name but a few. Chiropractic treatments are also available. Course leaders

---

14 According to information from Masesgården, the method is medically approved within the EU. However, there seems to be discussion about its scientific basis on a number of Internet forums. Objective information about its usability has been difficult to locate.

15 Ear candling involves placing the end of a hollow candle in the ear of the person being treated. Its other end is lit. It is said to clean the earway; bring about relaxation; relieve migraines and sinus infections; and, also, have the patient attain a sense of mental clarity. See http://oronljus.org/.

come from all over the country, with the courses varying in length from three to seven days.

When questioned about course listings, interviewees answered that they generally just test the waters to see what people want. Experienced course instructors who return year after year are often employed, but the importance is also felt of offering courses in areas that are both current and in demand. At the time of the interviews, Chakra Balance Dance was being offered, a course new to Masesgården. Decisions about what courses to hold are made by a 'scientific board'. The outcome may not always be as intended, which results in some courses and course leaders not returning.

At Masesgården, different worlds meet in interesting ways. Both holistic medicine and conventional medicine are used. Ulrika Wahlstedt, who manages the facility's treatments and health concepts, is trained in natural medicine and homeopathy, while Magnus Nylander, an allopathic doctor, also works at Masesgården. Our study shows that such mergers are becoming more frequent. Apart from Masesgården, there are a number of health institutes in Dalarna that can be categorized under natural medicine or holistic medicine, and yet in certain ways seem to be quite close to conventional health care. They work with nutrition, dietary supplements, measuring nutritional allergies, hair-mineral analysis, and exercise. However, they can also offer such treatments as acupuncture, Chinese massage, and kinesiology. These serve as bridging spaces – that is, places where people who have no prior experience of popular religious milieus are presented with techniques and practices that they otherwise would not encounter. Places such as Masesgården may well be significant in bringing together certain popular religious elements, and in making them more accessible to a larger public.

Coaching and Therapeutic Methods

There are many institutions and businesses in Dalarna working with coaching and other therapeutic methods whose goal is to help people deal with different life problems. In addition to providing conventional kinds of advice and counselling, they also use methods related to the alternative milieu that is the focus of our project. From our interviews, it emerged that a number of the entrepreneurs working in the area of coaching and therapy have a background in the popular religious milieu, and that the ways in which they work and think are, to some degree, inspired by courses and literature from this genre. Many use popular religious milieus as a resource – indeed, as a 'toolbox' – from which they take what they believe to be useful.

Professor Anne-Christine Hornborg examines the phenomenon of coaching and what she terms *layman therapy* and *self-certified therapists* in her recently published book (2012a). For a number of reasons, she is critical of these phenomena as well as of the fact that practitioners who lack the formal qualifications of a psychologist or psychotherapist are permitted to use the title 'therapist'. She maintains that coaching and lay therapy comprise aspects of a market culture in which entrepreneurs sell products at a price to relieve human suffering. In this way, states Hornborg, structural problems are individualized and left for the individual to deal with. She further discusses the relationships these practices have with religion, spirituality, and science (2012a: 11–14).

In our study, we found the reality to be more complex. Many such entrepreneurs actually do have socially-recognized qualifications. One example from southern Dalarna is a business run by two qualified psychologists. In addition to their degrees in Psychology, they also have instructor training in mindfulness and nonviolent communication. They offer courses in stress management, mindfulness, and communication. In other cases, entrepreneurs did not have such socially-recognized qualifications; however, in general they had received private training to become, for example, mindfulness instructors or Journey Therapists. We therefore feel that the term *self-certified therapist* is misleading as it gives the impression that somebody simply one day, on their own authority, decided to call him- or herself a therapist. Therapists and coaches in this area generally have diverse kinds of private training. Of course, the quality of such training might be questionable, since, as Hornborg states, neither the Swedish Higher Education Authority nor Sweden's National Board of Health and Welfare conduct any form of quality assurance (2012a: 46). However, not all private education is necessarily inferior, though it will likely never be socially endorsed since much of it focuses on existential strategies and life paths.[16] In

16 Here, training to be a priest in the Church of Sweden is an interesting exception.

this regard there are also related discussions about the ownership of various techniques and the important question of legitimization.

Many coaches and therapists in Dalarna work in the area of well-being of personnel, with clients in such organizations as the Church of Sweden, Arbetsförmedlingen (The National Unemployment Office), and the Swedish Social Insurance Agency. The people we interviewed often follow typical career paths, and many of them are both politically active and hold positions that grant them influence over many different social spheres.

Below, we present three case studies based on interviews with three entrepreneurs in this genre. One interesting point is that each of them describes a personal crisis that they overcame with the help of the very methods they now use to help others. This illustrates how *crisis* and *crisis management* form essential components of both popular religion and the personal life stories of individuals.

Case Study 1: Karin (respondent 12)

Karin has been running her business since 2004 in an average-sized town in Dalarna. She provides counselling, therapy, and training. In addition, she employs methods such as Journey Therapy,[17] The Work,[18] and mindfulness. Essential to her work is the idea that people have to let go of their pasts. She believes that a conflict exists between what she calls the ego and the soul or spirit: that is to say, between learnt survival strategies and the essence of a person. We must clear our minds of mistakes, blocks, and perceptions that are untrue. We need to begin taking responsibility for who we really are, for the choices we have, and for the choices we make. If we do this, Karin believes, the body will follow suit so that even our physical health will improve.

---

17 Journey Therapy is based on emotional memories, such as grief, anger, abandonment, and suppressed emotions, as well as memories that need to be confronted. Forgiveness is an important element in this process.

See www.resanterapeut.nu.

18 The Work is based on Byron Katie's method of posing four questions about a life situation or something that affects our life. The answers to these questions are then used as a basis for dealing with problems and analysing the situation.

See http://www.thework.com/index.php.

Among Karin's clients are business managers, project leaders, the Church, and the local council. She states that she never advertises, but her reputation – that of being skilled and able to help people who have problems – has spread to local businesses. They are not interested in the methods she uses, only in the results, she says. They know what she does is effective.

Karin's website has two parts: one, for the (private) individual and two, for businesses. The private individual is offered help with becoming the person he or she really is, finding his or her true potential, discovering what he or she wants from life and how to achieve that, and focusing on his or her personal success and growth. In turn, businesses can receive help developing their human capital, as well as developing and adapting programmes for individual, team, and managerial growth. Karin's business also trains life coaches. Her website states that upon completion of the training, life coaches can help people make decisions based on a sense of purpose and freedom rather than on powerlessness and crisis.

Karin describes how she adapts her methods according to the client. She offers job coaching to Sweden's government employment agency, and also has subcontractors who do the same. She is careful, in this case, not to include any methods that might be regarded as 'weird'. This job coaching is to help unemployed people become part of the workforce, and Karin considers it important that they do exercises to increase their self-confidence, as without self-confidence, she feels, one cannot secure a job. She also offers job interview training and helps the unemployed with their curriculum vitae.

Through the employment agency, Karin also works with a group of individuals with long-term illnesses. The plan is to get these people back to work. Karin stresses the importance of having them stop identifying with the sick part of their person. She normally begins by asking them what they are able to do and what they like to do. Some dare not even answer because they are scared of losing their government allowance. This forces them into a trap where they constantly have to describe what they are *unable* to do, states Karin – their weaknesses become the focus. The system thus forces them into an identity of being ill, which is not constructive. They must change their way of thinking. Karin states that, thanks to her input, several are successfully back doing at least part-time work.

Karin herself had a breakdown in the year 2000. Her job at the time had become too demanding and required a great deal of responsibility. Her employer paid for her to take the Journey course, as well as training as a relaxation instructor and mental trainer. These were the tools she needed to become well again. It was at that point she decided to leave her job and start her own business.

Case Study 2: Pernilla (respondent 13)

Pernilla is in her 60s and works in one of Dalarna's larger towns. She explains how she has always worked with vulnerable people or people requiring help. For example, she has been a teacher of dyslexic children, and she has also dealt with workplace issues. Pernilla believes that the workplace environment must be adapted to the individual and not vice versa. She has worked with problem-solving in the workplace for some years. This has involved, for example, dealing with employees who have alcohol-related problems and employees with disorders such as, for example, ADHD or Asperger Syndrome. Pernilla believes that crises trigger existential questions and that it is important as a therapist to discuss these.

Pernilla has been running her business since 2009. Its focus is on rehabilitation and the sustainable development of the human being. A former client was the Swedish Social Insurance Agency. Now she works with businesses and employers in the public sector who require help for their employees. Pernilla feels that her task is to find the inner strength of people and their true potential. She makes a point of ensuring that her premises are different from those of a conventional health centre – they have somewhat of a homely feel to them. The walls are green as a way of promoting a sense of quiet and relaxation.

Pernilla uses a number of different consultants, to whom she sends clients depending on their specific problem. She tailors the treatment to each client. Clients may be sent to physiotherapists, doctors, psychiatrists, or social insurance experts. She has also, at times, referred her clients to priests, deacons, or women's shelters. Existential counselling is an import feature of the treatment, as a way of reinstating the value of the individual. Pernilla says that a person needs to rediscover life before being able to return to work.

If Pernilla feels there is an imbalance in a person's body, she might also send that person to an acupuncturist, believing that this can complement conventional medicine. Tactile massage may be one form of treatment for people with, for example, fibromyalgia. She has also sent clients for stress management and visualization exercises. Pernilla herself has a background in mindfulness, Gestalt Therapy, and Rebirthing.

In 1998, Pernilla was diagnosed with an aggressive form of cancer. The treatment she received to fight it was extraordinarily tough. Her ill-health forced her to face her anxiety about death, which was an important turning point for her. She thinks that the treatment helped her 30 per cent in her recovery, but that it was her inner strength that supplied the remaining 70 per cent. Her experiences with this illness were extremely meaningful for her. At her sickest, she felt there was an angel by her bedside. He said he was her guardian angel and that his name was Michael. His message to Pernilla was that she should help others in need. Pernilla feels that now, whenever she is talking with a client, things come to her through a sort of hidden internal layer, which opens up to transmit important information.

Case Study 3: Arne (respondent 14)

Arne calls himself a mentor or advisor rather than a coach. Like Pernilla, he lives and works in one of Dalarna's larger towns. He was an active businessman in the construction industry for 25 years, but more and more his time has gone towards working with people. Among other things, he provides counselling and support to those who are looking for funding to start their own businesses. An important turning point in his life was when his son was born. His son is mentally challenged with serious physical complications. For Arne, this gave rise to many existential questions and also forced him to face many practical issues that came with his son's condition. Arne himself had suffered from a malignant tumour some years prior.

An event in the mid-1990s resulted in a complete change of life for Arne. He was a business manager and had been at a managerial meeting for which he had no enthusiasm. That evening, the group went out for dinner. On his plate, Arne was given a tomato cut into two pieces in the form of tulips. As he studied them, he began to wonder whether the two halves belonged together or whether they were separate. The noise around him began to fade until his complete focus was on the tomato pieces. Finally, he placed the two halves together and at that same moment realized something: this is my life! One half is an outer role, and the other half is the true soul. If the two halves do not fit together, then the result is chaos. At that point, his two halves did not fit together. He had been trying to adapt his inner-self to his outer-self. The inner half cannot be changed – the outer half, however, can. Arne resigned from his job.

After this, Arne started to work with helping people. From believing that his son was the problem, Arne realized that his role as a parent was his platform. He began working within organizations for the disabled and launched his own educational enterprise to support both the disabled and their families, as well as people experiencing any kind of life changes. He believes that crises can serve as a way for people to find their inner strength and develop new values. It is important to take control over our lives and find our inner power. It is so easy to become stuck in bitterness and sadness. Existential questions often become important for the family of disabled individuals – many struggle with this. It is essential to find meaning in life.

Arne believes that it is important to understand that everything has a purpose, even if we do not always immediately understand what that purpose is. With time, we will understand the meaning and value behind our suffering. Arne explains how his life today is extremely satisfying in a way that it would not have been without the experiences of the crises he went through. He states that spirituality is about understanding that there is a plan for everyone, to have trust to let life happen, to listen to one's intuition, and to follow one's feelings. When working with a client, Arne considers it important to be sensitive and to learn about the person. He often tells his clients about his experience with the tomato.

Arne states that he has always had a spiritual connection. Even as a child, he was reflective and wanted to look after others. He has tried many things himself, from shamanism to massage and energy healing.

Arne would like to incorporate what he terms *spiritual aspects* into the world of business. He does not believe there has to be any conflict between combining work with spiritual aspects and running a successful business. What we want to do must be grounded internally within ourselves. Arne states that people have an ego which drives them into external roles. There is also an inner-self – a sort of core which is genuine and purely spiritual. If there is a conflict with this inner core, the result can be ill-health, depression, and exhaustion. Arne describes spirituality as the inner ability we all possess to direct our own lives, to accept whatever happens, and to forgive. He has a strong belief in God, not as a physical form, but rather as a strength or power that exists within all people and that holds everything together.

Thus everything is based on finding internal motivation and on being internally grounded. We need to identify the situation as it is, have a goal, and take small steps. Each individual has the power to map out and direct his or her own life. Spirituality, states Arne, is the realization that we are in charge of our own lives.

Be Who You Are: Construction of the Authentic Self

In all three cases studies, there is a recurring essentialistic understanding of the human being. Many interviewees describe their view of the human being as one where an inner core exists within the person, something that he or she *actually* is. They describe this in slightly different ways, but many use terms such as inner potential or inherent strength or power, growth, and development. They also describe other, less constructive aspects of the inner person composed of roles and false concepts, and state that these cause us many problems. In brief, the individual should try to connect with his or her inner and more genuine part of the self, and from this take responsibility for who he or she is and do what he or she really wishes in life.

In numerous articles as well as in her book (2012a), Hornborg maintains that the field of therapy has been colonized by new spiritualized practices, encouraging people to find their inner-self and to develop their inner potential. She writes that despite the fact that this inner potential concept refers to the immanent strength of the individual, a concealed transcendent realm is presupposed that is larger than the ordinary, everyday life of the individual. According to Hornborg, this is often described as a higher self, and a further transformation is offered when one connects one's inner potential to this (2012b). Hornborg refers to this as being a notion of a universal spirituality within the individual, which, with guidance, should be developed so that the individual can live life to the full. The supernatural powers of atonement are deeply rooted in the individual, and this inner potential gives the individual undreamed of powers for maximum rewards in this life (Hornborg 2010: 83–6). Hornborg states that the use of the term *inner potential* is nothing but a strategic rewrite using non-religious language, and that this term belongs to a specific religious discourse that aims to sell solutions to the individual (2012a: 24). Further, she writes that a business that uses the term *soul* should be classified as spiritual and that we, regardless of whether our inner core is defined as spiritual or as our potential, are encountering a religious system of beliefs in such a business (2012a: 69–70).

However, we think it is a misconception on the part of Hornborg to say that an essentialistic understanding of the human being necessarily requires a 'concealed' transcendent realm. As with many other current phenomena, the term *inner potential* holds many different meanings that do not necessarily have anything to do with either religion or transcendent dimensions. The historical background to the current concept of an authentic self and an inner potential lies predominantly with the Human Potential Movement of 1960s' USA, with its basis in humanistic psychology.[19] The Human Potential Movement was much more practical in orientation than humanistic psychology, though both are based on a positive view of human life and the human being. Central to the movement was the idea that every individual has the capacity to achieve optimum mental health and complete self-realization, and to be authentic and free from internal and external limitations, such as defensive reactions and social roles. Feelings and emotional expression were

---

19 Humanistic psychology developed in response to psychoanalysis and to the psychology of the 1900s. Earlier connections also exist. During the Romantic period, for example, there was a belief in the idea of the authentic individual. One well-known spokesperson for this was Rousseau. The idea was that the human being has an inner nature – an authentic core – which he or she must become one with in order to realize his or her true self. These ideas are related to the human being alone and not to God. In Christianity, thoughts about the inner and outer human being existed, but the relationship with God was central, and there was no ideal of originality (Nilsson 2005: 49–50).

viewed as important, the idea being that certain feelings, such as anger, are suppressed due to social pressure and such suppression results in neuroses. Physical therapies of different kinds were key, given that the body was perceived as being an important part of the human being, and that the internal and external parts of the human being together formed a whole. The therapy focused on the here and now rather than the past in the hunt for the causes of problems, which is the case with certain other kinds of psychological therapies. Another characteristic of the Human Potential Movement was group therapy, as group processes were considered to be of therapeutic value. Thus therapy was not something simply between one patient and the therapist, but instead involved a whole active group. The Human Potential Movement was a syncretistic movement in which elements from many different areas of culture, including religion, were adopted and adapted. This merger of elements came to characterize the entire movement and was one reason why it developed as it did, that is to say in several different directions (Anderson 2004).

Today, the term *human potential* is not used as frequently as it once was; however, its dominant trends are well-known both in the popular religious milieu and in the social mainstream. In the 1970s, for example, the Osho movement – which has influenced three retreat centres in Dalarna – adopted elements of the Human Potential Movement which were reshaped and reinterpreted according to the special conditions of the movement. The idea behind human potential also interacted with other trends of thought, such as New Thought,[20] the so-called New Age, and, from the late 1960s, Eastern religions as well.

The notion that each individual has an inner essence that he or she does not always express in everyday life and that he or she may not even be aware of is well-known in contemporary secular spheres as well. The view of the individual has – owing to the influence of neoliberal and individualistic social trends – become increasingly positive in our times. The idea of the individual having responsibility for his or her own life and the capacity to achieve change

20 New Thought as an ideological current is represented in a number of diffuse movements. Historically, it is related to Christian Science. At its core is positive thinking, the belief being that 'correct' thinking has healing effects and that God (or the eternal intelligent principle) is accessible to human beings if their thinking is correct. See Wilson 1970: 153–6.

has become increasingly popular, something of which Hornborg is also critical. She states – and rightly so, to a certain extent – that if structural problems in society begin to be presented as the short-comings and responsibility of the individual, then the path is paved for permanent exclusion (2010: 95). It is also clear that in relation to unemployment or sick leave, such individualized views at a secular level are realized in a way that accords with the current social structure. On the other hand, these approaches can also benefit creativity, new perspectives, and changed interpretations of an individual's identity and value, something that Hornborg does not mention.

Thus, the belief that human beings have an inner potential can have religious dimensions, though this need not be the case. Beliefs about a 'higher self', as Hornborg terms it, can, though not necessarily, be a part of these structures of ideas. In actual fact, the notion of a higher self has a completely different background than the Human Potential Movement, and is more readily associated with the concept of *Advaita* (nonduality) within Hinduism, even if this has developed a completely different, more individualistic character in the West than in its culture of origin. In the Indian religious tradition, the focus is not on 'developing one's inner potential' in order then 'to do as one wishes in life'; rather, the focus is on the union of Atman and Brahman (individual soul and the Supreme Being) at a whole other level (Frisk 2002; also see Carrette and King 2005: 116). As such, ideas about an inner potential and a higher self are not at all automatically connected, which is the impression a reader gains from Hornborg. Nevertheless, it so happens that they sometimes exist in symbiosis. None of the three interviewees described here, meanwhile, use the expression *higher self*.

It is clear from the interviewees' stories that their work has what they term *an existential perspective*, even if it is only Arne who talks openly about spirituality. Yet it is unclear whether Arne's under-standing of spirituality – which he defines as the capacity to direct our own lives – can also be interpreted as connecting to a *concealed transcendent realm*, to use Hornborg's expression. Karin seems to equate the terms *soul* and *spirit*, but does not use the term *spiritual/ spirituality*. Pernilla too does not use the term at all.

The connection between ideas of an inner potential and ideas of a transcendent spirituality is thus not at all clear from our three case studies. As we did in chapter 4, we will here argue that the term *inner potential* can either include or exclude 'spirituality', depending on the person. Furthermore, we would like to argue that the question of whether spirituality should be included or excluded in ideas about human inner potential becomes quite unimportant as it is based on a constructed categorization that is seldom significant for people today. We would rather say that the idea of human inner potential ought to be analysed in a reflexive and independent manner without necessarily tying it to religious definitions, as this is an idea that is truly characteristic of contemporary culture and that can say a great deal about many different contemporary phenomena and ideals.

Health Fairs

The health fair has long been a meeting place for holistic medicine and popular religious techniques and practices for health and well-being. It is, however, difficult to establish details of its history, since organizers have not prioritized keeping any form of documentation of such events. Further, no academic overview in any form could be found. Since the early 1990s, Stockholm has hosted a festival by the name of Peace in Mind, and since 1999, Harmoni-expo – 'Sweden's largest alternative health fair for body and soul' – has been held twice a year. Harmoni-expo is impressive in size. It is held in two large gymnasium-sized halls and attracts producers from throughout Sweden. Participating in these health fairs (both of which we visited throughout the course of our project) were a number of producers from Dalarna. This demonstrated that the local producers in Dalarna are active in the national context as well and thus are coming into contact with other producers and clients beyond their area.

Similar but smaller health fairs are also organized in different places in Dalarna. We conducted our initial survey of such health fairs in Dalarna in 2009, at which time we found eight. We estimated the number of health fairs during our project to be between seven and nine per year. Annual health fairs took place in Rättvik (about two per year); Borlänge (about four per year); and Avesta (about two per year). Health fairs were also held irregularly in the towns and villages of Säter, Myckelby, Svärdsjö, and Mockfjärd. Acquiring reliable information about just how long these health fairs had been held proved difficult, but one organizer stated that hers was one of the oldest and that she had been organizing it for about seven or eight years (this information was attained in 2008, meaning that the first such health fair may have been held around the turn of the millennium). Each of these – all going by the name of health fair or harmony fair – received an estimated 100 to 200 visitors. However, exact numbers were hard to come by. Organizers of a health fair in Borlänge told us they had between 300 and 400 visitors at their fair, which they organized about four times a year. Attendance at a health fair in the town of Säter was estimated by the organizers to be about 500. In other words, these meetings are significant and attract quite a large number of individuals. The health fairs are organized by different entrepreneurs who use their networks to create such meeting places where the focus is on various forms of well-being and health.

The health fairs feature a significant number of healing and holistic medicine techniques, the selection being wide and varied. Products with no evident existential connection are also offered, although they still allow for certain personal interpretations. For example, there are skin- and hair-care products, as well as other personal-care and hygiene products such as creams and soaps (often homemade and organic). Other products frequently found at the health fairs include jewellery such as necklaces and earrings. Often these too are homemade or have a connection with ethnic peoples from different parts of the world, such as the jewellery associated with the indigenous people of North and South America. Home decor accessories can be included in this category – for example, candlesticks and metalwork. For anyone who so chooses, all of these can relate to identity creation and construction of meaning that may include or exclude existential dimensions.

Another category is constituted by products for well-being that have more than a simple aesthetic value and that can be used in different ways. One typical product is aloe vera and various types of juice extracts. Aloe vera, an extract from the thick-leaved plant *Aloe barbadensis*, has a number of different uses. It can be taken orally to alleviate internal problems and can be applied to the skin as an ointment or cream.[21] The drink Noni is also included in this category. It is made from the fruit of the *Morinda citrifolia* tree, which is found in Asia and Polynesia and considered to have healing and

21 See Schönström 2006: 125 and http://www.plants.usda.gov/java/.

restorative qualities.[22] Also in this category are magnets, stones, and crystals, which are said to have healing qualities, as well as CDs of sounds thought to restore balance in the body. Visitors can also find acupressure mats and different types of massage equipment, some simple, some advanced, such as electrical devices. The list is endless; the examples cited here, however, are enough to give the reader a sense of the phenomenon.

The third category covers purely practical activities that involve participation, treatments, and experiences. Visitors can take part in a séance; have tarot cards read; have a massage; or try out healing. The séances, in which a medium is supposed to contact dead relatives, often attract large audiences. In addition, divination and fortune-telling are popular activities. Visitors can schedule a time on a list drawn up by the practitioner. A large number of massage types are available: on occasion, classic Swedish massage. More often than not, massages are given some kind of association with healing beyond their purely muscular benefits, as discussed earlier.

The significance of the health fair as a place for meeting and inspiration cannot be underestimated. Here, large numbers of producers gather, and visitors are given the opportunity to try out all kinds of techniques, often at a reduced price. Space is invariably limited, and everyone must make the best of the small area available. Despite this, however, there is seldom any sense of chaos, the exhibitors working within their allotted areas. In the case of massage, or divination in the form of tarot cards, or counselling, small cubicles are often set up to create a sense of privacy.

Not only is it the visitors who come into contact with new or familiar forms of therapy and techniques; for the exhibitors too, these health fairs are hugely significant for networking. Producers meet each other and find out about new activities. This is important since one's own clientele often overlaps with that of other producers, so it is useful to know what else is available. One exhibitor stressed this aspect, saying that it was important to be able to refer her clients to others when they had problems with which she herself was unable to help. However, the same exhibitor also stated that much that was on offer at the health fairs was far from being good or even appropriate; indeed, some exhibitors, she felt, were only

22 http://www.plants.usda.gov/java/.

out for profit. This was interesting and confirms the impression we have from others who likewise did not agree with all of the other methods and techniques on display.

We can conclude, then, that health fairs are important meeting places. They do not simply afford producers the opportunity to increase their clientele; rather, they also offer an opportunity to meet other practitioners and learn about new products and techniques. Health fairs also allow people who might otherwise not come into contact with the popular religious milieu to learn something about it. Many of the producers in attendance have hardly any marketing resources. As mentioned earlier, we were surprised at just how few had their own websites. A health fair naturally attracts visitors who are aware of and, indeed, quite familiar with what will be exhibited, yet still it serves as an important avenue for reaching out to a wider audience and potential new customers.

Discussion

In this chapter, we have surveyed some of the arenas where religious expression takes place in contemporary Dalarna. What is especially apparent from our study is that activities with religious dimensions do not just take place in demarcated non-secular spaces, but in many places beyond these. Both the places and the activities can hold or be void of religious meaning, according to the wishes and inter-pretation of the individual, and depending on one's definition of *religion*. The identity of both the place and the activity is determined by the actors. The new arenas in fact mirror how the differences between the religious and the secular in contemporary society are becoming increasingly blurred and losing meaning. Occasionally, this process is termed *dedifferentiation*. The religious has become less clearly religious and the secular less clearly secular (Alver et al. 1999).

These new arenas – health centres, spa facilities, retreat centres, gyms, health resorts, health fairs – all contribute elements to world views, identity building, life experience, and life interpretation at the same time as they reinforce these in a particular social context. The fact that reiki healing and kinesiology can be found at the average exercise centre or gym helps to normalize and secularize these in the mind of the individual. Contemporary culture is to a great extent secular in orientation, which means that when parts of what, in the culture of origin, are perceived as religious activities migrate, it is often the case that they become secularized. Carrette and King (2005: 117) stress the fact that yoga, as a result of being decontextualized from its culture of origin, does not remain free-floating, but is instead reinterpreted based on modern psychological discourse and Western individualized values. The result is secularization. One form of yoga that has been to a great extent secularized in the West is, for example, power yoga. Initiated in the USA in the 1990s, power yoga incorporates exercises with a fitness orientation. Practitioners of power yoga nevertheless stress that it has both mental and spiritual components, and should not be regarded as a less powerful or less effective form of yoga.

Relation to Social Norms and Values

Above, we have discussed 'place', in particular geographical, imagined, and social place. However, 'place' may also relate to sociocultural context – place in relation to the norms and values of society (Huigen and Meijering 2005: 22). The degree of tension with the surrounding sociocultural environment is an important part of Stark and Bainbridge's theory on different forms of organization. A number of religious (as well as medical) forms of organization form part of the mainstream tradition, whereas other forms exist in differing degrees of tension with this. In the medical sector, conventional allopathic medicine represents the mainstream tradition in our culture; in the religious sector, Christianity and the Church of Sweden are dominant. Conventional allopathic medicine is based on science and empirical results. One criterion of treatments in a low state of tension (or none at all) with the mainstream medical tradition in Sweden is that they are covered by social insurance. Thus, doctors refer their patients to physiotherapists and psycho-therapists, but not to producers of Rosen Therapy or chakra massage. The divide between conventional and holistic medical therapies, however, is not written in stone. Methods that at one time were in a state of tension with the sociocultural mainstream can later move to become more acceptable or even completely accepted as a consequence of their having been scientifically tested and found to be effective. A good example of this is acupuncture, which in Stark and Bainbridge's terms would originally have been deemed an imported client cult, but which has (at least certain parts of it) now become part of the mainstream in terms of standard health care for pain relief.

One development we can detect in Dalarna is that the demarcations between what was considered mainstream and phenomena considered to be in a state of high tension with the dominant sociocultural context seem to have become less well-defined. The presence in secular arenas – such as in gyms and health centres – of different healing methods that might include components that are more or less religious is one part of this development. This is probably the result of the sociocultural mainstream becoming less apparent, as society becomes more pluralistic. In our globalized world, the number of imported and new phenomena within both the religious domain and the medical sector is increasing, and discussions about 'a mainstream' are becoming increasingly dated. Stark and Bainbridge developed their theories in the 1980s, at a time when the social mainstream still held a place and when it was still logical to discuss phenomena outside of it in terms of import and innovation. Today, on the other hand, innovative and imported influences have merged with elements that were once regarded as traditional, and as a result new and changeable traditions have been created. None of them, however, holds a dominant position in the same way Christianity once did. The former demarcations have consequently disintegrated, and new cultural phenomena have appeared. In this context, the question of tension with the mainstream sociocultural environment becomes increasingly problematic. Phenomena that were previously regarded as being either part of or external to the mainstream now exist side by side, merge, and are offered in one and the same place. For the individual, the demarcations between mainstream and alternative appear increasingly more constructed and artificial.[23] Important actors in this development are people who are personally involved in the popular religious milieu and who are now middle-aged and hold strategically important positions in our secular society. Karin, Pernilla, and Arne represent this group. For them it is natural, alongside their socially accepted qualifications, to also incorporate elements from the popular religious milieu in their professional work.

One researcher who examined the way in which ideologies and practices that a short time ago were perceived to be exotic and

23 See Frisk 2013.

divergent have now been de-exoticized is Christopher Partridge. Partridge opines that an important reason for this is that popular religious ideas today are often portrayed in popular culture – in films and television series. music and literature – in a way that makes them comprehensible and accessible in an entertaining manner. This, says Partridge, has the effect of de-dramatizing them so that they are decreasingly conceived of as being exotic or foreign (2004: 50–9).

However, Partridge does not mean that these popular religious ideas are, as a result, accepted by everybody; rather, he maintains that a high level of resistance exists towards many forms of therapy and world views that we discuss here (2004: 1–5). In Sweden, this opposition is exemplified in Vetenskap och folkbildning (The Swedish Sceptics' Association) and Humanisterna (The Swedish Humanist Association), as well as the works of critics such as Anne-Christine Hornborg. The fact that such resistance exists is, we would maintain, also an indicator that the popular religious ideas are spreading and gaining more acceptance. There is no longer consensus as to what is divergent or strange, and the popular religious milieu is contributing to the shift in boundaries. No longer is it the small alternative subcultures and oppositional cultures that alone challenge official versions of what is reality and truth; rather, this is happening on a large scale as a result of the mass-produced notions of popular culture.

Commercialization of Spirituality?

One of the sharpest criticisms of the current popular religious milieu is that it is a form of entertainment, superficiality, and consumerism. It is not just pronounced individual critics such as Richard Dawkins who are worth mentioning, but also more organized groups such as the Swedish Sceptics' Association and the Swedish Humanist Association.[24] Obviously, entertainment aspects are involved in parts of some practices, particularly in that sector of popular religion (religion 'everywhere', to refer to Gilhus) that we do not discuss in our study. This is apparent in books and popular television programmes in Sweden (such as *Sensing Murder* and *Ghost Hunters*). Jeremy Carrette and Richard King, two British scholars of religion who are especially critical of new spirituality, opine that

24 This is also discussed in Heelas (2008).

popular religion has become a cultural addiction and an alleged panacea for the anxiety produced by modern lifestyles (2005: 1). They criticize the commercialization of spirituality, stating that the market mentality has infiltrated all aspects of cultural expression in today's capitalist societies. They state that individualistic values expressed as 'spirituality' have come to replace questions about, for example, social justice (2005: x). They even call privatized spirituality a cultural Prozac, which offers a temporary sense of joy and self-affirmation without dealing with the underlying problems of social isolation and injustice (2005: 77). Spirituality, in other words, serves market and capitalist interests. Hornborg echoes this sentiment, deeming what coaches offer their clients as nothing more than a 'euphoric high' (2012a: 52). The illusion of being free within privatized spirituality is capitalism's prison, since it fails to recognize the dependence of the self on society and the ethical necessity of resisting the abusive aggression of a market society. Joel Haviv calls this phenomenon 'cosmic capitalism' (2007a: 11). In the book about religion in capitalistic society that he edited, he asks why and in whose interest employees engage in spirituality, energy, and the essential and sacred self as a means of being successful in working life (2007b: 150–1). Hornborg opines that new spiritual activities are presented as solutions even for structural problems, holding out the promise of freeing individuals from a grey, problem-filled everyday life to find new energy and the capacity to work towards better profit for both themselves and for their employers (2012a: 78).

We do feel that the critical approaches described here have some merit – it is clear that every society generates different kinds of religious manifestations and that social trends (for example, individualism) are also penetrating the religious sphere. However, the above perspectives are also strongly reductionistic: they disparage the contemporary search for religion or meaning, present people as victims of their illusions, and classify contemporary spirituality as a form of anaesthesia. This is an arrogant attitude with an open and clear political agenda, which, what is more, bolsters those ethnocentric perceptions we criticize in chapter 1, according to which certain religious views are labelled false and deceptive.

Responses to critiques of the popular religious milieu have been voiced by, among others, Marion Bowman, who asserts that commercial transactions can also be regarded as holy and valuable by the individual. She questions whether it is the alternative spiritual practices that have been caught up by capitalism, or whether it is instead spiritual entrepreneurs who are challenging, breaking down, and revaluing commercial actions (Bowman 2011).

In the next chapter, we will look more closely at a trend that has experienced increasing popularity in recent years: the use of mindfulness within conventional health care. We will discuss both how mindfulness has transformed from religious Buddhist practice into a secular activity for relaxation, awareness, and psychological problem-solving, as well as how it is used within Dalarna's health-care system. Mindfulness will thus be an example of a once religious phenomenon that has migrated to the secular sphere.

Chapter 6

Mindfulness in Dalarna: A Focused Area of Study

Over the last decade, mindfulness has become an everyday term in Western vocabularies. Shelves of self-help books have been published that recommend mindfulness as a method to combat a series of problems and to help people have a better life. Not only is it used in popular religious contexts, but it is also used within the conventional health-care sector. Even the small selection of such books that have been published in Swedish reveals how mindfulness is recommended for an array of ailments – weight issues, pain and stress management, anxiety relief, bulimia, depression, and also to help people with diagnoses like Asperger Syndrome. There are also books about mindfulness for childbirth; for parenting; for children and school; for care of the elderly; for healing; and for better relationships.[1]

Mindfulness is an attitude or method deeply rooted in Buddhism.[2] It is used in various Buddhist contexts but has spread to quite separate domains within Western culture. In Dalarna, the *vipassana* technique is practised in the Buddhist temple in the village of Ulvshyttan. *Vipassana*, meaning insight or seeing things as they are, is closely related to *sati*, of which mindfulness is one translation (Plank 2011). In contexts with a Zen Buddhist connection, such as at the retreat centre Berget and the Church of Sweden, meditation techniques are also used in which mindfulness training constitutes an important

---

1 See, for example: Ola Schenström, *Mindfulness i vardagen: Vägar till medveten närvaro* (2007), Titti Holmer, *Lycka nu: En praktisk guide i mindfulness* (2010), Maria Engström, *Förlossningsförberedelser för blivande föräldrar: Att föda med mindfulness* (2010), Mia de Neergaard, *Leva i nuet: Positiv mindfulness meditation* (2011), Vidyamala Burch, *Mindfulness: En väg att hantera smärta* (2011), Heidi Andersen and Anna-Maria Stawreberg, *Mindfulness för föräldrar* (2009), Lotta Byqvist and Anna Langer, *Kvinnorna som slutade banta: Mat, motion, mindfulness efter 45* (2011).

2 Mindfulness can be viewed as a technique, a number of techniques (a method), an attitude, a process, and a state of mind.

part, even if the actual term *mindfulness* is not always used. In our study of the popular religious milieu in Dalarna, we placed mindfulness in the category of Eastern Body-Mind Techniques. We found 17 producers in Dalarna who offer mindfulness training.

The focus of this chapter, however, is mindfulness as used within the conventional, secular health-care sector that did not feature in our survey. The book *Full Catastrophe Living: Using the Wisdom of Your Body and Mind to Face Stress, Pain, and Illness*, written by American Professor Emeritus of Medicine Jon Kabat-Zinn in 1990 (paperback edition 2009), has been a highly significant factor facilitating the breakthrough of mindfulness into the secular field of allopathic medicine. Kabat-Zinn initiated a number of studies on how his stress-reduction programme – which was based on mindfulness – was both medically and therapeutically useful. These studies are to a large extent responsible for the way in which mindfulness has come to be recognized as a so-called evidence-based technique – that is to say, a technique that works based on controlled studies which demonstrate that it has both medical and therapeutic benefits. Currently, mindfulness is used by caregivers at many levels, and in many areas within conventional health care by doctors, psychiatrists, counsellors and psychologists. In particular, mindfulness is used in various forms of treatment using cognitive behaviour therapy, CBT (Plank 2011: 200).

Here we discuss the migration of mindfulness from a religious context to a therapeutic context in the West. We examine how this occurred and how mindfulness has been justified and explained from a therapeutic standpoint. Of interest is the connection mindfulness has with religion, specifically with Buddhism. Through its acceptance in the health-care system, mindfulness has become part of the social mainstream and thus provides an excellent example of how religious practices can migrate from their original cultures, be reframed in secular terms, and then employed for therapeutic purposes in a new (here Western) culture. Katarina Plank talks about decontextualization as well as recontextualization in her study of Buddhist meditation techniques. Our small-scale study examines how mindfulness is employed within Dalarna's health-care system and includes interviews with professionals who use mindfulness in their work.

Mindfulness in Buddhism

In her thesis, Plank describes how the word *mindfulness* is a translation of the Pali term *sati* (2011: 187). *Samma sati* (Right Mindfulness) is the seventh element of the traditional Buddhist Eight-Fold Path, making it thus central to Buddhist discipline (Plank 2011: 195). The Eight-Fold Path forms the foundation of all Buddhist orientations. It is therefore easy to see how different varieties of *sati* have come to be practised in one or another way in most Buddhist schools.

Plank notes how the Buddha Siddhartha Gautama is said to have talked about *sati* as being the only way to reach the final goal *nibbana* (the Pali word for nirvana) in the Theravada scriptures, particularly in the *Satipatthana Sutta* and the *Mahasatipatthana Sutta*. The process of meditation leads to insight into the ultimate conditions of existence, which is why the term *vipassana* (insight) is sometimes used when talking about *satipatthana* (the basis of mindfulness) (Plank 2011: 188–90). Buddha's fundamental insights were that everything is continually changing (*anicca*), including the impermanent self (*anatta*), and that this situation results in dissatisfaction and suffering (*dukha*). The purpose of meditation is for the individual to transcend his or her sense of self through a realization that it is illusionary (Plank 2011: 42).

In this way, the concept of mindfulness in Buddhism is closely related to core Buddhist beliefs regarding the conditions of life and how one should respond to human existence. In traditional Buddhist milieus where mindfulness is practised, such basic beliefs are central as well as closely associated with the ethical dimensions of Buddhism (Plank 2011: 188–98).

Applications in Western Psychotherapy

Steven C. Hayes, a Professor of Psychology, describes the emergence and growth of behaviour therapy as a reaction against psychoanalytical approaches. First-generation behaviour therapy aimed to alleviate symptoms rather than to find far-fetched causes for problems in the unconscious. If somebody was suffering from anxiety, for example, the aim was to cure the person of the condition rather than find the ultimate cause. The second generation of behaviour therapy included cognitive methods, as there was a realization that individuals required help managing their thoughts, feelings, and cognitive mistakes or dysfunctional suppositions in a more direct way, and that there was a need to focus on ideas, beliefs, and suppositions. Thus, second-generation behaviour therapy became cognitive behaviour therapy (Hayes 2004: 2–3).

Hayes describes a third wave of behaviour therapy, which has been developing since the mid-1990s, as representing an insight into the significance of attention and metacognitive perspectives, in which the function of problematic cognitions, not their form, is understood to be the problem. The stress of therapy then shifts to contextual and experiential change strategies, and acceptance and mindfulness become important keywords. Psychological events are understood to be a set of ongoing interactions between the organism and historically and situationally defined contexts. A psychological event must thus be examined based on its function and context, and the perception of it as a problem can be changed if the context is changed. A 'negative thought' need not have a negative function if it is mindfully observed, even if it might have a negative function in other contexts – for example, if it is met with resistance or suppression (Hayes 2004: 5–9). Thus anxiety need not be a problem if dealt with in the correct manner (Hayes 2004: 17). The goal is not to challenge or change the content of thoughts; rather, it is to develop another approach to dealing with thoughts and feelings (Marlatt et al. 2004: 265).

There are many forms of therapy within the third wave of cognitive behaviour therapy. Psychologist Christopher K. Germer describes the four leading perspectives within which mindfulness is used. The first is Dialectical Behaviour Therapy (DBT), which is used as a treatment for borderline personality disorders as well as for other problems requiring treatment, such as eating disorders, drug abuse, and depression. The second is Acceptance and Commitment Therapy (ACT), in which the patient is encouraged to accept rather than control unpleasant sensations. The third is Mindfulness-Based Stress Reduction (MBSR), which is an eight- to 10-week course developed by Kabat-Zinn as a way of improving physical and mental health. Finally there is Mindfulness-Based Cognitive Therapy (MBCT), which is an adaptation of MBSR that teaches patients who suffer from depression to observe their thoughts and physical sensations (Germer 2005: 20; Plank 2011: 200–2).[3]

---

3 For a discussion of mindfulness, see Frisk 2012b.

The best-known method is MBSR. Its creator, Dr Kabat-Zinn, wrote his doctoral thesis on Molecular Biology. He has a background in a number of different Buddhist practices, and has trained with such Western instructors of *vipassana* as Jack Goldstein and Joseph Kornfield, as well as the Vietnamese Buddhist Thich Nhat Hahn and a number of Tibetan Buddhist teachers.[4] Using these experiences, Kabat-Zinn aimed to isolate one technique, mindfulness, from the Buddhist context. He is of the opinion that mindfulness is about attentiveness and awareness, and defines the phenomenon as 'the awareness that emerges through paying attention on purpose, in the present moment, and nonjudgmentally to the unfolding of experience moment by moment' (Kabat-Zinn 2003: 145). Mindfulness can be expressed in a range of forms, from a series of formal exercises that are performed regularly at certain times to informal exercises that aim to cultivate a continued sense of awareness in all everyday activities (2003: 147).

Kabat-Zinn's position is that mindfulness may derive from Buddhism, but that does not make it Buddhist. The essence of the technique, he maintains, is universal and independent of any faith and ideology, which is why it can be practised by anyone. However, he also states that it is not simply by coincidence that mindfulness has its origins in Buddhism, since the aim of Buddhism is, as with mindfulness, to alleviate suffering and dispel illusions (2009: 12–13).

Kabat-Zinn developed MBSR at the University of Massachusetts as a way of treating chronic pain and stress-related disorders (Plank 2011: 200). The fact that it is today used throughout the world, he explains, is a result of the tremendous attention it received on television and other forms of media in the early 1990s (Kabat-Zinn 2009: xxix–xxx). MBSR is an eight- to 10-week programme composed of various mindfulness and relaxation techniques. Participants meet once per week, receiving instructions, learning about the techniques, and discussing, for example, stress and strategies to deal with various problems (Plank 2011: 200–1). Participants are expected to practise mindfulness at home for 45–60 minutes, six days per week (Kabat-Zinn 2009: 141). Patients who are referred to the clinic may be suffering from any of the following: heart problems, cancer, lung disease, high blood pressure, headaches, chronic pain, sleeping

4 In his foreword, he also expresses his gratitude towards several other Eastern teachers from whom he seems to have drawn inspiration (see Kabat-Zinn 2009: xxi).

problems, panic attacks, st_ess-related digestive disorders, and skin ailments (Kabat-Zinn 2009 7).

The book *Full Catastrophe Living* – for which Thich Nhat Hanh wrote the foreword – describes the mindfulness techniques used in the stress-reduction programme. Kabat-Zinn labels stress, pain, and sickness as life's total catastrophes, maintaining that the strategy for dealing with these is the art of living consciously and in the present (2009: 1). He states that we must be aware of the present moment, which includes the whole spectrum of our experiences, both good and bad, and that we must be comfortable in our own skin (2009: xxviii–xxix). Stress and pain cannot be avoided: we must face them. Escape and avoidance are not solutions (2009: 2–3). Everything in life is temporary and can change at any time (2009: 6). We must learn to allow ourselves to live in the moment with everything as it is without trying to change anything (2009: 20). Kabat-Zinn stresses the importance of having a non-judgemental attitude and of being witnesses to our experiences. We must be aware of the constant stream of judgemental thoughts and reactions in which we are normally caught up and instead learn to take a step back (2009: 33). Acceptance means seeing things as they really are in the present moment. If we have a headache, we must accept it. We must also learn to let go of thoughts and feelings that the mind wants to cling onto (2009: 38–9).

The techniques that are described include sitting meditation, awareness of the breath, yoga positions, walking meditation, and everyday mindfulness. The relaxation techniques of body scanning and the Raisin Consciousness exercise are also described. The latter is well-known in the mindfulness culture, and deals with experiencing a raisin in its entirety, from various perspectives, and with all senses (Kabat-Zinn himself writes [2009: xxi] that he learnt this technique from Kornfield). One further meditation technique deeply rooted in Buddhism and presented in the book is the so-called Loving Kindness Meditation (*metta*):[5] its aim is to arouse feelings of kindness, generosity, love, and forgiveness towards oneself as well as towards other people (Kabat-Zinn 2009: 182).

The clinical psychologist Christopher K. Germer, who, like Kabat-Zinn, has a background in various Eastern meditation

5 This is also practised in various Buddhist schools, with principal reference made to the Theravada scriptures

techniques, defines mindfulness as (1) awareness (2) of present experience (3) with acceptance (Germer 2005: 7). Germer describes mindfulness as a skill that provides us with a strategy for relating to all manner of experiences – positive, negative, neutral – in such a way that our level of suffering decreases and our sense of well-being increases. Mindfulness is about focusing on the present moment. We do not become stuck in the past or in the future, and we do not judge or reject what is happening at any given moment. We are present. This type of awareness generates energy, clarity, and joy, and can free us from conditioning. Germer describes non-judgement and acceptance as important ingredients in therapeutic mindfulness; intense feelings such as shame, anger, and fear must be faced with an open mind (2005: 4–7).

Many studies have been conducted into how mindfulness works. The Swedish doctor Ola Schenström, one of the best-known advocates of mindfulness in Sweden, refers to studies of MBSR that demonstrate how the method is able to significantly help alleviate pain and sleep disorders. Physical symptoms decreased by on average 30 to 35 per cent, and psychological symptoms, such as worry, anxiety, and depression, by 40 to 50 per cent. Schenström further maintains that an important effect was the improved quality of life for the majority of patients. Other positive effects of MBSR are lower blood pressure and reduced stress, as well as relief from chronic headaches, inflammation, and irritable bowel syndrome (Schenström 2007: 71–72). Schenström also refers to studies of self-destructive patients with borderline personality disorders who were successfully treated using DBT. Furthermore, a combination of cognitive therapy and mindfulness training reduced episodes of depression by 50 per cent in those patients who had previously suffered three or more bouts of depression (Schenström 2007: 73–4; also see Lazar 2005).[6]

6 Yet these studies have been questioned. Mindfulness is, for instance, often simply one element of many in a given treatment routine, and the effect of mindfulness in itself is not always clear. Depression, for example, can come in different forms and have different causes. Mindfulness may well help in a number of cases, though perhaps not all (email from Mehrdad Beigi). Neurosurgeon Pekka Mellergård maintains that most of the studies on mindfulness are flawed because of their lack of random patient selection and relevant control groups. Mellergård states that similar effects of other changes in the patient's life cannot be ruled out: for example, structured listening to classical music (Mellergård 2012).

Other Swedish doctors have also made use of mindfulness. One such doctor is Åsa Nilsonne, a psychiatrist and Professor of Medical Psychology. She has authored several books in Swedish on the subject. Nilsonne describes a model for mindfulness, deeply rooted in DBT, in the following terms: observe, describe, do not judge (2009: 16). The chapters in one of her books discuss, in this order, thoughts, feelings, the body, sleep, and relationships with other people. Nilsonne stresses how mindfulness can improve quality of life – both for people in general who are simply trying to manage and cope with the everyday, as well as for those who have psychiatric issues (2011: 10–13). She defines therapeutic mindfulness as the ability to be aware in the present moment (2011: 14) and specifies four key components: observation, description, non-judgement, and participation (2011: 22).

Interesting to note is the fact that many key figures from the field of mindfulness in Western therapy talk openly about its connection with Buddhism and have personal experience with both Buddhist and other Eastern religious systems. Buddhism differs in a number of ways from Christianity; indeed, certain Buddhist trends that do not stress belief in God or other theological doctrines are relatively easy to reconcile with secular and psychological perspectives. The core teaching of Buddhism emphasizes human suffering and the transience of the human being, and Buddhist philosophy offers many theories as to how the human mind functions and generates a sense of suffering. Scholar of Buddhism Andrew Olendzki writes that the human being has a reflexive desire for what is pleasant to continue and for what is unpleasant to cease, and that the reason why we experience problems is the conflict that exists between our desires and the realities of life. The instinct to cling to our desires is automatic and leads to an attitude of clinging or grasping, as described in Buddhism, which in turn gives rise to a construction of 'me' and 'mine' and consequently to an illusory construction of the self. What users are looking for from the mindfulness technique is another level of understanding, from which they can see reality as it *is*, without classifying it as good or bad and consequently wishing that life be different (Olendzki 2005: 250–1).

Mindfulness is about reprogramming body and mind so as to avoid the suffering that the human being's inner driving forces generate. These driving forces are described within Buddhism and can be connected with Western psychotherapeutic perspectives in different ways. Both are interested in how people function and in how suffering can be alleviated. However, there are some essential differences between Buddhist and Western psychological perspectives. One is the view of the self: Buddhism believes that the human being does not have a permanent self, whereas the larger goal of Western psychotherapy is to promote the development of a healthy self. A further difference is that the goal of Buddhism is enlightenment, a state of being that cannot adequately be described in psychological terms. Some scholars, however, state that the differences may not actually be as great in practice as they are in theory (see Fulton and Siegel 2005; Olendzki 2005).

Applications in the Health-care Sector in Dalarna

Mindfulness is used in various contexts within Dalarna's health-care sector. This became apparent from phone calls we made to health-care centres throughout the county. Since 2009, the counselling unit in Falun, to which the different health-care centres refer patients, has offered courses in mindfulness for patients with stress-related symptoms. Four to eight such courses are usually held every year, with eight patients in each. Groups meet once every week, and the patients learn exercises to do at home. Patients provide an estimate of their stress level at the start and at the end of the course. Results show that the courses are beneficial in terms of patient stress reduction, as perceived by the patients themselves (telephone interview with Elisabeth Nyberg).

In other areas of health care, mindfulness is used to help with panic and anxiety attacks, depression, sleep problems, marital problems, and self-harming tendencies. At the hospital in Mora, for example, patients who have suffered heart attacks are introduced to mindfulness alongside lectures on lifestyle change. The rehabilitation clinic for chronic pain in the small town of Säter holds mindfulness workshops which draw inspiration from Ola Schenström.

It proved impossible to conduct any quantitative survey of exactly how many patients are exposed to mindfulness throughout the health-care sector in Dalarna each year, which was our original aim. Every counsellor, psychologist, and psychiatrist has his or her own 'toolbox' from which he or she is free to use or not use different aspects of the mindfulness concept/practice. Further, it is worth considering the exact definition of mindfulness: a number of therapists employ relaxation exercises and term these mindfulness even when these techniques do not strictly comply with the concept.

Despite this, it remains apparent that mindfulness is widely used within Dalarna's health-care system. Often, an introduction to mindfulness forms part of CBT courses, which are offered at different levels, from introductory to advanced. Psychologist and psychotherapist Mehrdad Beigi, who works at the psychiatric unit in Falun, uses both DBT and ACT forms of mindfulness in his work, as well as techniques from MBCT. He describes the mindfulness trend as being part of third-wave cognitive behaviour therapy that began in the 1990s, in which the basic perspective is that it is not the symptoms themselves that are the problem but rather the patient's attitude towards the symptoms. Mindfulness is about adopting a sort of metacognitive perspective, becoming aware of the witnessing self, and being in the position of observing instead of reacting to psychological pain. Mindfulness involves a sort of exposure to what we normally flee from. Through mindfulness, we are forced to face this at the same time as we maintain distance (telephone interview with Mehrdad Beigi). The Exposure Technique, often used in CBT with or without mindfulness, forces the patient to face what is difficult and to remain in the feelings that the difficulty provokes until it no longer gives rise to such reactions. To a great extent, psychopathology, according to Beigi, perpetuates mental health issues since it is more about avoiding and fleeing painful experiences – so-called experiential avoidance. Another mechanism close to cognitive therapy is so-called *decentration* – the idea that thoughts are only thoughts and not truths. Other interviewees mentioned *urge surfing*, a CBT method used to prevent relapses in cases of addiction, which is similar in certain ways to mindfulness and which can be combined with other techniques.

Mindfulness: Religious or Secular?

Mindfulness as an attitude and a method has migrated from a Buddhist (and thus religious) context to a Western therapeutic context. One of the most important Western institutions, namely science, has legitimized the technique and as such it has gained inroads into another of Western society's most important institutions: the medical and health-care sector.

The interesting question that arises here is whether mindfulness as it is used within the health-care sector should be regarded as a religious technique or not, and what the difference is between the ways mindfulness is used in Buddhist and secular contexts respectively. There seems to be a consensus on the historical relation mindfulness has to Buddhism: this is mentioned in most books about therapeutic mindfulness. However, therapists generally hold that mindfulness is simply a special way of being attentive, which in itself lacks religious associations.

Nevertheless, Anne-Christine Hornborg, a historian of religion, expresses doubt that a traditional religious practice such as mindfulness can be reduced to a secular technique. She writes that, should a Christian priest choose to hold prayers in a secular school and say that the act is secular, most would argue that it is impossible for a prayer to be non-religious. According to Hornborg, this is comparable to the therapeutic and secular use of mindfulness (2012b). In another work (2012a: 201), Hornborg seems rather to question whether mindfulness really is a traditional religious technique or whether it is a purely Western method that refers to ancient Asian traditions simply as a guarantee of quality.

Another historian of religion, Katarina Plank, describes and discusses *sati* as a much more complex process than simply 'attentiveness' as used in the contemporary therapeutic sense, which she argues is a simplification at a number of different levels. In a Buddhist context, *sati* is an important component of the path to the attainment of *bodhi* (awakening or enlightenment) and ultimate liberation (*nibbana*). According to Plank, different states of mind should, in traditional Buddhism, not only be accepted – as is the case with therapeutic mindfulness – but rather should also be seen and understood, and replaced with states of mind that are more constructive. *Sati* in traditional Buddhism has important ethical dimensions as well (Plank 2011: 188–98). Plank uses the term *mindfulness appropriator* for those individuals who take elements of Buddhism as a means of strengthening their own views and legitimizing their own positions minus a genuine interest in the religion itself (2011: 209–10). She summarizes criticisms from several prominent Buddhist figures, pointing out that mindfulness in the contexts of therapy and the popular religious milieu is used for worldly purposes, the result being a confirmation and solidifying of the self instead of insight into the transience of the self and spiritual awakening (Plank 2011: 216–27). In such a way, Plank indicates that mindfulness as used in therapy corrupts genuine Buddhism and cannot be regarded as being part of Buddhist tradition.

As with many other techniques, methods, and practices we examine and discuss in our project (for instance, yoga and coaching), mindfulness is an activity that, depending on the individual, may or may not hold religious import. The question itself, 'religion or not', becomes meaningless in a contemporary context. Being 'attentive' is not in itself a religious act – however one might define religion – but such an attitude can, depending on the individual, connect to world views, perceptions, values, experiences, and identities that are religious in character. Whoever practises mindfulness in a traditional Buddhist context can thus understand both the method and its result differently than the person practising mindfulness within a traditional health-care setting.

These, however, are *possible* and not *self-evident* differences. Producers and consumers of mindfulness within health care may perceive mindfulness in many different and individual ways. In response to a direct question, a few of our interviewees working in Dalarna's health-care system made reference to 'spiritual' dimensions (see the discussion about the term *spirituality* in chapter 4). However, unlike Plank, we do not mean – insofar as there may be religious elements in therapeutic mindfulness for some individuals – that this should be interpreted as 'corrupted' religion. Religion and religious techniques are continuously being reinterpreted and changed according to the context. It is therefore to be expected that when a technique such as mindfulness enters a secular context, it is going to be interpreted according to other cultural parameters. At the same time, however, it is important to point out that when a practice, technique, or concept enters a new cultural context, those who see themselves as representing its original, historical tradition may feel that it has been stolen or that it is less genuine in the new context.

One difference between therapeutic and Buddhist perspectives which is widely discussed is the attitude to the self. Buddhism regards the self to be illusory, whereas Western therapy regards the self as important and worth enhancing. Hornborg discusses this when she writes about the conscious adaptation of mindfulness into a Western context, where she claims that emphasis is on the confirmation of the self instead of on the insight that the self is transient

(2012a: 44). However, when reading the literature on the subject of mindfulness in therapeutic contexts, it is striking how seldom the self is mentioned. The impression is that the self seems to be a non-question within mindfulness. Mehrdad Beigi corroborates this observation in an email. He writes that schools of behaviour therapy generally regard the self as a construction and instead focus on the interplay between the individual and environment. Therefore, discussions on the subject of the self are rare within mindfulness. Mindfulness is about being able to observe, describe, and be present in the moment without judging, and the question of self and non-self becomes insignificant.

This position is, however, somewhat different in the case of ACT. Here, the discussion is mainly on the self as 'context', meaning a perspective or an arena in which one's experiences can be observed from a distance. This perspective is constant and remains unaffected by content (inner experiences). It is about the observant self, which is an experience and not a tangible 'thing'. In contrast, the self as 'content' is about becoming one with the experiences, which can have both positive and negative aspects: for example, that life becomes limited and suffering occurs. Consequently, it is the self as context that is discussed in positive terms in ACT. Beigi states that mindfulness exercises can lead to an experience of the observing self. This theory takes its point of departure in RFT (Relational Frame Theory), which is a psychological theory based on language. The important aspect of ACT is to create distance from one's experiences (email from Mehrdad Beigi).

Thus, there is no evidence for Hornborg's interpretation that therapeutic mindfulness would fit within what she terms new spiritual beliefs about the inner essence of the individual (2012a: 64). As we saw in the previous chapter, an increasing individualism and essentialization of the individual exists within our culture, which is at times expressed in religious and therapeutic contexts. However, this does not mean that this is the universal criterion for new spirituality or that all new therapies can be pressed into this structure (and thus be called new spiritual). Above, we demonstrated how mindfulness in many contexts takes a completely different view of the self.

An interesting fact is that some doctors and therapists who are key figures in the field of mindfulness within health care are completely open about its connection to Buddhist contexts. A parallel can be drawn here with some of the coaches in Dalarna we interviewed. In addition to their accredited training, they have also taken privately arranged courses and subsequently implemented methods from the popular religious milieu in their professional work. For ideas to become socially mainstreamed, it is clearly important that they are implemented by those people who are active within the mainstream. After incorporating mindfulness into their medical practices, Jon Kabat-Zinn and Ola Schenström, both doctors, began offering their own mindfulness training courses. These courses are not socially sanctioned in Sweden; rather, they are regarded as private affairs. There are no social controls as to who can use the term *mindfulness* in his or her work or what educational background is required of the mindfulness course leader, something Hornborg points out.

One final interesting observation, which Hornborg also discusses, is that links to Buddhism, at least in Sweden, are more likely regarded as positive rather than negative by the potential practitioner, since the practice of mindfulness is often related to traditional Eastern wisdom (2012a: 43). It cannot be ruled out that such a link might also influence the individual's experience of the technique. Another more Westernized name, such as 'attention training', might well not provide the same positive association. In such a way, references to religion can reinforce the positiveness, even in our secular culture.

Chapter 7

The Church of Sweden: Its Response to Religious Pluralism

The county of Dalarna is included in the diocese of the large town Västerås, which is located in the county of Västmanland. The diocese also encompasses Västmanland, and in Dalarna is divided into five deaneries. There are some 40 parishes in Dalarna, which vary greatly in size: from small rural parishes, such as Djura with 569 members in 2010, to the significantly larger urban parishes – for example, Stora Tuna, which in 2010 had 34,636 members.[1]

During the course of the project, we gathered material from various parish offices and churches, and examined the websites of each parish to obtain an overview of the different activities offered by the Church of Sweden in Dalarna. A review of the material demonstrates that the Church offers a diversity of activities, many of which are inherently religious in nature, such as Sunday worship, baptisms, weddings, funerals, and confirmations, but also many of a more social and secular character. Deacons offer and organize family support, grief support, walking groups, activities for the hearing impaired and for the hearing and visually impaired, family counselling, and youth groups. There are also discussion groups and support groups for people living on the fringes of society; meetings for the unemployed; cafés; and handicraft groups (whose products are sold to raise money for charity). It is clear that the Church has lost members over recent years, but the impression we obtained of the Church of Sweden's position in Dalarna is that it is far from being marginalized. It is visibly present in a number of places and offers a wide spectrum of services and activities.

The Church of Sweden operates within a society that is often described as being one of the world's most secularized (see, for example, Zuckerman 2005, where a review of various studies

---

1 All information about the Church's statistics was gratefully received from Peter Brandberg, Church of Sweden, Analysis Centre.

shows that up to 85 per cent of the Swedish population declare themselves either atheist or agnostic). Naturally, these figures need to be analysed in terms of what they are actually telling us and what secularization really means. The fact that Sweden consistently scores high in other similar studies, however, demonstrates that the Church is facing great challenges.

Currently, one such challenge is the growing pluralism. Sweden is a society in which, as this project clearly demonstrates, there are a great number of different world views, techniques, practices, and beliefs. Many people who have recently made Sweden their home bring with them different religious practices and perspectives from their countries of origin. The increasing diversity and constantly changing range of belief systems are circumstances with which the Church must deal, and which offer both opportunities and challenges. Immigration and the demographic changes are clearly nothing new; however, in our globalized times, they are more widespread and apparent (see chapter 8).

When older religious traditions that have dominated the landscape for an extended period of time meet newly introduced or newly visible religious elements, there are several possible positions groups can take. One standard model – often used in contemporary theological contexts to examine the relationship a group of one religion may have with other religions – is based on three approaches: exclusivism, inclusivism, and pluralism. A group's affiliation with one of these categories can be examined in terms of its position in three areas: (1) Soteriology – that is to say, how one views salvation or enlightenment. An exclusionary approach would then be the view that there is only one way to achieve this (these) goal(s). The inclusionary position would be that everything is interconnected and that all religions actually have the same aim. Lastly, a pluralistic viewpoint is the belief that there are different forms or objectives for different religions and that each has its own validity. (2) How outer reality is perceived (e.g., the nature of God, and whether God and Brahman – for instance – can be perceived as different names for one and the same thing). An exclusionary approach is thus the belief that there is but one true way to regard the nature of God. An inclusionary approach is the belief that regardless of the term used by the different religions to refer to the divine, the same thing is intended. According to a pluralistic approach, there can be different deities depending on the religion, and each of them is legitimate in its own way. (3) Interreligious dialogue – that is to say, the group's attitude towards taking part in such dialogue and the reasons it gives for this. An exclusionary approach would be to completely reject such dialogue in the belief that one has nothing in common with other religions. In the case of groups with an inclusionary or pluralistic approach, the grounds for interreligious dialogue can differ depending on the level at which they accept theological differences and variations (McCarthy 1998: 74–5).

In literature produced by the Church of Sweden, we find clues to its position on these issues. For example, the Church publishes texts that discuss its relationship with other faiths: examples of titles are *True to Oneself – Open to Others: Discussions about Theology in the Church of Sweden* (2001); *Church Sacraments in a Pluralistic Context* (2012); and *Meeting Islam* (2011) (our translations). All of these discuss the importance of dialogue with other religions, both in the context of church services as well as within society at large. There is a certain focus on other Christian-based religions and Islam. Although secular society in Sweden is discussed, the popular religious milieu is barely mentioned: this is something to which we will return. The Church of Sweden also publishes through Sveriges kristna råd (The Christian Council of Sweden). The following publications all discuss the meeting of religions and ways in which Christians should relate to other faiths: *Can We Pray Together?* (2007); *The Meeting of Religions* (2006); *Charta Oecumenica* (2001); and *The Coming Together of Religions Through Marriage* (2011) (our translations).

The picture presented in these documents is of a church that, to a certain extent, may be described as inclusionary, in the sense that it believes the Christian message holds clear significance for the salvation of humankind, but further believes that this salvation is also accessible to those who have not heard its message. However, there are also pluralistic features, as the Church does not regard Christianity as being the sole road to salvation. It is difficult to find any indicators to suggest the Church might be exclusionary, although far from all religious forms and orientations are discussed in these texts. There are certainly limitations to what the Church of Sweden accepts as being religious – for example, many of the beliefs that we discuss in this study would not be so regarded. However, the Church can, for the most part, be characterized as being inclusionary and pluralistic, and open to ecumenism and dialogue.

Another way to regard the meeting of these different religious domains, which deals more with the level of willingness to be innovative and to include new ideas in one's own traditions, is to differentiate between a view that rejects and a view that integrates. This has much to do with boundaries and delimitations. One extreme position is to completely reject new ideas and consequently strengthen one's own boundaries and identity. The other extreme is to indiscriminately embrace the new, integrate it into one's own traditions, and allow these to be remoulded and renewed. In practice, however, it is more reasonable to talk about a continuum along which many different positions exist between these extremes. The Church of Sweden embraces a large number of different approaches, both to other traditions as well as to popular religiosity, which can manifest themselves in many forms of expression in different places and which can also change drastically over time. Being too open to other views can result in a loss of identity, yet there is also a risk of losing relevance if one is too closed to change.

Below, we examine how the Church of Sweden approaches the new pluralism. We do not present a comprehensive survey; rather, we give point by point examples of where the various approaches of the Church are visible. To begin with, we provide an example of dialogue, principally with Islam, and then continue with the retreat movement and Zen meditation within the Church of Sweden. We then examine the Indian Oneness movement and its encounters with the Church. Finally, we discuss sacred dance.

Dialogue that Challenges and the Potential for Collaboration

Jakob's Chapel and the House of Jakob, both of the Church of Sweden, can be found in the town of Borlänge. The priest Anders Litborn, who works there,[2] is interested in ecumenical collaboration as well as meaningful dialogue, especially with the Muslim community, which has grown to be extensive within the municipality. Borlänge is described as multicultural and is home to many Muslims (an estimated 10,000) as well as a number of Yazidi (an estimated 500 to 600). Yazidi are Kurdish followers of Mazdeism with ties to Zoroastrianism. The latter have no organization in this geographical area.

---

2 This text is based on an interview with Anders Litborn.

A few years ago, Litborn began his involvement with religious dialogue. A concrete example was the exhibition 'God Has 99 Names' hosted by his parish. The Church of Sweden in Borlänge has ongoing contact with both Muslims in Borlänge and Buddhists in the rural community of Ulvshyttan. This contact has resulted in, for instance, themed weeks, panel debates, and lectures. The purpose of all these has been to promote interest in relevant questions, for religious dialogue.

Litborn's view is that if one is clearly aware of one's centre, then there is no need for sharp boundaries. He himself readily takes part in Ramadan, and many Muslim children are involved at some level within the Church. One area of collaboration is teaching – of children who require language and cultural instruction and of women who learn Swedish with kitchen utensils as instructional tools. There is also help available in times of crisis, and assistance is provided to families whose Swedish is limited. This is all appreciated regardless of religious affiliation.

However, certain limits do exist and are maintained. Litborn states, for example, that baptism cannot be carried out simply as a blessing. The principal rule is that the individual being baptized will subsequently belong to the Church. This also applies to Holy Communion, though nobody is asked whether or not they are members of the Church or whether or not they have been baptized. Litborn invites everyone to take part in Holy Communion and turns nobody away. This is then an indication of a process of change currently taking place within the Church of Sweden. Previously, the Church's position on this matter was significantly stricter.

In terms of the religious groups that have immigrated to Sweden, it would seem that all collaboration is positive. Representatives from different groups try to find themes they can discuss and places where they can meet without there being any compromise of faith.

The picture changes somewhat when we look at dialogue with the popular religious milieu. Litborn indicates that he would consider certain kinds of cooperation, but not, for example, renting out Church premises for New Age activities. Scepticism exists about some popular religious methods – for example, meditation and other Eastern techniques. Litborn says that the problem may not lie with the technique itself but rather with its purpose. Meditation as a way to increase a sense of well-being is not an issue, since the Church also employs meditation. However, if the motivation is for something else – for example, for building merit (which can be the case in a Buddhist context) – then the Church would not be able to endorse it.

Retreats: Foundation Berget and the Stiftsgård in Rättvik

The Swedish word *stiftsgård* refers to a conference centre and hotel facility owned by the Church of Sweden. The first such facility in Sweden was the *stiftsgård* in the town of Rättvik, which was established in 1942 on the initiative of the Swedish Bishop John Cullberg. The purpose of the facility was to create an environment focused on youth activities. The facility aimed to offer a place for meetings and courses, and to serve as a centre for the instruction of youth as future leaders, as well as a place for recreation and holidays (Jonson 1982: 11). The *stiftsgård* in Rättvik became a model for other such facilities that were established around the country. The fundamental idea was to welcome everybody, regardless of faith and belief. With respect to our project, the Rättvik *stiftsgård* is interesting for two reasons: one, because it leads us to the House of St David at Foundation Berget and, two, because it serves as a place of contact for people who have no interest in formal church activities, since it also offers other spiritual and religious features than those typically offered by the Church. For example, it has held weekend retreats involving yoga, meditation, and prayer; courses in church music; as well as courses that are more secular in character (bird-spotting weekends and weekends for senior citizens).

The Rättvik *stiftsgård* functions in three ways. First, it holds its own events and activities, most of which are social in character. The facility collaborates with a number of different agencies, such as social services, the Swedish Social Insurance Agency, and relief centres for women, while also offering services for people with various social needs. In addition, it has a close working relationship with job centres, organizing courses in vocational training. Second, it works closely with the diocese in Västerås and holds courses with more direct ties to the Church, such as further training for priests and deacons. Third, it rents out its facilities for conferences and meetings to local authorities and businesses in particular, but also to those individuals offering activities with potentially religious features, such as courses in yoga and meditation. However, the *stiftsgård* does not advertise these, and it proved difficult to gain more information as to who has held activities or courses there in the past as no register exists. Characteristic of the organization is, nonetheless, its sense of openness. The official position is that all are welcome, even if there is an unofficial evaluation as to what fits with the ideology of the *stiftsgård*. This open attitude is partially due to the fact the facility is independent, and as such is somewhat of a separate entity from the Church.[3]

In the 1930s, the first retreat in Sweden was organized by the Methodists Göte Bergsten and David Sandberg, who found their inspiration in England in the Oxford movement. Bergsten also arranged retreats at the offices of the bishop in Västerås, where the vicar Evert Palmer, inspired by the Anglican Franciscans, was interested in creating a much richer liturgical retreat. This idea spread throughout the diocese, and since 1952 such retreats have been organized regularly at the *stiftsgård* in Rättvik. The warden at that time was Nils-Hugo Ahlstedt. By the mid-1950s, the retreats had become so popular that there was a clear need for a new location as they were preventing other events and activities from being held (Jonson 1982: 24). In 1956, it was determined that the retreats required their own premises. Ahlstedt, together with the Franciscan Father Hugh, initiated the building of the House of St David, the construction of which was completed in 1962. The House of St David was included in the *stiftsgård* up until 1974, when the Foundation of the House of St David was established. In 1978, there was a reorganization, and Foundation Berget was formed (Garmo and Mases 2002: 20).

In 1973, the House of Meditation was established as a complement to the retreat activities at the House of St David. It was led by the Rättvik meditation centre the chair of which was Hans Hof, who was Professor of Philosophy of Religion at Uppsala University, as well as a close friend of Ahlstedt. For many years, Hof had been keenly interested in Zen meditation. In the early 1980s, Rättvik's meditation centre ceased its collaboration with Berget and in 1984 the House of Meditation became part of the House of St David. One reason for this was that Rättvik's meditation centre was having financial issues, but there were also questions as to whether and to what extent activities at the centre could be considered Christian. It is interesting to observe the difficult balancing act that existed

3 Telephone interview with a representative from the *stiftsgård* (respondent 15).

between the clearly Christian identity of the House of St David and the openness and responsiveness the meditation centre took towards people's questions and different interests, a balancing act that ultimately failed (Garmo and Mases 2002: 18). Here we see an example of the problems that can arise when there is experimentation with change and attempts to integrate new elements. When new elements are integrated on a large scale, it can result in confusion of identity. This problem was, however, solved when the House of Meditation was incorporated into the House of St David in 1984. Here, there was a return to clearer Christian roots, where integration of new elements could be better controlled.

The House of St David and the House of Meditation continue to serve as important bridges between the Church and the popular religious milieu (and, it should be added, the Catholic Church as well, since there are sisters at the House of St David from the Community of the Holy Trinity). Berget is owned by a trust and as such has a somewhat complicated relationship with the Church of Sweden. Over the years, the Church has both questioned activities at Berget and found inspiration from them, especially when it comes to the retreats, which have had a broad impact on the Church of Sweden (Garmo and Mases 2002: 21). Yet there is more to the House of Meditation than simply retreats, with a wide diversity of courses having been held there over the years. A quick review shows that courses on everything, from literature and Internet use to care for dementia patients, have been held. Of most interest for our project are those connected to the popular religious milieu. For example, the centre has organized courses in spirituality, the Alexander Technique (see note 4, page 84), Eutony (an alternative health therapy that works with different areas of tension in the body to create balance www.alternativmedicin.se), the enneagram (a symbol with nine points that, according to the teachings of Gurdjieff, is seen as fundamental to universal cosmic laws),[4] meditation, yoga, qi-gong, mysticism, and sacred dance. The list is long and varied. We put the question to the warden Per Mases and one of the sisters working at the facility as to what limits exist that determine

4 Russian-born George Ivanovich Gurdjieff developed an influential system of ideas about cosmology and psychology which included the belief that human beings live their lives as sleepwalkers. They can be awakened from this state and transcend to a higher level by way of certain exercises such as sacred dance, work, and spiritual exercises. See Ouspensky 1986.

whether a course can or cannot be held there. They answered that the courses must have a Christian basis and that a Christian world view of humankind is a prerequisite.[5] This is an interesting attitude if we look back at the many activities that have been arranged there over the years and that, at least in terms of ideas, are quite distant from Christian teachings.

The sister we spoke with told us that in 1983, when the five Catholic sisters arrived at Berget, there was a clear divide between the House of St David and the House of Meditation. She explained that the Christian basis was not adequately clear and that this was the main reason for disagreements. Since 1984, when the two became one, the aim has been to list all activities under four themes: Finding Oneself, Spiritual Guidance, Care of People and Humanitarian Values, and Cultural Sources (respondent 16, Sister at the House of St David).

Foundation Berget, with its House of St David, the House of Meditation, and the Catholic Community of the Holy Trinity, serves as a meaningful place where different worlds can come together and an exchange of ideas can take place. Those coming to the retreats can learn about Catholicism and have the opportunity of acquainting themselves with a great number of techniques from the popular religious milieu, techniques that normally would not be found within the framework of the Church. Over the years, many different activities have taken place there. It is, however, interesting to note that limits exist as to what can be arranged, and these limits seem to have been renegotiated on a number of occasions. It is possible to regard the House of St David as a door through which elements from popular religion can pass so that they might receive acceptance within the Church. Anything regarded as not having a Christian basis is rejected; however, one also finds here the beginnings of the integration of elements that might later be found in other places within the Church. One example of this is Zen meditation, which is nowadays practised in many churches throughout Sweden.

Meditation and Zen

Meditation in a Christian context is becoming increasingly commonplace. On Berget's website, Christian meditation is listed

5 This conversation with respondent 16 and Per Mases took place on March 6, 2009. Mases died on December 24, 2010.

as being offered at 83 places in the country. More often than not, this refers to so-called 'deep meditation'. *Kristen djupmeditation* (Christian Deep Meditation) was also the title of Sten Rodhe's 1976 book, but, by all accounts, the term had been used even earlier than that. Meditation has been traditionally used within certain strands of Christianity for many years, despite there being hot debates on blogs and webpages about whether or not it even has a place in Christian tradition. Today a link has been established with certain Buddhist forms of meditation, principally Zen.

Growth in the popularity of Zen meditation in Sweden has been attributed to Elin Lagerkvist, daughter of Pär Lagerkvist, the Nobel Prize-winning Swedish writer. She translated the book *Zen: en Zenbuddhistisk antologi* (1963) [Zen: a Zen Buddhist Anthology], an important book since it was one of only a few publications on the subject available in Swedish at that time. However, when it comes to a direct link between Zen meditation and the Church of Sweden, there is a clear connection to Dalarna and more precisely to Rättvik: Hans Hof and the House of St David.

Meditation expanded as part of the retreat movement as early as the 1930s, by all accounts in a form adapted to Christianity and the needs of the Church. In the 1970s, however, great interest grew in different forms of meditation, and German Jesuits became interested in Japanese Zen meditation. They adapted the method so that it could be practised without any particular religious content on the one hand and used by Christians on the other. These two forms were of huge significance for the development of meditation both within and outside Christian contexts (Jonson 1982: 26).[6] The reason that interest in Zen meditation grew within a Christian context in particular can likely be explained by the fact that this form of meditation is not as dogmatically demanding as many other forms.

In the early 1970s, the House of St David held courses in Zen meditation. These were well-received, and Per Mases subsequently travelled throughout Europe to learn more on the subject. Professor Hans Hof was, in this respect, a driving force, and it was with his help that the meditation centre in Rättvik was founded in 1972,

---

6 Jonson does not discuss the exact difference between these two forms; however, other authors write that it is the *focus* of the meditation – not the *technique* – that distinguishes them. It can be said that the first form centres around the experience of unity with the all, whereas the Christian form stresses the personal experience of (or unity with) God (or Jesus) (see, for example, Stinissen 2008).

which then led to the building of the House of Meditation. The House of Meditation was set up to offer meditation without any particular religious character and thus the form of meditation the German Jesuits had developed suited it particularly well. However, since this form of meditation could also be adapted to Christian contexts, it came to be part of the retreats and was practised at the House of St David (Jonson 1982: 26–7) – an illustrative example, then, of how a religious practice from something as distant from Christianity as Buddhism could be adapted to both Christian contexts and contexts more characteristic of the popular religious milieu (or even the secular domain). Subsequently, interest in Buddhist Zen meditation as taught at the House of St David spread to other contexts, partly because many Christians throughout the years had attended retreats there. Thus, with time, Zen meditation gained increasing acceptance within the Church as a whole.

A clear example of this acceptance is the fact that Zen meditation is currently practised in other contexts affiliated with the Church of Sweden in Dalarna besides Berget and Rättvik's *stiftsgård* – for instance, in Falun's Stora Kopparberg Church. At the time of our project, Zen meditation was being offered there every week. The session began at 18.30 with an introduction for those who did not have prior experience with meditation. They were told, for example, about the importance of sitting comfortably. To help with this, meditation stools, which were clearly Eastern in appearance, were available for use. Participants gathered at the very front end of the church, close to the altar. During our visit, there were 19 participants – four of these men. A female priest led the meditation. She began by directing focus towards the light and good, while also stressing the importance of Jesus for these concepts. Then the meditation itself began. It was organized into two sessions, each 20 minutes long, with a break during which time participants walked slowly around the altar. The meditation concluded in complete silence, and the participants vacated the church, still in silence.

The reason given for meditating is, as in the popular religious milieu, that it is a useful means of dealing with stress. However, in Christianity, meditation is also 'a tool to contemplative prayer or prayer free of conceptions that leads to knowledge about God based on experience and shared knowledge'.[7] The fact that meditation

7 Text from the Falun parish website: this can be found on the Church of Sweden's homepage www.svenskakyrkan.se.

within the Church originates in Buddhist Zen meditation is clear, even if it is referred to at times as simply meditation. In the Church of Sweden, however, it has been adapted and has taken on a form that fits within a Christian context. We have not examined the extent to which meditation practised in the Church of Sweden differs from the original form. What is interesting to note is the same process that we describe earlier in the case of other techniques – that is to say, the change in their content depending on context. In the case of mindfulness, secular significance replaces Buddhist significance, and when it comes to meditation, Christian significance replaces Buddhist significance.

Thus, an obviously foreign technique such as Zen meditation, which is more often associated with the popular religious milieu, has over a period of just 40 years come to be accepted and integrated so that it can now be practised in one of Falun's most central churches.

The Oneness Church Service in the Village of Vikmanshyttan

The ambivalent position of the Church of Sweden when it comes to new influences is exemplified by the Church hierarchy's response when one of their priests organized a Oneness church service in the rural community of Vikmanshyttan one Friday in March 2010. Normally, Oneness is not a technique found in the Church of Sweden, though in the Stockholm diocese Oneness features regularly in the Engelbrekt Church.

The Oneness movement has its origins in southern India and began in 1994 with a married couple whose followers refer to them as Sri Bhagavan and Sri Amma. In 1996, the movement began spreading throughout the world, and in 2000, the Oneness University was founded. Its foremost activity is diksha, the laying of hands on another person's head, as done by trained diksha practitioners. Within the movement, the term *diksha* translates as divine blessing. The act itself is quite simple: hands are laid on a person's head where they remain for a couple of minutes. On the movement's website, diksha is described as being a divine gift that activates an energy known as kundalini as well as the body's chakras. This results in a higher level of consciousness and finally in a state of what is described as Oneness. It is believed that this higher level of consciousness in an enlightened person can be transferred to another person, again through diksha. The aim is to spread this state of consciousness to as many as possible (preferably before the year 2012, which was seen as a year of particular importance for humanity). According to its webpage (www.onenessuniversity. org), diksha embraces every faith and spiritual tradition, and is felt to awaken the personal divinity of the individual.

The priest behind the Vikmanshyttan initiative described how normally only one or two people attended church services. She hoped that the Oneness church service would reach out to a greater number of spiritually interested people. At the 2010 service, more than 30 people attended, and many of these (an estimated 30 per cent) gave diksha. The service began with the priest's sermon, in which she explained what had led to the Oneness service and, very openly, the issues that this particular church service brought with it. She referred to the Father, the Son, and the Holy Spirit, maintaining that despite the changes to the day's service, Jesus remained central to the Church. She also talked about how the Church is there for everybody, especially the least privileged people in society.

After this, the service continued in a format that cannot be described as traditional. Further, many elements of the service were clearly non-Christian. Christian hymns merged with Hindu religious songs with references to Hindu religious mantras.

Participants were encouraged to move about freely, light candles, and write down their prayers on slips of paper. After this, most people sat down, and a number of people began to give diksha. Despite this physical movement and apparent free form, the service never felt chaotic. On the contrary, it progressed calmly, and everyone in attendance seemed to understand and respect its form. Afterwards, many gathered to talk over coffee and tea.

The priest who officiated at the service had herself been initiated in the Oneness movement and after more than 20 years as a Christian priest had developed an increasing interest in what unites different religions and religious traditions. She stresses that God can be found in every person. Her interest is in how different traditions can come together. If the Church shuts the door to other traditions, she believes it will lose its relevance in the modern world. She compares Oneness blessings to a form of intercession, a tradition deeply rooted in Christianity.

There is a story behind this Oneness church service. The vicar gave permission to the priest to go ahead with the service, but then the vicar fell sick before the service had taken place and was replaced. Some days prior to the service, a number of critical emails were received by the parish office, which resulted in a meeting being called. Those who sat on the church council were informed about the plans and expressed their concerns. The decision was made that the service would be allowed to go ahead but that it would be the first and last time that such a Oneness church service would ever take place in Vikmanshyttan. The priest found this regrettable, since she felt it to be an exciting way to encourage more people to attend church services.[8]

To dare try something novel and different in such a significant organization as the Church of Sweden – given how steeped in tradition it is – constitutes a risky venture. It is possible that in the future a Oneness church service may once again be allowed in the church in Vikmanshyttan, but for now there are no such plans.

Sacred Dance

In Sweden, a key person for the practice of circle dancing is Maria Rönn. Rönn was ordained as a priest in 1991, at a time when she was already strongly interested in dance. In her work at the Markus Church in Björkhagen outside Stockholm, Rönn, through Marie Louise von Malmborg, came into contact with the Findhorn Foundation in Scotland. In 1992, she trained to be an instructor of what is termed *sacred dance* or *circle dance*. A German dance professor by the name of Bernhard Wosien had developed this form of dance, which is why Rönn continued her training in Germany with Wosien's daughter, Maria Gabriele Wosien. In 1994, Rönn began working as a priest once more, bringing the dancing with her to the Church by holding courses for dancing instructors, along with Lisbeth Gustavsson, both within and outside the Church (for instance, in the towns of Sigtuna, Lund, and Härnösand) (www.mariaronn.com and Rönn 1997: 13–15).

Dalarna has an interesting connection with the Findhorn Foundation – the Fridhem retreat centre (Stiftelsen Stjärnsund), at which sacred dances also take place. In 1985, Lucie Minne arrived in Stjärnsund. She had a keen interest in sacred dance and was partly responsible for Bernhard Wosien being invited to the centre.

8 Interview after the Sunday church service as well as a telephone interview (respondent 22).

Minne went on to lead courses herself in what she termed *sacred circle dances*, continuing with these until 2002 when she moved to England. Despite her move, the practice of sacred dance seems nonetheless to have continued close to the Fridhem retreat centre. The retreat centre in Stjärnsund is situated in the parish of Husby, and, even as recently as 2010, sacred dances were being held in Stjärnsund's parish office.[9]

Sacred dances – or, as they are sometimes called, movement meditation, healing circle dancing, universal peace dancing, or community dancing – are currently held throughout Sweden, both within and outside the Church of Sweden, including in Dalarna. A network has grown and, in 2012, courses were being offered in about 55 places in Sweden, including a large number in the Stockholm area (www.heligadanser.info).

One of our interviewees, whom we will call Susanne, has been organizing sacred dances and teaching the technique for many years in Dalarna. Susanne, who prefers call it movement meditation, has been active in the practice for over 15 years and has run her own dance business for many years as well.[10] She describes the humble beginnings of the business when she was a study circle instructor in the mid-1990s. After a few years, the Church became more seriously involved, and the first church services were held that included sacred dance. First came evening mass, but the concept soon spread to other forms of church service. Between 2004 and 2009, Susanne worked together with Christian-based study groups, holding on average one church service including sacred dance per term, all of which attracted large groups. At the same time, she organized retreats both in Sigtuna and at Berget, which included meditation as well as movement meditation.

Susanne describes in detail the significance of the dances and their long tradition. Sacred dance is mainly a form of community expression, which is believed to have its origins in early human history. Dancing in circles and groups can be observed in contemporary folk dances. Susanne feels that prayer, meditation, and sacred dance are one and the same form of expression, sacred dance

---

9 Interview with Susanne (respondent 17) as well as information from the Husby parish website: http://www.svenskakyrkan.se/husby/.

10 Susanne, as well as others in this movement, writes Sacred dancing with a capital S. We have chosen not to do so here.

being a form of movement meditation. Susanne states that today we spend too much time sitting. We are not designed to do so which is why so many of us do not feel well, she explains. Through movement, we can find both inner peace and relaxation. Dancing is basic to our needs and has a positive impact on our whole being. It is through dance, states Susanne, that people find the strength not only to recover their sense of well-being but also to attain a sense of presence. Sacred dance, in other words, has many positive effects. Not only is it physically beneficial, but it also unites the body and soul, thus making the individual whole.

Sacred dances have thus been organized for many years in collaboration with the Church of Sweden in Dalarna. However, this process was not always a straightforward one. In 2009, Susanne organized the final church service that included sacred dance when the Church ceased working with her. Initially, she was unable to find out why this had happened, but over time she learnt that there were concerns about the inclusion of sacred dance in church services – though what these concerns were, she never discovered. If we consider the other examples discussed earlier in this text, we might suspect that the Church had doubts about how such dancing aligned with basic beliefs held by the Church of Sweden. This, however, is not Susanne's opinion, nor is it her explanation.

Discussion

We have above examined some of the meetings between the Church of Sweden and other belief systems in Dalarna. It is apparent in several ways that the Church has approached such meetings with a certain ambivalence. Litborn's observation that as long as one is aware of one's centre, then there is no need to have defined margins is telling. If one has a strong and clearly defined identity, it is easier to be open to new ideas. This perhaps lies at the basis of all forms of ecumenism and dialogue, which are in actual fact about mutual respect and understanding. Yet, it appears to be easier for the Church of Sweden to be in dialogue with representatives from Islam, which in many ways resembles Christianity, than with representatives of the popular religious milieu, which is more amorphous and whose boundaries are less clearly defined.

The Church of Sweden can be described as inclusive for the most part as well as pluralistic. It advocates theological discussion with other religious groups about, for example, faith and ethics. Yet it moves along a continuum where it both rejects and integrates new elements. The relation that the Church has with the popular religious milieu clearly exemplifies this problem. The Church is rather dismissive of many of the beliefs and practices featured in the popular religious milieu. With respect to these elements, it would thus be more correct to describe it as exclusionary.

Nevertheless, in some cases the Church has sought innovation and demonstrated a willingness to include new elements in its institution. Innovation and change are natural stages in the development of a religion, and it is easy to stagnate and lose relevance in the contemporary world if doors are completely closed to new phenomena that large segments of the populace perceive to be important. This is nothing new; rather, it has been an important question throughout time. The retreat movement described above is one such outcome of prior deliberation and influence from other traditions.

The problem is, where is the line of demarcation to be set? This has clearly varied over time and between different geographical areas. Representatives of the Church have varying opinions regarding to what degree and in what way they can include elements that cannot be directly tied to the tradition of the Church.

One strategy in many cases is to differentiate between ideology and technique, applying a technique but giving it another meaning. This is the case with, for example, Zen meditation, which has functioned well, whereas there has been more scepticism with respect to yoga, sacred dance, and, to a larger extent, with diksha. There is also the timeframe to consider: Zen meditation has had a longer relation with the Church than have the other phenomena. It might just be a matter of time before more practices originating in other cultures also gain inroads into the Church.

A further aspect to the relationship the Church has with the popular religious milieu is who it permits to use its facilities. One example is the health fair that took place in Säter in March 2009. Two organizers had gathered 29 exhibitors in the parish office belonging to the church in Säter. In a small space, exhibitors displayed their products and techniques, and offered visitors the chance to experience healing and massage. In addition, lectures were held on the top floor on such diverse subjects as previous lives and activation of the light body before the coming ascension.

According to event organizers, the fair attracted many visitors and was declared a success, which is why, one year later, they began planning for a similar fair. They contacted the parish office once more about renting the space, but this time their request was declined. The organizers were both surprised and annoyed. When we contacted the parish office, staff members there were rather reserved in their responses and did not want to discuss what had happened. What was clear, however, was that there had been some negative reactions to the March 2009 fair, which is why permission was not renewed for a second time.

At an individual level, we discovered that a few among our informants (besides those at Berget) were quite active in both the Church of Sweden as well as in the popular religious milieu. These were priests and members of church councils, and others who in different ways were deeply engaged with the Church but who were also involved with diksha, healing, yoga, automatic writing, or UFO spotting. Their number was too small to enable us to describe it as a trend; nevertheless, we were surprised. We concluded that there are people who simply do not see any problem with involvement in the Church of Sweden alongside involvement in the popular religious milieu. Heelas and Woodhead discuss this, stating that the individualization process that is happening in society at large is being felt by the Church and that a changed stance on religion can be observed, one that more clearly than before places focus on the individual. In this respect, church contexts have begun overlapping with the holistic milieu. Heelas and Woodhead nonetheless state that there is a long way to go before we can talk about one and the same position within these milieus (2005: 67–8).

One possibility, meanwhile, is that the relaxation of divisions between different religious milieus is a phenomenon that is affecting Dalarna more than urban areas, since the social context of rural counties is smaller and more condensed. In Dalarna, the Church is less marginalized than it is in urban communities. We also noticed that people who were socially active were often also active within the Church. Being active in the Church seemed to be part of a more general social engagement – an engagement that could also be expressed in popular religious ways.

However, it might also be the case that one result of the current process of globalization is to dismantle previously clear divisions and that the boundaries between Christianity and the popular religious milieu are becoming less sharp. Globalization with its myriad effects is thus worth exploring for the light it potentially sheds on the context of the popular religious milieu in Dalarna. This will be the theme of our next chapter.

Chapter 8

Dalarna: A Local Place in a Global World

Globalization refers to a world that is becoming ever more compressed as a result of increasing modes and levels of worldwide communication. This reality has led to surging flows of ideas, people, products, and services between all regions of the world. Thus, several of the world's cultures and societies have become interconnected at many levels, and there is an increased awareness of the world as a whole. This phenomenon has in recent decades been discussed from a number of different perspectives (see, for example, Martikainen 2004: 42–3; Frisk 2001: 31; Beyer 1994: 2). Globalization has been problematized in the areas of finance, politics, and culture (see, for example, Waters 1995: 7). The media – specifically the Internet – and migration – specifically global relocation, the phenomenon of refugees, and tourism – are important explanations for many of the great cultural changes we have experienced in recent times (King 1995: 6–7; Appadurai 1996: 3).

A number of researchers, such as Roland Robertson, talk about *glocalization* – that is to say, the interaction between global phenomena and local phenomena as part of a process by which the global becomes significant at the local level (1995: 40). When the term *local* is used, it can refer to anything from a small village to a whole continent (Massey and Jess 1995b: 226).

In this chapter, we will examine some examples from Dalarna that illustrate the effects of globalization on the popular religious milieu and the ways in which global influences are expressed through adaptations at the local level – in other words, *glocalization* if we adopt Robertson's term.

Hälsogränden: The Holistic Health Centre in Hedemora

In many towns and communities in Dalarna, groups of people, predominantly women, have joined together to rent premises from which they can offer their respective services. Often their focus is health. One explanation for the increasing number of such establishments in Sweden over recent years might be the fact that the long-term unemployed are able to apply for business start-up grants. In addition, becoming a collective and renting space together has a number of benefits, one naturally being financial. Besides, customers visiting one business will find brochures and information about the others in the same location and, what is more, one business will more often than not recommend the others. This form of collaboration – holistic health centres offering a number of different services at one and the same place – can be regarded as a local structure for globalized activities.

Hälsogränden is an example of such entrepreneurial collaboration. Located in the small town of Hedemora,[1] it began in November 2009 when five businesses opened in shared premises.[2] From a globalization perspective, these five businesses exemplify how cultural elements have spread throughout the world, coming together in mixed forms at one place (Rawlinson 1998: xviii). Here one also finds examples of local adaptations. The first entrepreneur we describe exemplifies this. She holds courses in *livsyoga* (life yoga), which is a local (Swedish) development of Yogi Bhajan's kundalini yoga from India and the USA.[3] She is also a stress therapist, which in her case involves the practice of breathing exercises, relaxation, body awareness, affirmation, visualization, and coaching as part of her services. In addition, she holds courses in yoga both for people who have been registered as sick for long periods as well as the long-term unemployed, in collaboration with the Swedish Social Insurance Agency and Arbetsförmedlingen, Sweden's employment office.

---

1 The text that follows is based on interviews with the founder of the holistic health centre (respondent 18). See also Frisk 2013, where Hälsogränden in Hedemora is discussed along with Western Esotericism.

2 Since then, the holistic health centre has undergone many changes in terms of its businesses and activities.

3 The parent organization for Yogi Bhajan's kundalini yoga is 3HO (Healthy, Happy, Holy Organization), which was founded in the USA in 1969. The founder came from India. This yoga form was introduced into Sweden in the 1990s by Tomas Frankell, a well-known New Age figure here. He chose not to involve himself in the 3HO organization and nowadays calls his form of yoga *livsyoga* (life yoga), which, he explains, is a Western adaptation of yoga (see Frisk 1998).

Business number two works with mindfulness, light therapy, Rosen Therapy, essential movement, and classic massage. It also sells Fair Trade cotton clothing from Africa. Rosen Therapy is a massage technique that focuses on the mind and the emotions. Its aim is to awaken unconscious feelings and memories that are locked within the body. Essential movement is a development of this. Mindfulness has its origins in Buddhism (see chapter 6), whereas the other activities are rooted in the American Human Potential Movement, which in turn has a historical background in humanistic psychology.[4] Key characteristics of the Human Potential Movement – of which most are apparent in Rosen Therapy, essential movement, and massage – are a focus on the inner potential of the human being, the significance of expressing feelings by way of body therapies, a focus on the here and now, as well as group therapy. Also characteristic of the Human Potential Movement is syncretism, which aims to bridge divisions between East and West, inner and outer dimensions, as well as science and religion.[5]

The third entrepreneur is a dietician, who works in the area of physical exercise and who also sells nutritional supplements.

The fourth is a hairdresser whose team, besides offering the expected services, also does 'spiritual haircutting'. This is a sort of hair-balancing where, it is explained, acupuncture energy is stimulated, chakras are balanced, and imbalances in the body rectified. The hairdressing team also offers reiki healing alongside head massage. (Reiki healing developed in Japan in the very early 1900s, but healing techniques there date much further back.) There is a certain degree of creativity and innovation involved, and possible inclusion of theosophical elements (Theosophy was inspired by Eastern religions), as indicated by the use of such terms as aura and chakra. The hairdressing team also mentions using Chinese acupuncture, though to what extent is not clear.

The fifth therapist employs psychodynamic psychotherapy, a form of treatment within the tradition created by Sigmund Freud, of psychoanalysis that focuses on revealing the unconscious and conflicting forces of the client's psyche in order to relieve mental tension.

4 Classic massage also has its origins in the Swedish health movement of the 1900s.

5 See also Anderson (2004).

The above account clearly demonstrates that Hälsogränden is a site where many cultural elements from a number of different parts of the world have come together and merged. Today's globalized world is what has enabled Hälsogränden to form in the way that it has.

Yet do these elements really come from all over the world? Global currents typically do not move from all places to all places (Ritzer, 2011: 154). Just as there are financial currents that for the most part move in certain directions, there are also cultural currents that are significantly stronger in some directions. Thus, when we scrutinize our empirical data from Dalarna – for which Hälsogränden serves as an illustrative example – we find many phenomena related to the American Human Potential Movement, which itself was inspired by Central European psychological trends and Eastern trends, especially Indian. In various yoga groups we find direct trends from India – as well as indirect ones, considering how a number of them first arrived in other countries, in particular the USA. We can find certain Chinese and Japanese influences, as with traditional Chinese medicine and reiki, and some influences from indigenous peoples (this, however, was not clear at Hälsogränden). That said, trends from the African continent are conspicuous by their absence. Nor did we find much related to Islam or Arabic countries, apart from the Muslim communities within Dalarna that have been established by immigrants and that as such result from human rather than cultural currents.

The key terms at Hälsogränden are inner and outer health. Our interviewee (the first entrepreneur, who is also a yoga instructor) states that these are closely related. If we are in contact with our inner-self, we naturally become more interested in looking after our outer-self, and vice versa. Inner health, she believes, is the same as spirituality. It is interesting to observe the mix of conventional, secular activities that the dietician, psychotherapist, and, to a certain extent, the hairdressing team represent at Hälsogränden. Clients can be referred to the dietician and psychotherapist from the regular health-care system, and there are no super-empirical notions forming the basis for treatment. It is also interesting to note the collaboration that the Swedish Social Insurance Agency and the national employment office have with the yoga instructor, collaboration that demonstrates how divisions between the official and the alternative are being erased in our contemporary world.

The Shaman from Azerbaijan

In 2010, a shaman from Azerbaijan held activities at an art gallery in a small town in Dalarna. He had sought asylum in Sweden in 2009. When we interviewed him, he told us that he wanted to spread the secret knowledge of the ASSA people from the lost city of Atlantis (this had been taught to him by a master in Russia some 20 years prior). These people were the original and secret people from Atlantis, not to be confused with the Atlanteans who are more generally known. He carried out his activities through the use of a yoga system and shamanistic drum journeys. In our interview, he stated how his yoga differs from traditional Indian yoga since the physical movements come to him intuitively when he relaxes, something he believes happens when there is a change in energy. Healing is one purpose of his activities. As with many of our interviewees, he talked about the challenges that the current world is facing, which he nonetheless believes will result in an increase in understanding of who we are beyond our bodies, minds, and personalities – it will be a golden age. He would very much like to form a group, perhaps a school (respondent 19).

When we consider this shaman from Azerbaijan, we find he represents many features of globalization. On the one hand, he himself emigrated from a country that to the average Swede would seem rather exotic; as such, it would be arguably easier to conceive of some ancient wisdom preserved there – in other words, a sort of 'wisdom of the Orient' conception. On the other hand, he himself draws elements from different cultures, from yoga to neo-shamanism and Western Esotericism. Cultural influences are partly about which cultures hold *power* in the world – and as such have a better chance of being visible and spreading – as well as about the way in which we collectively *perceive* other cultures and places. Oriental cultures have long appealed to Westerners seeking ancient wisdom and mystical realization. This is the case on both a global and a local scale. A church, retreat centre, or place in natural surroundings can also begin to be perceived as special and find connections with beliefs that in turn form our experiences.

The clear individualism of this shaman from Azerbaijan was interesting to note. The yoga movements he uses cannot be associated with any particular yoga style. As he states, they appear to come to him intuitively. We also found other people in Dalarna who, like the shaman, have developed their own forms of yoga.

Global versus Local in Gravendal near Ludvika

In Dalarna, there are no fewer than three retreat centres with ties to Osho or, as he was formerly known, Bhagwan Shree Rajneesh. Their level of independent orientation in terms of the Osho movement varies. Oshofors near Olofsfors (www.oshofors.nu) seems to have the closest ties with the movement. The retreat centre holds a few courses each summer, but is described as being a place where people can live together for set periods of time. Baravara outside Rättvik (www.baravara.se) offers courses led by international Osho therapists, but also draws inspiration from other sources. It has developed an independent profile that might be described as having been locally adapted to suit its Swedish context.

Lastly, there is a retreat centre in Gravendal outside Ludvika (www.uniomystica.se), where Shanti Kristian (born 1929) offers a variety of courses. Shanti Kristian has a background in the Osho movement, but the website explains how he also found inspiration elsewhere. Originally from Denmark, he has lived in several places throughout the world. By way of example, he lived in Norway as well as at the Osho collective in Oregon in the USA during the 1980s. Having also visited India a number of times, he is an example of a global individual who has firsthand experience of a number of different cultures. His background is in psychoanalysis and Human Potential therapy. In 1982, he is said to have become enlightened, a designation given to him personally by Sri Bhagavan of the Oneness movement, and in recent years, he has also made use of the diksha method. He is presented as an independent individual who has created his own profile in these contexts.

Retreat centres exemplify how global trends can and do establish themselves in local contexts. This is not always a smooth, straight-forward process. In February 2012, disagreements between the retreat centre in Gravendal and the local community were made public in a series of articles in the local newspaper.[6] People with close ties to the retreat centre had been buying up nearby buildings, and local community residents were afraid that 'the cult' would take over the village. The residents were critical of the way those running the retreat centre kept to themselves and showed no interest in helping preserve local sites of cultural interest. One

6   http://www.dt.se/ludvika/1.4396227-rorelse-vill-byta-namn-pa-by-invanare-oroliga; http://www.dt.se/dalarna/1.4397265-drommer-om-goldendal.

person active at the retreat centre wrote on the web that if more people were to buy houses in the village, then the village could be renamed Goldendal (after Golden City in India, the location of the headquarters of the Oneness movement). This was met by protests from the local community. Yet the idea, according to Shanti Kristian himself, came from a dream of one of the persons affiliated with the centre, which was joked about and had nothing to do with any genuine plans (interview with Shanti Kristian and his partner Sharya).[7] Such incidents clearly illustrate how conflicts of interest can arise between the local population and outsiders who have a more global perspective. It is not uncommon for people engaged in retreat centres in Dalarna to also buy their own houses close by. They settle there because they are attracted by the activities held at the retreat centre. Not all are interested in other activities that the local community regards as important. This gives rise to disagreement that is sometimes openly expressed but most often remains an undercurrent. In fortunate cases, new arrivals to a community are seen as contributing to the life of an area with their creative ideas. Most often, the responses are likely to be mixed.[8]

Alexander Markus: World Teacher in Dalarna

Alexander Markus, born in Hungary in 1939, lives in Dalarna. His wish is to create a place in the county for his school for life sciences, known as AIC or L'Académie Internationale de Culture Humaine Intégrale (translated as The Universal Academy for Global Human Culture, Philosophy, Science and Technology), which was founded in 1989. According to the webpage (www.celestemetoden.com), he had memories of previous lives even as a child, many in gnostic contexts; in one of these, in the 1700s, he was Saint Germain.

Alexander Markus narrates that at the age of 14, he met a light being, his consciousness was lifted to a higher dimension, and a

7 According to an email from Sharya on February 25, 2013, the disagreement was quickly resolved, and today there are no conflicts between the retreat centre and the local community.

8 In Oregon in the 1980s, a major conflict situation arose when the Osho movement deliberately attempted to take over political power within a local community. This, however, was a very different situation from the one in Gravendal. In Oregon, the number of members of the Osho community Rajneeshpuram was much greater than the local population. Additionally, this came at a time when opposition to the Osho movement was particularly strong (Frisk 1998; 2007). None of these conditions was present in Gravendal.

voice urged him to leave Hungary for Sweden and there to establish a centre for the development of higher consciousness. Thus he was chosen to be a world leader, his task to start in Scandinavia.

From the late 1950s, according to the website, Alexander Markus was active in different free-church, spiritualistic, theosophical, and similar contexts in Sweden, yet found no satisfactory answers. A further meeting with the light being urged him to travel to Ecuador. There, in the 1970s, he met a teacher by the name of Johnny Lovewisdom, who is said to have initiated him into Gnosticism and Mahayana Buddhism. In 1981, he was also initiated into the Sant Mat (Teachings of the Saints) by the Sikh Maharaj Charan Singh Ji of the Radha Soami Satsang in north India.

Through such experiences, Alexander Markus formulated 'CelesteMetoden', which he calls a gnostic life science. The intention with this is to distance negative thoughts and feelings that are held within our unconscious and unite our higher self with the central universe. We must change our consciousness so as to achieve a society full of love and wisdom.

The number involved in the group Alexander Markus has set up is not stated; however, information suggests that there may be about 100 who attend seminars, though most do not come from Dalarna (interview with Alexander Markus).

Here as well we see a person with an international background who has brought together various global trends. What is interesting in this case is the special significance given to Scandinavia and Dalarna, to such an extent that it is stated that a world teacher will come from the North. Similar thoughts are presented by the group we describe next: Siljans Måsar (the Gulls of Lake Siljan).

Siljans Måsar (The Gulls of Lake Siljan)

The snow fell softly over the old family home and outbuildings, covering them and the tall pine trees with a thick, white blanket. Everything was silent and still. Lake Siljan lay frozen at the bottom of the slope, its surface glistening in the white glow. It was close to midnight. Everyone was sound asleep; everyone, that is, except seven individuals who, elated to the point of tears, sat around a fire. This evening was to change their lives forever. The time had come for them to fulfil their mission – to awaken humanity in preparation for receiving the message.

In times gone-by when there was no time, the Creator sowed a seed along the shores of Lake Siljan. This seed germinated and grew and is today everything you see on Earth. You have lived through all stages of the growth of this seed and have now reached the final examination for your enlightenment here on Mother Earth [...] Our message to you in this book is a gift from the Universe, to be used as a tool in all stages of your life [...] You are never alone. You are Gods on your way home – and we accompany you. The Lords of Lake Siljan.[9]

In October 2009, the group known as the Gulls of Lake Siljan (Siljans Måsar) held its first official meeting in Rättvik.[10] There were about 25 people, including us, in attendance, mostly women in their 50s and older. The meeting was led by a woman who we shall call Astrid. She played a key role since it was she who had written down the messages from the Lords of Lake Siljan using automatic writing. She explained that it was exactly one year to the day that the event described above had taken place; it was at that time that she, with the help of another key person in the group of seven, who we call Osman (from Turkey), used automatic writing for the first time. Astrid explained that she does not know what she is writing. When she reads the texts aloud during the meetings, it is the first time she is seeing and comprehending them.

Many of the messages that appeared by way of automatic writing are now published on the group's website. Not all of them, however, are ascribed to the Lords of Lake Siljan. Some, for example, are ascribed to Archangel Gabriel, Maria Magdalena, or 'the Sisters from Sirius'. In the very first message, the group was urged to start a website and spread the message using printed materials and the Internet (first in Swedish, then in English). The significance of the Internet was frequently stressed. Many of the messages explain how those who are listening are the chosen ones, their mission being to serve as light-workers and spread by example light and love. The

9 Back-cover text of the book *Ljus från norr: Budskap från Universum genom Siljans Måsar* [Light from the North: Messages from the Universe Through the Gulls of Siljan: *our translation*], no publishing house or author name provided, 2009.

10 The information below was gleaned from the group's website (www.siljans-masar.se); observations from two meetings, in 2009 and 2010; and interviews and informal discussions with attendees at the meetings. The information about the World Brotherhood Union Mevlana Supreme Foundation was gathered from its website (www.dkb-mevlana.org tr); an interview with the leader Vedia Bülent Çorak in Istanbul; and a short description by Gail M. Harley (2002) in *Religions of the World: A Comprehensive Encyclopedia of Beliefs and Practices*.

light shall come from the North. Mother Earth, a common theme in the messages, helps by giving signs in nature. What is also clear is that there is an expectation of some kind of catastrophe, before – according to the Plan – the Golden Age can begin, an existence in harmony with Mother Earth. The task of Siljans Måsar is to unite humanity. They have begun their work but this will continue for many centuries. Belief is in one god, a creator. Nine people should be central to Siljans Måsar, but they go unnamed, and it became apparent during the meetings we attended that nobody knows exactly who these nine are.

According to the messages, there are seven groups similar to Siljans Måsar in the world today, although Siljans Måsar is the largest and most important. It is not stated who the other groups are.

During the two meetings in which we took part, the belief that every human being can be his or her own channel was stressed. Osman, who appeared to have a central role in the group and yet was external to it, helped to 'open the channel to the universe' so that those who so chose could begin to receive messages themselves and record these through automatic writing. This opening itself was ritual-like, with special gestures and words. According to Osman, not everybody has the correct DNA code required for them to be able to open the channel.

By March 2010, Siljans Måsar had over 70 members.

Lake Siljan and Siljans Herrar (The Lords of Lake Siljan)

According to Siljans Måsar, the light shall come from the North, and it is the area around Lake Siljan that is of particular significance for the group. One message states that Siljan is the place where beauty will grow forth and it is from there that goodness will spread, first within Sweden and then throughout the Nordic countries and Europe. In addition, the Siljan area holds ritualistic significance for the group. During one of the gatherings in which we took part, group meditation was held right beside the lake, where the energy was 'taken down'. Osman explained – and we have heard it similarly said, though in different words by other interviewees from other milieus in Dalarna who have nothing to do with Siljans Måsar – that Lake Siljan is the site of a meteorite strike, that the rocks there have a special structure, and that energy waves of the highest frequency therefore can descend exactly there.

Siljans Herrar describe themselves in some of the messages. They call themselves a group 'of the Highest Assembly within the Central Solar System' comprising 11 people (five women and six men, who are named and whose latest incarnation is described in message 41 on the website) who have been incarnated on Earth.[11] The word *herr* (lord) does not indicate maleness but should rather be interpreted to mean those who are in control of their situation and life plan. Their mission is to 'awaken humanity and report to the Highest of places'.

What Preceded Siljans Måsar?

The written history of Siljans Måsar began with the midnight meeting at an old farm in Dalarna in 2008, when Astrid began receiving messages using automatic writing. Yet there is a story that pre-dates this event. What is not clear from the back-cover text quoted above is that the meeting at the Dalarna farm concerned a book called *The Knowledge Book*. Astrid recounted at the first Siljans Måsar meeting how she had received this book as a gift during a course in the town of Växjö in southern Sweden before receiving messages for the first time and using automatic writing. It was not made clear when this event had taken place, but the book, having been translated from Turkish into Swedish, was published in 2006. After the course in Växjö, Astrid and her family moved to Falun, where she learnt about the shop that Osman runs in the centre of the town. She entered the shop and began talking to Osman. When she heard that he was from Turkey, she explained how she had read *The Knowledge Book*. Osman was rather surprised, explaining that he too had read it and had not known about its translation into Swedish.

The history of the Turkish group World Brotherhood Union Mevlana Supreme Foundation, which published *The Knowledge Book*, began on New Year's Day in 1966 in Istanbul.[12] Vedia Bülent

---

11 Nine are said to have lived in European countries (one in Sweden), one in the USA, and one in Canada.

12 The question as to when phenomena 'begin' is complex. Our guess is that older roots for the group would be found if it was possible to investigate the founder's background more closely. Harley is the only academic who has approached this movement. She states in a very short introductory text in an encyclopedia that the main source of inspiration for the group is Theosophy and Western Esotericism, but that it has integrated teachings about UFO beliefs in an attempt to bring religion and science together, and that the teachings have also taken on a certain Turkish and Muslim character. No numbers exist about group size (Harley 2002: 1424–5).

Çorak (born in 1929), a well-to-do doctor's wife and mother of one daughter, awoke with a nasty cough. Later in the day, feeling better, she went to the cinema with her husband to see a Frank Sinatra film. During the showing, her whole body began to shake and her heart to pound. She returned home, where her husband gave her some medicine. After this, she took up a pen and suddenly began to write a poem using automatic writing. She did not herself know what she was writing and was naturally astonished. She received many messages. She learnt that it was the 'Highest Assembly' that was writing through her and that she would be the new missionary who would unite religions and people. However, she believed she was the wrong person and tore up the paper. The same message, nonetheless, kept coming to her, and again and again she would tear up the paper until eventually she consented. After this, there began a period of some years when she, according to her own testimony, left her body during the night to visit other dimensions. In 1981, she began – using automatic writing and according to instructions – to write *The Knowledge Book*, an impressive work of some 1,000 pages which took her 12 years to complete. In 1993, the World Brotherhood Union Mevlana Supreme Foundation was founded. Mevlana is a name of the Sufi mystic Rumi who lived in the thirteenth century, and Vedia Bülent Çorak is believed to be an incarnation of him.

The Knowledge Book is written in a very complex language that is far from easy to understand. Those who wish to read it must meet every Tuesday evening to read the book in groups (of at least three people) located all over the world. First, a call must be made to Istanbul. Those present must read one chapter aloud, then afterwards recount the chapter for one another. The text is considered to be coded, which means that the significance can be other than the literal, and readers are said to gain a higher consciousness simply from reading it (this is also said to be the case with the literature of Siljans Måsar).

In brief, the teachings of the movement state that our planet is about to enter a golden age, when humanity will be united. After this, a better age will come when the order of Allah will be directly active. There is only one god. Prior to all this, however, chaos will reign on Earth. *The Knowledge Book* is dictated through 'the alpha channel', which can now be found directly over Turkey and which is said to be the direct reflection mechanism of Allah. All holy books – the Old Testament, the Book of Psalms, the New Testament, the

Qur'an[13] – were revealed through this channel. *The Knowledge Book*, which is also called the Cosmic Book of this Last Age, reveals all secrets and contains the frequencies for all known holy books up to the present day. If the cipher in an individual's genes accords with the hidden ciphers in the book, a direct connection is established between the human being and the message in the book. The world view includes many different cosmic dimensions and planets where different beings exist. The world is said to be going through different periods of development with different people who have appeared in accordance with where the alpha channel was active at the time. Examples are Moses, Jesus, and Mohammed. By way of *The Knowledge Book*, the foundations for the world state have been set, according to Allah's fourth order. It is only Vedia Bülent Çorak who can receive the messages using automatic writing.

The emergence of Siljans Måsar ties in with *The Knowledge Book*. Many in the group have read it. The book was brought to and shown at the meetings we attended. Otherwise, however, it was not used. One member during an informal conversation told us that the group had discussed *The Knowledge Book* and concluded that it was too difficult and could not therefore be widely distributed. She believed that the guides from other dimensions had realized this and had instead formed the material of Siljans Måsar, which is easier to understand and, she states, better suited for Sweden and the Nordic countries.

The Ongoing Story of Siljans Måsar

It was not long before Siljans Måsar split up. Astrid and others in leadership positions have gone their own way and formed smaller groups. Many of these have a strong presence on the Internet – for example, in Facebook groups, where anybody can publish messages received through automatic writing. In Siljans Måsar, much emphasis was placed on establishing one's own channels and receiving one's own messages. The question is whether or not this particular feature played a role in the break-up of the group. Regardless, there do seem to have been different wills at play and disunity as to whom the group should follow. The balance between hierarchy and equality can at times be difficult. Some interviewees

13 Eastern religions and writings are mentioned sporadically, but do not appear to be significant.

expressed a sense of disappointment with the fact that they could not agree. According to the Plan, they should have been united and gone forward together in their work. However, human beings have their own free will and consequently this group was unsuccessful. Many feel that one of the smaller groups should take over and continue with the mission that Siljans Måsar initiated.

Siljans Måsar: A Local Adaptation

Siljans Måsar is a representative example of so-called glocalization, that is to say ideas that spread globally but adopt local features. Place-bound beliefs can be linked to the individual's place and purpose in the world – and thus also concern identity. We see examples of this in the special place Turkey holds for the Mevlana Brotherhood and in the central role that Lake Siljan plays in Siljans Måsar. That places or countries are ascribed a particular significance in terms of the new world order is not unusual. For example, this was once the case with Sweden when in the 1600s Johannes Bureus believed this place to hold particular significance in upcoming eschatological events (Karlsson 2010: 244–54). In Siljans Måsar, we see how the area around Lake Siljan replaces Turkey as a significant place, and how Astrid and other local women replace Vedia Bülent Çorak as contacts for the spiritual leaders. Even these spiritual leaders become somewhat local. In the case of Siljans Herrar, most of the 11 leaders by way of their latest incarnations have connections with Europe and the Nordic countries. Instead of *The Knowledge Book*, members of Siljans Måsar read their own messages received through automatic writing and make much use of the Internet as a channel of communication. The example of Siljans Måsar also demonstrates how a movement can take on different forms through relocalization and in this case adopt a more democratic structure where there is more than just one leader believed to channel all messages.

One important aspect of globalization is that both cultures and cultural currents are constantly moving and changing as a consequence of different influences. Some of the discussion about globalization talks about how Western culture is spreading throughout the world as a result of uneven power distribution. It has here been pointed out that Western culture itself is a blend of different cultures, that there are strong counter movements from other cultural currents, and also that Western elements are adapted and changed according to local influences (Pieterse 1995: 45–54). We can name, for example, the Mevlana Brotherhood, which may well have been influenced by theosophical currents, which in turn were influenced by both Western esotericism and Eastern currents, but which in Turkey assumed certain Muslim features. In the theoretical debate about globalization, discussions touch on hybridization, creolization, as well as syncretism (Pieterse 1995: 62; Hannerz 1996: 66). Ulf Hannerz describes creolized culture as being a combination of diversity (historical roots on different continents), creative collaboration, and innovation against a backdrop of global centre-periphery relations (1996: 67–8).

The Indirect Consequences of Globalization

Up to this point, we have discussed the direct consequences that globalization has had in terms of migration, communication, and the meeting of different cultural currents. Yet globalization has also indirectly affected how religion is expressed in the present and could be regarded as being one of the processes that have most influenced the formation of current forms of religious expression. The discussion that follows focuses on globalization, although many of the changes described are also reinforced by other processes in contemporary society.

Relativization, the Experience Dimension, and This-worldliness

Characteristic of our globalized world is the fact that cultural elements from many parts of the world can be found in one and the same place. Sociologists of religion Roland Robertson and Peter Beyer opine that this leads to a process they term *relativization*. As a result of globalization, a society or culture is perceived as being simply one of many in the world, the result being that all cultures, and even religions, are relativized. Individuals form their religious identity knowing that their religion is but one of many (Beyer 1994: 9, 26–30). William Paden states that the ability not only to understand the world but also to understand *how* we understand the world – that is to say, the ability to step back and see our perspective as one of many – is an indicator of contemporary thinking and an effect of the new pluralistic situation. Paden terms this *self-reflexivity* (1992: 3).

Through this process of relativization, different cultural elements are presented as being of equal worth, which when combined with individualism, as discussed in chapter 9, opens the way for choice and combinations according to likes and dislikes. Paden notes that different possibilities are perceived like alternative pairs of glasses; that one should not be truer than the other (1992: 4). In the long term, boundaries between different religions may also become less clear and less essential (Frisk 2002). This tendency is apparent in the Dalarna study. We met several people who worked within the Church, such as wardens, even a priest, who were also deeply engaged in the popular religious milieu. Relativization can, additionally, result in religions that claim to have a *particular* truth – for example, Christianity – being undermined and losing their credibility (Frisk and Nynäs 2012), which will ultimately benefit popular religiosity.

A further consequence of relativization is that the credibility of *all* beliefs is, to a certain extent, undermined. When many belief systems and ideologies exist side by side, it must be clear to the individual that not all can be true.[14] This might be one reason the ideological dimension in contemporary popular religiosity is becoming less significant, whereas orientations to other aspects such as experience, feelings, and practice dominate. These aspects are also clear in popular religiosity as a whole. Examples discussed in earlier chapters were yoga and mindfulness, which are activities that can hold different kinds of cognitive understanding, but where the focus is on experience and corporeality. The world here and now, belonging to the domain of experience, is stressed at the expense of existence after death, which has more of a place in the sphere of belief.[15]

Globalization and relativization have further consequences that we do not discuss in this book since they characterize popular religiosity in Sweden to a significantly lesser degree. A common perspective is that globalization brings with it two types of religious response: one that encourages the creation and revival of particular identities, the *particularistic* response; and one that focuses on the global culture as such and that relativizes cultural, personal,

14 This also gives rise to much uncertainty about the question of beliefs. The questionnaires show that answers such as 'don't know', 'somewhat', and 'maybe' are frequent. This is also the case with 'typical' new religious beliefs such as reincarnation and belief in God as a life force (http://www.worldvaluessurvey.orgwvs.jsp).

15 Another reason for the this-worldly orientation is the excessive materialism of our culture, which can create a need for religious legitimacy.

and religious identities, the *universalistic* response. One aspect of contemporary religious change is thriving fundamentalist religious movements, which aim to restore tradition and make religion influential in society. While these movements can be perceived as particularistic responses to globalization, Western popular religious phenomena can mainly be viewed as universalistic responses (Frisk and Nynäs 2012).

Globalization is a complex process that has varied consequences in different cultures. The response that is triggered seems to be linked with economic and historic development, as well as power structures. Those parts of the world where universalistic responses to globalization dominate are characterized by fast-paced and stable socio-economic development, which according to Ronald Inglehart leads to individualistic values and democracy (Inglehart and Welzel 2005). In such societies, there is no recent history of oppression. These societies also hold more power (economic and otherwise) than those in other parts of the world and lack, as a rule, a glorified past. Those societies with contradictory characteristics – weak socio-economic development, limited power, a glorified history – as well as parts of cultures with these characteristics are often more open to particularistic responses to globalization (Rajagopal 2001; Castells 2004).

To a certain extent, affirmation of local identities can also be perceived as being a particularistic response or, as Manuel Castells calls it, resistance identities, whose representatives oppose global processes and seek to return to local historic traditions. In Dalarna, we can see this to a certain extent with Siljans Måsar, as well as with other phenomena such as the few women we met who call themselves witches who want to connect with older, local traditions – for example, healing with medicinal herbs. Some refer to local folklore. This is exemplified by a medium in the village of Älvdalen, who told us the following:

> Gnomes or small people came just as I was about to hold a large séance. Instead, the small people came through, in a number of groupings. They were very angry because the people were going to move a small building and the people's dogs were urinating in their holes (respondent 20).

One goal of larger, particularistic religions in the world – such as, for example, certain Islamic and nationalistic Hindu movements – is often the securing of political influence.

The Equal Worth of Everybody and the Inner Authority of the Self

Peter Beyer maintains that, from a liberal perspective, a globalized society rejects the notion of outsiders as representing evil or chaos in a social sense. Those who were previously outsiders are now neighbours. In contrast, in a conservative understanding, the reality of evil is affirmed, and other peoples and cultures are often viewed as manifestations of evil. Liberal religious orientations, according to Beyer, readily include everybody in the global community (1994: 85–7).

Popular religious trends are for the most part liberal in the sense in which Beyer uses the term, even if contrary examples do exist. The general tendency, however, is to be inclusive and, ideologically speaking, there is little discussion about evil. Linda Woodhead (2001) notes that themes such as punishment, hell, and the devil in contemporary times have all but disappeared from popular spirituality and institutionalized religion, a fact substantiated by our empirical material from Dalarna.

A further aspect of an inclusive approach is that all voices are given equal worth. Popular religiosity is principally a lay movement (Sutcliffe 2003), where authority and hierarchy are not highly valued. Every individual can be as authoritative as any priest or spiritual leader – not by way of studies and knowledge, but rather by way of his or her own inner experiences. We see this with Siljans Måsar, where each individual is supposed to be able to learn to receive automatic writing, which distinguishes it from the parent movement in Turkey. This is a strong tendency in popular religiosity, though not universal, given the authorities of different kinds in this milieu. Yet the producers in our survey of popular religiosity in Dalarna represented a form of authority, being, as they were, teachers, leaders, or lecturers. Nonetheless, Paul Heelas observes that the authority and celebration of the self are the most characteristic features of contemporary New Age trends (1996).

Social, political, and economic changes over recent decades have also greatly increased the value of the individual and his or her self-determination, the effect being less influence on the part of institutions (Woodhead 2001; Roof et al. 1995: 244). We will discuss this in the next chapter, where we will also examine individualism in popular religiosity.

Chapter 9

Secularization, Individualism, and Identity

Globalization, as discussed in the previous chapter, is an important factor in the way religion is currently expressed. There are, however, other processes that are also important and that ought to be included in discussions about contemporary popular religiosity. Below, we have chosen to examine three concurrent themes, which we discuss in relation to our empirical material from Dalarna: secularization/ sacralization, individualism, and identity.

Secularization, Sacralization, and Post-Secular Culture

The decline in organized religion (especially Christianity) in Europe, Australia, and, to a lesser extent, the USA is well-documented.[1] Many theorists have described and attempted to explain ways in which this process of secularization should be understood. Many, such as Stark and Bainbridge, and Christopher Partridge, opine that theories about secularization are not enough to explain the religious landscape in the West, stressing that a process of sacralization is occurring at the same time (Stark and Bainbridge 1985: 2–3). Partridge asserts that 'spiritualities' are constantly appearing and assuming new forms and expressions that differ radically from traditional religions. There are many ideas and practices that have their origins well beyond the Christian cultural domain but that are no longer foreign to a Western audience. This domain, which Partridge terms *occulture,* is supported by and based in large part on popular culture and popular cultural beliefs (Partridge 2004: 4).

Partridge bases his argument on Colin Campbell's discussions about 'the cultic milieu' (Campbell 1972). Campbell maintained in

1 For a discussion on the situation in Great Britain and the USA, see Heelas and Woodhead 2005: 49–76. A useful overview of research into secularization in the West can be found in Bruce 2002. For a problematization of theories on secularization, see Partridge 2004: 8–16 and Zuckerman 2005.

a number of articles during the 1970s that the process of secularization leads not only to religion losing its significance and becoming less interesting, but also to a departure from 'churchly religion' towards 'spiritual and mystical religion'. He opined that in discussions about secularization, little heed was paid to either the interest in less organized forms of religious or the interest in mysticism. Going further, he stated that the Enlightenment and the resulting secularization neither made the cult milieu impossible nor precluded it: on the contrary, it instead supported the cultic milieu's critique of the importance that traditional religion places on dogmas and doctrines. According to Campbell, this had paradoxical implications, to say the least, since Enlightenment secularism, which rejected religion, dualism, and dogmatic teachings, at the same time laid the ground for both spiritual as well as mystical forms of religiosity (1978: 152).

Partridge espouses this view, opining that the processes of secularization and sacralization occur simultaneously, in parallel to each other. He describes this process as being a shift from what is objectively revealed to subjective experience, from what is exclusive to what is inclusive and relative, and as a process where what once belonged solely to the religious field is being increasingly decoupled and reaching a wider public. This results in spiritual beliefs becoming more accessible and also to their being interpreted and used in completely secular ways (Partridge 2004: 42–50; see also our discussion about globalization in chapter 8). Partridge takes Campbell's argument a step further, maintaining that, far from vanishing or collapsing, religious world views are instead most definitely alive in Western society. Personalized alternative spiritualities have always existed, though mostly in the background. Only now are they becoming more visible and contributing to the shaping of Western society and culture (Partridge 2004: 53). Nevertheless, the process has been both slow and irregular (Partridge 2004: 58).

What, though, does this personal alternative spirituality involve, and what are its consequences? Partridge presents his theory in his voluminous *The Re-Enchantment of the West* (published in two volumes, in 2004 and 2005), where he demonstrates that so-called occulture can be found in many different forms. He provides numerous examples of how world views relating to religion or spirituality are a recurring theme within many different popular cultural genres. He examines film and television, music, literature, the organic movement, psychedelic phenomena, cyber spirituality, UFO milieus, the occultic milieu, the holistic milieu, and eschatological beliefs. In all of these, Partridge finds various examples of how beliefs he associates with the term *occulture* are portrayed in popular culture in an entertaining and accessible manner. It is Partridge's opinion that such beliefs are apparent in both conventional and alternative milieus. He consciously avoids giving occulture a strict and restrictive definition, choosing instead to define it in a more metaphorical manner:

> Occulture is the spiritual *bricoleur's* Internet from which to download whatever appeals or inspires; it is the sacralising air that many of our contemporaries breathe; it is the well from which the serious occultist draws; it is the varied landscape the New Age nomad explores; it is the cluttered warehouse frequently plundered by producers of popular culture searching for ideas, images and symbols. (Partridge 2004: 85)

What Partridge aims to show is that all of these techniques, practices, symbols, and beliefs are accessible to an ever wider public and that their broad cultural impact is growing. Increasing numbers are embracing them and they are being perceived as less exotic than before. The fact that religious symbols and pictures appear in popular cultural literature and music has often been interpreted as an indication of secularization, since religious content has been reinterpreted and presented as entertainment. Partridge, however, disagrees with this interpretation. Rather, in his view what has happened is that the divisions between what is regarded as sacred or holy and as profane or entertainment have been erased or have at least become blurred, and this need not be interpreted as secularization (2004: 60–8).

Our material from Dalarna clearly demonstrates that alongside the process of secularization, other counter processes are occurring, processes that are engaging relatively large parts of the population. Like Partridge, we see, as discussed earlier in the book, that the divisions between the religious and the profane are becoming less clear. Mindfulness or yoga can be practised with few or no explicitly religious elements and without thought being given to these, since the question of whether it is religion or not has lost its significance. In contrast to Partridge, however, we wish to maintain – based on our empirical material – the importance of secularization in this development. The fact that the differences between what is religious and what is profane have become less apparent undoubtedly has to do with the new ways in which religion is currently being expressed; however, these forms of expression are strongly influenced by secular phenomena – for example, by psychology and therapy. What we see from the material from Dalarna can clearly be interpreted as religious expression, but this kind of religion is expressed in a secularized culture and has secularized features. The surrounding culture strongly affects how religion is expressed, and our culture is no exception.

One term that is increasingly used is *post-secular*: its definition is not particularly clear, but it includes the idea that secularization theories are not (any longer) unequivocally sustainable. The fact is that the religious landscape is also undergoing a process of sacralization. The theme of the 2011 Donner Institute Symposium was post-secular religious practices, and in the publication that developed out of the symposium, the announcement read: 'A post-secular society is that which combines a renewed openness to questions of the spirit with the habit of critical enquiry ' (Ahlbäck 2012: 5). Religion has not disappeared as a result of processes of modernization. It is rather the case that new and unexpected relations between social actors and the sacred have developed. Religion today is part of a new cultural framework, where individualism, pluralism, and new conditions for identity and belonging ('deterritorialization') are important components (Giordan and Pace 2012: 1–3). The secularization process has not distanced religious expressions in our culture; rather, it has converted them (Giordan and Pace 2012: 5). Based on the various phenomena we have examined throughout this study, we would like to suggest that perhaps what is most important in the current process of religious change is that the differences between 'religious' and 'secular' are becoming less obvious and less significant. Our opinion is that this is an important indicator of post-secular culture.

Individualism

A distinct feature of our culture that has been noted by many researchers (Ahlin 2007; Heelas 1996; Heelas and Woodhead 2005) is growing individualism. The value of the individual and his or her right to self-determination, responsibility, and opportunities are stressed, both in political neoliberal trends as well as in psychological and therapeutic trends that expanded predominantly during the latter part of the 1900s. Freedom of choice of the individual is encouraged and external authorities lose their significance. Within the health-care sector, patient-centred care is gaining more ground, just as a student-centred perspective is in the field of education. Collective activities and group membership, as found in clubs, churches, and political parties, are losing popularity. With its emphasis on the creative potential of the individual, the Human Potential Movement in the 1960s was an expression for individualism and has gone on to influence and bolster individualistic tendencies ever since. These tendencies have led to a more essentialist understanding of the human being, as discussed earlier.

Religious expression has also been affected by individualism. In his 1996 book, Paul Heelas discussed the sacredness of the individual as one of the most distinctive characteristics of the New Age. Together with Linda Woodhead, he expanded on this argument in a later work (2005), which we have discussed in chapter 4, where they talk about subjectivization – that is to say, the ever-increasing individualistic, subjective orientation in Western culture. Contemporary culture is ever more person-centred, the subject being the focus. This is the case in education, work, health, and more or less all cultural sectors. This development has also affected the relationship the individual has to religion in such a way that subjective-life has gained ground while the opposite is true of life-as (Heelas and Woodhead 2005: 2–5). According to Heelas and Woodhead, this subjective turn of modern culture is a root cause of both secularization and sacralization; it favours and reinforces the spirituality of subjective-life, while undermining other forms of religion (2005: 77–8). As a result of contemporary pluralism, religions that present a single truth lose their authority, and people look inwards instead in their search for a deeper truth (2005: 130).

Above all else, Linda Woodhead (2001) highlights a change she terms *turn to life*. She maintains that this process is two-sided. The first side is personal and is about living life to the full. She calls this *selfing* – going about life on one's own terms. The second side is cosmic and concerns turning to the life force and realizing that one's individual self is but a single aspect of something much greater. To turn to life also encompasses a stronger emphasis on nature and human relations. This approach is holistic and involves an orientation towards this world. Further, it emphasizes equality and fairness. There is also a strong focus on the strength and ability of the individual (Woodhead 2001: 111–13). Woodhead opines that this approach – this turn to life – is gaining a place not only within the domain of alternative spirituality, but also within the Christian churches of Western society. This is especially apparent in liberal religious trends as well as in theological trends that are more feminist in theological orientation. Punishment, hell, damnation, and beliefs in demons are Christian concepts that have all but vanished along with ideals of asceticism and self-sacrifice. Older beliefs of sacrifice and self-deprivation, which were once presumed to prepare people for the next life, have been replaced with experience, equality, and focus on this-worldliness (Woodhead 2001: 113–17). Woodhead describes this turn to life as a 'flight from deference' and argues that religion is no longer about subordination to a higher authority or asceticism. This orientation of no longer being willing to subordinate oneself to higher powers is not the case in the religious sphere alone. A study of values (World Values Survey) conducted in 1990 indicates that respect for institutions and authorities is on the decline. Woodhead opines that one result of this is the continuously declining trust in government authorities, political parties, and religious institutions (2001: 117–21).

Our material from Dalarna demonstrated the importance of the individual in a number of areas. The popular religious milieu in its entirety can be seen to be an expression of individualism where the freedom of choice of the individual is central and the idea of the buffet table is prominent. There is also a general emphasis on relativization, in such a way that the individual is encouraged to choose from different practices based on his or her personal preferences. A large proportion of popular religious practices involve individual sessions – massage, therapy, healing, private séances – all of which involve one client spending private time with a producer. The health of the client is clearly the focus. Elements of healing dominated our study. Furthermore, the inner authority of the individual outweighs the authority of others and of tradition. Courses exist in which participants learn different things – but at the end of the day, it is up to the individual what he or she takes away from the course and how this learning is applied in everyday life. A clear example of this is the form of yoga developed by one of our interviewees who called it (when translated) My Spirit Yoga. Another yoga instructor knew intuitively which movements he would teach his pupils. Then there was the case of a female healer who had all but completely moved away from traditional healing techniques she had learnt and instead sensed the needs of her clients on an individual basis.

Naturally, popular religious practices are not completely univocal. The very existence of healers, mediums, and therapists demonstrates that there are authorities at different levels in this domain. Some of these can be quite powerful, and the leader may be perceived as enlightened or spiritually advanced.

Based on our empirical material, we can also confirm Woodhead's thesis about this-worldliness being a prominent characteristic of the popular religious milieu. The body is the focus in a number of the techniques we surveyed, whereas there is little sign of asceticism. A sense of feeling better in the here and now dominates, with little thought given to the next life. Yet not even this is univocal: the spiritualistic movement partly concerns life after death, even if it seems to be more about confirmation that the deceased are present among us rather than about how we should prepare ourselves for death. The this-worldly trend is most likely a result of the material welfare of current society. While the increase of material welfare of the 1960s and '70s generated protests that were ascetic in nature, the religious conceptions of the present seem rather to affirm and validate materialistic reality.

Religion and Identity

A number of researchers maintain that the new role of the individual as the final authority has brought with it a demise of traditions – including religious traditions. Currently, it is the individual him- or herself who is responsible for creating his or her own religious identity. The individual is unconstrained by tradition in his or her desire to find fulfilment and his or her true self (see, for example, Giddens 1997; Ahlin 2007). The choice of religious components depends on which self-identity we wish to present.

The American religious scholar David Chidester has examined the connection between religion and identity. For him, religion means 'ways of being a human person in a human place' (2005: vii). As he specifies in the following passage:

> I define religion as discourses and practices that negotiate what it is to be a human person both in relation to the superhuman and in relation to whatever might be treated as subhuman [...] religion entails discourses and practices for creating sacred space, as a zone of

inclusion but also as a boundary for excluding others. [R]eligion [...] is the activity of being human in relation to superhuman transcendence and sacred inclusion, which inevitably involves dehumanization and exclusion. (Chidester 2005: vii–viii)

According to Chidester, religion is thus mostly about being human. A human phenomenon can be said to have religious qualities if it involves 'religious work': that is to say, if there is negotiation about what it means to be human. Chidester opines that all cultural expressions that classify individuals into the three categories of human, subhuman, and superhuman, orientate the human being in time and place, and negotiate the right of ownership of these orientations and classifications can be deemed religious. Therefore, religion exists in contexts where negations about what it means to be human take place, and religion is one means of understanding what this involves. Chidester's categories of human, subhuman, and superhuman are classifications that he argues always exist in religious contexts even if they are not readily discernible. What it means to be human can often be found in descriptions of what is deemed a good and worthy life. This includes beliefs about how a person should live if he or she wants to reach his or her full potential, though it can also be about ethical rules or, in more traditional religious contexts, how to live to achieve salvation. Statements and categorizations concerning the subhuman are often the opposite, and concern bad and wrong ways of living or not being human. This may be connected to an ethic that prescribes certain acts to be bad or wrong; however, it can also be about criticism of a stressful and unworthy existence, which results in an inability to find time to be 'human' or to realize our potential. Chidester's third category, superhuman, concerns role models and ideals that are worth striving for. Here, for example, different gurus, leaders, and particularly insightful individuals are highlighted. Such people are said to have found an honourable and good way of living; reached their full potential; and attained wisdom from which we should all learn. It is not solely about messianic figures such as Jesus; living individuals can also belong to this superhuman category.[2]

2 Over the years, Chidester has discussed his categories and classifications on a number of occasions. What we present here is our interpretation of these. See, for example, Chidester 2005, as well as Chidester 1991: 51–78.

On this basis, it is clear for Chidester that there is no need to look for what is traditionally associated with religion. Certainly, Gods, Goddesses, sacrifices, rites, and myths can be included in religion, but religion is about much more than these. Religion negotiates what it means to be human, and it is this religious 'work' that we should seek if we are interested in what religion truly is:

> In my view, something is doing religious work if it is engaged in negotiating what it is to be human. Classification, orientation, and negotiation – these are the processes that I look for when I study religion and religions: the processes of classifying persons into superhuman, human, and subhuman; the processes of orienting persons in time and space; and the contested negotiations over the ownership of those classifications and orientations. (Chidester 2005: 18)

Chidester is also interested in cultural phenomena that are clearly false and fabricated but that nonetheless purport to be religions. In the context of popular culture, it is not uncommon for elements of religions to be borrowed or used as inspiration as a means of creating playful societies and websites, or of interpreting other cultural phenomena. Chidester studies Coca-Cola as a lifestyle and attempts to understand those individuals who claim Coca-Cola to be a holy drink, the result of which is somewhat fanatical behaviour: they collect Coca-Cola paraphernalia and lead lives in which Coca-Cola is the central aspect. Chidester also examines those who describe McDonald's as being their 'holy church', regarding the fast-food chain's meals as a sacrament. There is no doubt that these 'religions' are fabricated, often as a means of provoking religion. However, despite this, they do nonetheless engage groups of people,[3] and, according to Chidester, they can fill the same function as more traditional religions.

Chidester's way of viewing religion is open to many different arguments. For example, he leans towards a functionalistic view, which brings with it a reductionalistic view of religion, even though a 'soft' one. However, what is arguably the most provocative aspect of his view is that it goes against what we 'intuitively' perceive as religion and religiosity, and results in a very broad definition of religion that includes a great many human activities and cultural phenomena. For example, political organizations could very well be

---

3 Chidester appears not to have studied the exact number of individuals who devote themselves to such fake religions and thus provides no figures.

said to fall within his definition. An important point for Chidester is that everything should be examined based on the criteria he proposes. For Chidester, religion is not some exclusive cultural activity that is easily or even necessarily separate from other such activities. Naturally, this is his point when he examines so-called fake religions. Yet what Chidester does above all is question the limitations of the concept of religion – that is to say, our tendency to apply the term to a set type of phenomenon based on tradition or sheer habit.

Chidester argues that when we seek religion, we need to look for what can classify, orient, and negotiate what it is to be human. In our empirical material from Dalarna, we find numerous examples of this. Chidester's definition of religion can be split in three aspects: the first is his classification of what is human life. Many of our informants had clear beliefs about what is worth striving for and how one could best go about reaching one's full potential. Many described their practice as a path that gave them purpose and an opportunity to grow, progress, and develop to their full potential.

Many of our informants were also critical of the lifestyles they observed all around them, lifestyles that they had themselves once led. They often described their former lives in terms of unsustainability: they involved stress and commercialism; leading such a lifestyle caused many of them to have breakdowns or to experience crises. They were critical of both society and contemporary ideals and lifestyles.

Many of our informants had clear ideals that they strove for. Course leaders, mediums, healers, therapists, and coaches were described in quite positive terms. In addition, there were several individuals in Dalarna whom many regarded as charismatic leaders. One example was Alexander Markus; another Shanti Kristian (both were interviewed for this study).

The second aspect of Chidester's description of religion, that religion orients people both in time and in space, can also be found in the popular religious milieu. It is about context and practices that create 'places', partly as a means of including those who belong there and partly as a means of excluding those who do not. This has already been discussed in detail in the chapter on contemporary religious arenas and here we will only mention by way of example the popular view of Dalarna, and above all the area around Lake Siljan, as ideal both for living and for personal growth.

The third aspect of Chidester's definition of religion is negotiations about ownership of classifications and demarcations. Precisely as in other religious contexts, negotiations take place here where participants fight for their idea as to what constitutes a good 'human' life. We found many examples of this within the popular religious milieu among the producers we interviewed, and it was not just a case of, as Chidester is perhaps primarily interested in, claiming one perspective to be the best or perhaps even the only one. Rather, it was more about gaining a broader social acceptance for one's services. As discussed earlier, the relationship between what is socially accepted and what is alternative is constantly changing. Many of the practitioners we met in Dalarna find themselves in the midst of what can be described as an ongoing negotiation. There are a great many practices that are gaining ever more ground and acceptance beyond the popular religious milieu as well. Examples that we took up in previous chapters are mindfulness and yoga. Yet, this is not happening without discussion, and the debate is taking place in a number of places. It might be a case of ideological, political, economic, or religious interests, or about power. That subject, however, is simply too vast to discuss within the framework of this book.

Conclusion

Religious expressions mirror their times. Contemporary popular religion, the theme of this book, is being shaped by the great forces of our time, such as globalization, secularization, and individualism.

Above all, the popular religious milieu is syncretistic, containing elements from many different parts of the world. The degree to which different cultures are represented in this blend depends on a number of different factors, among them global power structures and beliefs that are spreading by way of cultural currents. Eastern and North American cultures frequently serve as sources of inspiration for developments in European popular religion.

We live in a secular culture that tends to be dominated by secular interpretations of religious practices. In addition, individualism has a secularizing effect on religious organizations though, perhaps paradoxically, it has a sacralizing effect on popular and individual forms of religion. Though the popular religious milieu addresses super-empirical and existential questions, at the same time these forms of religion are hybrids, which allow room for individual interpretations of meaning. The focus is on personal experience, on corporeality and presence, on aesthetics and the creation of places and activities that are meaningful, individualistic, and social.

At the same time, the popular religious milieu embodies clear links with older traditions. Healing and divination have an age-old history, yet are currently used in innovative ways as a result of globalization and the influence from psychological and therapeutic traditions. Individual human beings, who in contemporary popular religion are perceived in essentialist terms, are in focus and are viewed as having unique and powerful potentialities. Women are clearly over-represented in this subculture, perhaps because of the opportunities for finding meaningful social positions in this milieu that tie in with traditionally female roles involving caring, healing, and relationships.

The place of popular religion in Dalarna must be considered with one crucial factor in mind: the status and position of the Church of Sweden. In this rural county, the status of the Church remains relatively strong, despite congregational numbers declining here as in other parts of Sweden. We have demonstrated how the Church of Sweden is subject to innovation. It is engaged in dialogues with representatives of newer trends and ideologies, even if at times the Church sets boundaries and rejects some of these. The retreat movement and Christian meditation – in which inner experience is central – is an example of such engagement.

Our study has further demonstrated that certain cultural demarcations are becoming less evident, and that there exist tendencies to transcend traditional boundaries. This applies to the boundaries between the secular and the religious, as well as between the mainstream and alternative. Like Christopher Partridge, we are able to observe ongoing processes, the result of which is an increased acceptance and mainstreaming of world views, beliefs, and practices that were once regarded as alternative and different. Instead, they are now very much live options.

Religion can be defined and analysed in a number of ways. We favour multidimensional studies so that religious phenomena might be viewed from a number of different perspectives. We feel that Benson Saler's ideas hold great potential, and, to a certain extent, we have adopted his theoretical perspective in this book. David Chidester's focus on identity and religion is also of great interest, allowing as it does for new angles of analysis.

Popular religion constitutes an ongoing challenge for the field of Religious Studies. It not only presents problems as to what should or should not be regarded as religious, but also forces us to question the entire concept of religion as it is currently understood and demarcated as a field of study. Much research remains to be done; The Meditating Dala Horse Project is our contribution, and is merely a beginning.

References

Printed Sources

Ahlbäck, T. (2012). 'Editorial Note', in T. Ahlbäck (ed.), *Post-Secular Religious Practices*. Åbo: Donner Institute for Research in Religious and Cultural History, p. 5.

Ahlin, L. (2004). 'Alternativ behandling og spiritualitet i Århus', in M.C.Q. Fibiger (ed.), *Religiøs mangfoldighed: En kortlægning af religion og spiritualitet i Århus*. Århus: Systime Academic, pp. 471–88.

Ahlin, L. (2007). *Krop, sind – eller ånd? Alternative behandlere og spiritualitet i Danmark*. Höjbjerg: Forlaget Univers.

Ahlstrand, K. and G. Gunner (eds.) (2008). *Guds närmaste stad? En studie om religionernas betydelse i ett svenskt samhälle i början av 2000-talet*. Stockholm: Verbum.

Ahlstrand, K., B. Palmer, and E. Willander (2008). 'Guds närmaste stad?', in K. Ahlstrand and G. Gunner (eds.), *Guds närmaste stad? En studie om religionernas betydelse i ett svenskt samhälle i början av 2000-talet*. Stockholm: Verbum, pp. 9–24.

Alver, B.G., I.S. Ingvild, L. Mikaelsson, and T. Selber (1999). *Myte, magi og mirakel: I møte med det moderne*. Oslo: Pax Forlag.

Andersen, H. and A.-M. Stawreberg (2009). *Mindfulness för föräldrar*. Stockholm: Bonnier existens.

Anderson, W.T. (2004). *The Upstart Spring: Esalen and the Human Potential Movement: The First Twenty Years*. Lincoln: iUniverse, Inc.

Andersson, D. and Å. Sander (eds.) (2009). *Det mångreligiösa Sverige: Ett landskap i förändring*. Lund: Studentlitteratur.

Appadurai, A. (1996). *Modernity at Large: Cultural Dimensions of Globalization*. Minneapolis: University of Minnesota Press.

Asad, T. (1993). *Genealogies of Religion: Discipline and Reasons of Power in Christianity and Islam*. Baltimore: Johns Hopkins University Press.

Ashworth, G.J. and B. Graham (2005). 'Introduction to Theme One', in G.J. Ashworth and B. Graham (eds.), *Senses of Place: Senses of Time*. Aldershot: Ashgate, pp. 15–17.

Barker, E. (2004). 'The Church Without and the God Within: Religiosity and/or Spirituality?', in D.M. Jerolimov, S. Zrinaak, and I. Borowik (eds.), *Religion and Patterns of Social Transformation*. Zagreb: IDIZ (Institute for Social Research in Zagreb), pp. 23–47.

Beyer, P. (1994). *Religion and Globalization*. London: Thousand Oaks, New Delhi: SAGE Publications.

Bjerström, M. (2008). 'Waldorfpedagogik i förskoleåldern', in *En introduktion i Waldorfpedagogik: Barnets utveckling från förskola till gymnasium. Kursplanen i Waldorfskolan*. Stockholm: Levande Kunskap Stockholm AB, pp. 4–6.

Bogdan, H. (2007). *Western Esotericism and Rituals of Initiation*. Albany, NY: State University of New York Press.

Botvar, P.K. and U. Schmidt (eds.) (2010). *Religion i dagens Norge: mellom sekularisering og sakralisering*. Oslo: Universitetsforl.

Bowman, M. (2011). 'Understanding Glastonbury as a Site of Consumption', in G. Lynch, J. Mitchell, and A. Strhan (eds.), *Religion, Media and Culture: A Reader*. London: Routledge, pp. 11–22.

Bromander, J. (2008). 'Enköpingsstudien: En religionssociologisk analys', in K. Ahlstrand and G. Gunner (eds.), *Guds närmaste stad? En studie om religionernas betydelse i ett svenskt samhälle i början av 2000-talet*. Stockholm: Verbum, pp. 53–102.

Bruce, S. (2002). *God is Dead: Secularization in the West*. Oxford: Blackwell.

Burch, V. (2011). *Mindfulness: En väg att hantera smärta*. Stockholm: Bonnier Fakta.

Burke, P. (2009). *Popular Culture in Early Modern Europe*. Farnham: Ashgate.

Byrne, R. (2007). *The Secret = Hemligheten*. Orsa: Energica.

Byqvist, L. and A. Langer (2011). *Kvinnorna som slutade banta: Mat, motion, mindfulness efter 45*. Stockholm: Forum.

Campbell, C. (1972). 'The Cult, the Cultic Milieu and Secularization', in M. Hill (ed.), *A Sociological Yearbook of Religion in Britain*, Vol. 5. London: SCM Press, pp. 119–36.

Campbell, C. (1978). 'The Secret Religion of the Educated Classes', *Sociological Analysis: A Journal in the Sociology of Religion* 39(2). De Kalb, IL: Northern Illinois University, pp. 146–56.

Carlbaum, C. (2008). 'Waldorfskolan – en utvecklingsväg: En vandring genom årskurserna', in *En introduktion i Waldorfpedagogik: Barnets utveckling från förskola till gymnasium. Kursplanen i Waldorfskolan*. Stockholm: Levande Kunskap Stockholm AB.

Carrette, J. and R. King (2005). *Selling Spirituality: The Silent Takeover of Religion*. New York: Routledge.

Charta oecumenica. Riktlinjer för det växande samarbetet mellan kyrkorna i Europa (2001). Sundbyberg: Sveriges kristna råd.

Castells, M. (2004). *The Power of Identity. The Information Age: Economy, Society and Culture* (2nd ed., Vol. II). Oxford: Blackwell Publishing.

Chidester, D. (1991). *Salvation and Suicide: An Interpretation of Jim Jones, The Peoples Temple, and Jonestown*. Bloomington: Indiana University Press.

Chidester, D. (2005). *Authentic Fakes: Religion and American Popular Culture*. Berkeley, CA: University of California Press.

Engström, M. (2010). *Förlossningsförberedelser för blivande föräldrar: Att föda med mindfulness*. Stockholm: Gothia.

Fibiger, M.C.Q. (2004). 'Indledning', in M.C.Q. Fibiger (ed.), *Religiøs mangfoldighed: En kortlægning af religion og spiritualitet i Århus*. Århus: Systime Academi, pp. 8–17.

Fitzgerald, T. (ed.) (2007). *Religion and the Secular: Historical and Colonial Formations*. London: Equinox.

Frisk, L. (1993). *Nya religiösa rörelser i Sverige. Relation till samhället/världen, anslutning och engagemang*. Åbo: Åbo Akademis förl.

Frisk, L. (1997). 'Vad är New Age? Centrala begrepp och historiska rötter', *Svensk religionshistorisk årsskrift*, pp. 87–97.

Frisk, L. (1998). *Nyreligiositet i Sverige: Ett religionsvetenskapligt perspektiv*. Nora: Nya Doxa.

Frisk, L. (2000). 'New Age-utövare i Sverige: Bakgrund, trosföreställningar, engagemang och "omvändelse"', in C.-G. Carlsson and L. Frisk (eds.), *Gudars och gudinnors återkomst: Studier i nyreligiositet*. Umeå: Institutionen för religionsvetenskap, pp. 52–90.

Frisk, L. (2001). 'Globalization or Westernization? New Age as a Contemporary Transnational Culture', in M. Rothstein (ed.), *New Age Religion and Globalization*. Aarhus: Aarhus University Press, pp. 31–41.

Frisk, L. (2002). 'The Satsang Network: A Growing Post-Osho Phenomenon', *Nova Religio* 6(1), pp. 64–85. http://dx.doi.org/10.1525/nr.2002.6.1.64.

Frisk, L. (2007). *De nya religiösa rörelserna – vart tog de vägen? En studie av Scientologi-kyrkan, Guds Barn, Hare Krishna-rörelsen, Moon-rörelsen och Bhagwan-rörelsen och deras utveckling över tid*. Nora: Nya Doxa.

Frisk, L. (2012a). 'The Anthroposophical Movement and the Waldorf Educational System', in C. Cusack and A. Norman (eds.), *The Brill Handbook of New Religions and Cultural Production*. Leiden: Brill, pp. 193–211. http://dx.doi.org/10.1163/9789004226487_010.

Frisk, L. (2012b). 'The Practice of Mindfulness – From Buddhism to Secular Mainstream in a Postsecular Society', in T. Ahlbäck (ed.), *Post-Secular Practices*. Åbo: Åbo Akademi, pp. 48–61.

Frisk, L. (2012c). 'Spirituality and Everyday Life in Sweden', in G. Giordan and E. Pace (eds.), *Mapping Religion and Spirituality in a Postsecular World*. Leiden: Brill, pp. 27–41. http://dx.doi.org/10.1163/9789004230231_004.

Frisk, L. (2013). 'A Small Town Health Centre in Sweden: Perspectives on the Western Esotericism Debate', in K. Granholm and E. Asprem (eds.), *Contemporary Esotericism*. Sheffield: Equinox, pp. 372–91.

Frisk, L. and P. Nynäs (2012). 'Characteristics of Contemporary Religious Change: Globalisation, Neoliberalism and Interpretative Tendencies', in P. Nynäs, M. Lassander, and T. Utriainen (eds.), *Post-secular Society*. New Brunswick, London: Transaction Publishers, pp. 47–70.

Fulton, P.R. and R.D. Siegel (2005). 'Buddhist and Western Psychology: Seeking Common Ground', in C.K. Germer, R.D. Siegel, and P.R. Fulton (eds.), *Mindfulness and Psychotherapy*. New York: Guilford Press, pp. 28–54.

Färnlöf, Å, K. Svedros, and P. Frisk (2007). *I hälsans tjänst: Hälsorörelsen och hälsobranchens historia*. Stockholm: Hälsokostrådets förlag.

Garmo, S. and E. Mases (2002). *Gud, vi tackar dig. 40 år på Berget i Rättvik. En jubileumsskrift*. Rättvik: Stift Berget.

Germer, C.K. (2005). 'Mindfulness: What is it? What Does it Matter?', in C.K. Germer, R.D. Siegel, and P.R. Fulton (eds.), *Mindfulness and Psychotherapy*. New York: Guilford Press, pp. 3–27.

References   183

Giddens, A. (1997). *Modernitet och självidentitet: Självet och samhället i den senmoderna epoken*. Göteborg: Daidalos.

Gilhus, I.S. (2012) 'Angels in Norway: Religious Border-Crossers and Border-Markers', in M. Bowman and Û. Valk (eds.), *Vernacular Religion in Everyday Life: Expressions of Belief*. Sheffield: Equinox, pp. 230–45.

Giordan, G. and E. Pace (2012). 'Introduction: Mapping Religion and Spirituality in a Postsecular World', in G. Giordan and E. Pace (eds.), *Mapping Religion and Spirituality in a Postsecular World*. Leiden: Brill, pp. 1–8.

Gustafsson, G. (1997). *Tro, samfund och samhälle: Sociologiska perspektiv*. Örebro: Libris.

Hammer, O. (1997). *På spaning efter helheten: New Age – en ny folktro?* Stockholm: Wahlström & Widstrand.

Hammer, O. (1999). *Profeter mot strömmen: Essäer om mystiker, medier och magiker i vår tid*. Stockholm: Wahlström & Widstrand.

Hanegraaff, W. (1996). *New Age Religion and Western Culture: Esotericism in the Mirror of Secular Thought*. Leiden, New York, Köln: Brill.

Hannerz, U. (1996). *Transnational Connections: Culture, People, Places*. London: Routledge.

Harley, G.M. (2002). 'World Brotherhood Union Mevlana Supreme Foundation', in J.G. Melton and M. Baumann (eds.), *Religions of the World: A Comprehensive Encyclopedia of Beliefs and Practices*, Vol. 4. Santa Barbara, California: ABC-CLIO, Inc., pp. 1424–5.

Haviv, J. (2007a). 'Introduktion', in J. Haviv (ed.), *Medarbejder eller modarbejder – religion i modern arbejdsliv*. Århus: Klim, pp. 11–24.

Haviv, J. (2007b). 'Medarbejder eller modarbejder – religion som legitimering af ökonomisk handlen', in J. Haviv (ed.), *Medarbejder eller modarbejder – religion i modern arbejdsliv*. Århus: Klim, pp. 147–73.

Hayes, S.C. (2004). 'Acceptance and Commitment Therapy and the New Behavior Therapies', in S.C. Hayes, V.M. Follette, and M.M. Linehan (eds.), *Mindfulness and Acceptance: Expanding the Cognitive-Behavioral Tradition*. New York: Guilford Press, pp. 1–29.

Heelas, P. (1996). *The New Age Movement: The Celebration of the Self and the Sacralization of Modernity*. Oxford: Blackwell Publishers.

Heelas, P. (2007). 'The Holistic Milieu and Spirituality: Reflections on Voas and Bruce', in K. Flanagan and P.C. Jupp (eds.), *A Sociology of Spirituality*. Aldershot: Ashgate, pp. 65–80.

Heelas, P. (2008). *Spiritualities of Life. New Age Romanticism and Consumptive Capitalism*. Malden, MA: Blackwell Pub.

Heelas, P. and L. Woodhead (2005). *The Spiritual Revolution: Why Religion is Giving Way to Spirituality*. Malden, MA: Blackwell.

Holmer, T. (2010). *Lycka nu: En praktisk guide i mindfulnes*. Stockholm: Månpocket.

Hornborg, A.-C. (2010). 'I coachningland – på spaning efter den inre potentialen', *Chaos* 1(53), pp. 79–101.

Hornborg, A.-C. (2012a). *Coaching och lekmannaterapi: En modern väckelse?* Stockholm: Dialogos.

Huigen, P.P.P. and L. Meijering (2005). 'Making Places: A Story of De Venen', in G.J. Ashworth and B. Graham (eds.), *Senses of Place: Senses of Time*. Aldershot: Ashgate, pp. 19–30.

Höllinger, F. and T. Tripold (2012). *Ganzheitliches Leben: Das holistische Milieu zwischen neuer Spiritualität und postmoderner Wellness-Kultur.* Bielefeld: Transcript Verlag. http://dx.doi.org/10.14361/transcript.9783839418956.

Inglehart, R. and C. Welzel (2005). *Modernization, Cultural Change, and Democracy: The Human Development Sequence.* Cambridge: Cambridge University Press.

Johansson, L. (2004). 'Martinus kosmologi', in C. Partridge, P. Beskow, and L. Johansson (eds.), *Nya religioner: En uppslagsbok om andliga rörelser, sekter och alternativ andlighet.* Örebro: Libris, pp. 335–40.

Jonson, J. (1982). *Mötesplats till glädje: En bok om stiftsgården i Rättvik.* Rättvik: Stiftsgården.

Kabat-Zinn, J. (2003). 'Mindfulness-Based Interventions in Context: Past, Present, and Future', *Clinical Psychology: Science and Practice* 10(2), pp. 144–56.

Kabat-Zinn, J. (2009). *Full Catastrophe Living: Using the Wisdom of Your Body and Mind to Face Stress, Pain, and Illness.* New York: Delta Trade Paperback. First published 1990.

Karlsson, T. (2010). *Götisk kabbala och runisk alkemi: Johannes Bureus och den götiska esoterismen.* Stockholm: Stockholms universitet, institutionen för etnologi, religionshistoria och genusstudier.

King, R. (1995). 'Migrations, Globalization and Place', in D. Massey and P. Jess (eds.), *A Place in the World? Places, Cultures and Globalization.* New York: Oxford University Press, pp. 5–44.

King, U. (ed.) (2001). *Spirituality and Society in the New Millennium.* Brighton, Portland: Sussex Academic Press.

King, W. (1987). 'Religion (First Edition)', in L. Jones (ed.), *Encyclopedia of Religion.* Detroit: Macmillan Reference, pp. 7692–701.

Knott, K. (2005). *The Location of Religion: A Spatial Analysis of the Left Hand.* Oakville, CT: Equinox.

Kraft, S.-E. (2011). *Hva er nyreligiøsitet.* Oslo: Universitetsforlaget.

Kunin, S.D. (2003). *Religion: The Modern Theories.* Edinburgh: Edinburgh University Press.

Lagerkvist, E. (trans. and ed.) (1963). *Zen: En zenbuddhistisk antologi.* Stockholm: Natur och kultur.

Lazar, S.W. (2005). 'Mindfulness Research', in C.K. Germer, R.D. Siegel, and P.R. Fulton (eds.), *Mindfulness and Psychotherapy.* New York: Guilford Press, pp. 220–40.

Liebendörfer, Ö. (2008). 'Lek, konst och levande kunskap', in *En introduktion i Waldorfpedagogik: Barnets utveckling från förskola till gymnasium. Kursplanen i Waldorfskolan.* Stockholm: Levande Kunskap Stockholm AB, p. 3.

Ljus från norr: Budskap från Universum genom Siljans Måsar (2009). No author or publisher mentioned.

Lužný, D., Z.R. Nešpor, et al. (2008). *Náboženství v menšině: Religiozita a spiritualita v současné české společnosti.* Praha: Malvern.

Löwendahl, L. (2002). *Med kroppen som instrument: En studie av New age med fokus på hälsa, kroppslighet och genus.* Stockholm: Almqvist & Wiksell International.

Martikainen, T. (2004). *Immigrant Religions in Local Society. Historical and Contemporary Perspectives in the City of Turku.* Åbo: Åbo Akademis förlag.

Marlatt, G.A., et al. (2004). 'Vipassana Meditation as a Treatment for Alcohol and Drug Use Disorders', in S.C. Hayes, V.M. Follette, and M.M. Linehan (eds.),

Mindfulness and Acceptance. Expanding the Cognitive-Behavioral Tradition, New York: Guilford Press, pp. 261–87.

Massey, D. and P. Jess (1995a). 'Introduction', in D. Massey and P. Jess (eds.), *A Place in the World? Places. Cultures and Globalization.* New York: Oxford University Press, pp. 1–4.

Massey, D. and P. Jess (1995b). 'Places and Cultures in an Uneven World', in D. Massey and P. Jess (eds.), *A Place in the World? Places, Cultures and Globalization.* New York: Oxford University Press, pp. 216–39.

McCarthy, K. (1998). 'Reckoning with Religious Difference: Models of Interreligious Moral Dialogue', in S.B. Twiss and B. Grelle (eds.), *Explorations in Global Ethics: Comparative Religious Ethics and Interreligious Dialogue.* Boulder, CO.: Westview, pp. 73–117.

McGuire, Meredith B. (2002). *Religion: The Social Context.* 5th edition. Belmont, CA: Wadsworth.

McGuire, M.B. (2008). *Lived Religion: Faith and Practice in Everyday Life.* New York: Oxford University Press. http://dx.doi.org/10.1093/acprof:oso/978 0195172621.001.0001.

Mellergård, P. (2012). 'Mindfulness som medicin', *Nod 1*, pp. 20–25.

Melton, J.G. (1988). 'A History of the New Age Movement', in R. Basil (ed.), *Not Necessarily the New Age: Critical Essays.* Buffalo, NY: Prometheus Books, pp. 35–53.

Mikaelsson, L. (2000). *Religionsbyen Bergen.* Bergen: Eide forlag.

de Neergaard, M. (2011). *Leva i nuet: Positiv mindfulness meditation.* Malmö: Human Potential.

Nilsson, S. (2005). *Den potentiella människan: En undersökning av teorier om självförverkligande. Uppsala Studies in Social Ethics 30.* Uppsala: Uppsala Universitet.

Nilsonne, Å. (2009). *Mindfulness i hjärnan.* Stockholm: Natur & Kultur.

Nilsonne, Å. (2011). *Vem är det som bestämmer i ditt liv? Om mindfulness.* Stockholm: Natur & Kultur.

O'Connor, C. (2011). '"Becoming Whole": An Exploration of Women's Choices in the Holistic and New Age Movement in Ireland', in O. Cosgrove, L. Cox, C. Kuhling, and P. Mulholland (eds.), *Ireland's New Religious Movements.* Newcastle upon Tyne: Cambridge Scholars Publishing, pp. 220–39.

Olendzki, A. (2005). 'The Roots of Mindfulness', in C.K. Germer, R.D. Siegel, and P.R. Fulton (eds.), *Mindfulness and Psychotherapy.* New York: Guilford Press, pp. 241–61).

Olivestam, C.E., M. Eriksson, and S. Lindholm (2002). *Från kyrka till wellbeing: Handbok i kyrkokunskap.* Lund: Studentlitteratur.

Orsi, R.A. (2004). *Between Heaven and Earth: The Religious Worlds People Make and the Scholars Who Study Them.* Princeton, NJ: Princeton University Press.

Ouspensky, P.D. (1986). *The Fourth Way: The Teachings of G.I. Gurdjieff.* London, Henley: Arkana.

Paden, W. (1992). *Interpreting the Sacred: Ways of Viewing Religion.* Boston: Beacon Press.

Palmer, B. (2008). '"Ryck ut jackan!" Andlighet som paus i livsstressen', in K. Ahlstrand and G. Gunner (eds.), *Guds närmaste stad? En studie om religionernas betydelse i ett svenskt samhälle i början av 2000-talet*. Stockholm: Verbum, pp. 277–92.

Palmer, S.J. (1994). *Moon Sisters, Krishna Mothers, Rajneesh Lovers: Women's Roles in New Religions*. Syracuse, NY: Syracuse University Press.

Partridge, C. (2004). *The Re-Enchantment of the West*, Vol. 1: *Alternative Spiritualities, Sacralization, Popular Culture and Occulture*. London: T & T Clark International.

Pieterse, J.N. (1995). 'Globalization as Hybridization', in Mike Featherstone (ed.), *Global Modernities*. London: Sage, pp. 45–68. http://dx.doi.org/10.4135/9781446250563.n3.

Plank, K. (2011). *Insikt och närvaro: Akademiska kontemplationer kring buddhism, meditation och mindfulness*. Göteborg, Stockholm: Makadam förlag.

Rajagopal, A. (2001). *Politics after Television: Hindu Nationalism and the Reshaping of the Public in India*. Cambridge: Cambridge University Press. http://dx.doi.org/10.1017/CBO9780511489051.

Rawlinson, A. (1998). *The Book of Enlightened Masters: Western Teachers in Eastern Traditions*. Chicago: Open Court.

Restall, M., and A. Solari (2011). *2012 and the End of the World: The Western Roots of the Maya Apocalypse*. Lanham: Rowman & Littlefield Publishing Group, Inc.

Ritzer, G. (2011). *Globalization: The Essentials*. Chichester, West Sussex: Wiley-Blackwell.

Robertson, R. (1995). 'Glocalization: Time-Space and Homogeneity-Heterogeneity', in M. Featherstone (ed.), *Global Modernities*. London: Sage, pp. 25–43. http://dx.doi.org/10.4135/9781446250563.n2.

Rodhe, S. (1976). *Kristen djupmeditation*. Stockholm: Verbum.

Roof, W.C., J.W. Carroll, and D.A. Roozen (1995). *The Post-War Generation and Establishment Religion: Cross-Cultural Perspectives*. Boulder, San Francisco, Oxford: Westview Press.

Rosander, G. (1994). 'Hur Dalarna blev svenskt ideal', in *Saga och sed: Kungl, Gustav Adolfs Akademiens årsbok 1993*. Annales Academiae Regiae Gustavi Adolphi MCMXCIII, pp. 57–73.

Rothstein, M. (1997). *Gud är blå: De nya religiösa rörelserna*. Nora: Nya Doxa.

Rönn, M. (1997). *Heliga danser: Dans som rit och bön*. Stockholm: Verbum.

Saler, B. (2000). *Conceptualizing Religion: Immanent Anthropologists, Transcendent Natives, and Unbounded Categories*. New York, Oxford: Berghahn Books.

Saler, B. (2009). *Understanding Religion: Selected Essays*. Berling, New York: Walter de Gruyter. http://dx.doi.org/10.1515/9783110218664.

Schenström, O. (2007). *Mindfulness i vardagen: Vägar till medveten närvaro*. Stockholm: Viva.

Schönström, S. (2006). *Från akupunktur till schamanism: Guide till komplementär- och alternativmedicin*. Stockholm: Natur och kultur.

Selberg, T. (2011). *Folkelig religiøsitet: Et kulturvitenskapelig perspektiv*. Oslo: Spartacus Forlag AS.

Smith, J. (2004). *Relating Religion: Essays in the Study of Religion*. Chicago: University of Chicago.

Stark, R. and Bainbridge, W.S. (1985). *The Future of Religion: Secularization, Revival, and Cult Formation*. Berkeley: University of California Press.

Stark, R., and W.S. Bainbridge (1996). *A Theory of Religion*. New Brunswick, NJ: Rutgers University Press.

Steiner, R. (1995a). 'Anthroposophical Spiritual Science and the Great Questions of our Present Civilization (Spiritual Science and Waldorf Education I). The Hague, February 23, 1921', in *Waldorf Education and Anthroposophy 1. Nine Public Lectures. February 23, 1921–September 16, 1922*. Hudson, NY: Anthroposophic Press.

Steiner, R. (1995b). 'Education and Practical Life from the Perspective of Spiritual Science (Spiritual Science and Waldorf Education II). The Hague, February 27, 1921', in *Waldorf Education and Anthroposophy 1. Nine Public Lectures. February 23, 1921–September 16, 1922*. Hudson, NY: Anthroposophic Press.

Steiner, R. (1995c). 'The Fundamentals of Waldorf Education. Aarau, November 11, 1921', in *Waldorf Education and Anthroposophy 1. Nine Public Lectures. February 23, 1921–September 16, 1922*. Hudson, NY: Anthroposophic Press.

Stinissen, W. (2008). *Kristen djupmeditation*. Örebro: Libris.

Stridell, E. (2008). *Dormsjöskolan: Återblick på ett lärorikt halvsekel*. Garpenberg: Föreningen Dormsjöskolan.

von Stuckrad, K. (2005). *Western Esotericism. A Brief History of Secret Knowledge*. London: Equinox.

Sutcliffe, S.J. (2003). *Children of the New Age: A History of Spiritual Practices*. London, New York: Routledge.

Sutcliffe, S.J. (2006). 'Re-Thinking "New Age" As a Popular Religious Habitus: A Review Essay on The Spiritual Revolution', *Method & Theory in the Study of Religion* 18(3), pp. 294–314. http://dx.doi.org/10.1163/157006806778553552.

Svanberg, I. and D. Westerlund (eds.). (2008). *Religion i Sverige*. Stockholm: Dialogos.

Voas, D.and S. Bruce (2007). 'The Spiritual Revolution: Another False Dawn for the Sacred', in K. Flanagan and P.C. Jupp (eds.), *A Sociology of Spirituality*. Aldershot: Ashgatem, pp. 43–61.

Waters, M. (1995). *Globalization*. London: Routledge.

Willander, E. (2008). 'Avslappnad och berörd. Synen på hälsa och andlighet bland hälsofrämjande företag i Enköping', in K. Ahlstrand and G. Gunner (eds.), *Guds närmaste stad? En studie om religionernas betydelse i ett svenskt samhälle i början av 2000-talet*. Stockholm: Verbum, pp. 241–76.

Wilson, B.R. (1970). *Religiösa sekter: En sociologisk studie*. Stockholm: Aldus, Bonnier.

Woodhead, L. (2001). 'The Turn to Life in Contemporary Religion and Spirituality', in U. King and T. Beattie (eds.), *Spirituality and Society in the New Millennium*. Brighton, Portland: Sussex Academic Press, pp. 110–23.

Woodhead, L. (2002). 'Women and Religion', in L. Woodhead, P. Fletcher, H. Kawanami, and D. Smith (eds.), *Religions in the Modern World*. London: Routledge, pp. 332–56.

Woodhead, L. (2007). 'Why so Many Women in Holistic Spirituality? A Puzzle Revisited', in K. Flanagan and P.C. Jupp (eds.), *A Sociology of Spirituality*. Aldershot: Ashgate, pp. 115–25.

Woodhead, Linda and Ole Riis (2012). *A Sociology of Religious Emotion*. Oxford: Oxford University Press.

Zuckerman, P. (2005). 'Atheism: Contemporary Rates and Patterns', in M. Martin (ed.), *The Cambridge Companion to Atheism*. Cambridge University Press: Cambridge, pp. 47–68.

Electronic Sources

Electronic Articles

Cook, J. (2012). 'Not All Yoga is Created Equal', *Yoga Journal*, http://shar.es/pz2wW. Accessed April 13, 2012.

Hanegraaff, W. (2005). 'Spectral Evidence of New Age Religion: On the Substance of Ghosts and the Use of Concepts', *JASANAS* 1, pp. 35–8, http://www.open.ac.uk/Arts/jasanas/. Accessed December 1, 2012.

Hornborg, A.-C. (2012b). 'Designing Rites to Re-enchant Secularized Society: New Varieties of Spiritualized Therapy in Contemporary Sweden', *Journal of Religion and Health* 51(2), June, pp. 402–18, http://link.springer.com/article/10.1007%2Fs10943-010-9356-5?LI=true. Accessed January 25, 2013. http://dx.doi.org/10.1007/s10943-010-9356-5.

York, M. (2005). 'Wanting to Have Your New Age Cake and Eat It Too', *JASANAS*. 1, pp. 15–34, http://www.open.ac.uk/Arts/jasanas/. Accessed December 1, 2012.

Websites

Note: These websites were accessed during the course of our study and it is possible that some of them may have since changed or may no longer be functional.

www.alternativmedicin.se – Accessed February 13, 2013
www.banerskolan.se – Accessed January 2, 2012
www.baravara.se – Accessed February 7, 2013
www.berget.se – Accessed February 7, 2013
www.celestemetoden.com – Accessed February 13, 2013
www.chiball.com – Accessed April 13, 2012
www.dalarna.se/sv/Mer-om-lanet – Accessed July 3, 2012
www.dkb-mevlana.org.tr – Accessed February 13, 2013
www.druidorden.org – Accessed December 11, 2011
www.dt.se/nyheter/ludvika/1.4396227-rorelse-vill-byta-namn-pa-by-invanare-oroliga – Accessed February 25, 2012
www.dt.se/nyheter/dalarna/1.4397265-drommer-om-goldendal – Accessed March 5, 2012
http://frid.nu/ – Accessed February 7, 2013
www.frimurarorden.se – Accessed December 11, 2011
www.heligadanser.info – Accessed February 13, 2013
www.lantmateriet.se – Accessed July 3, 2012
www.lesmills.com/global/bodybalance/bodybalance-group-fitness-class.aspx – Accessed April 13, 2012
www.livshalsa.se – Accessed February 7, 2013
www.mariaronn.com – Accessed February 13, 2013

www.onenessuniversity.org – Accessed February 14, 2013
www.oshofors.nu – Accessed February 7, 2013
http://oronljus.org/ – Accessed February 13, 2013
http://www.plants.usda.gov/java/ – Accessed February 13/2 2013
www.poweryoganu.nl – Accessed April 13, 2012
http://www.regiondalarna.se/dalafakta/befolkning/ – Accessed July 4, 2012
www.resanterapeut.nu – Accessed February 13, 2013
www.sanktakatarina.se – Accessed September 20, 2011
www.siljansmasar.se – Accessed February 13, 2013
www.solsokehem.se – Accessed February 7, 2013
www.svenskakyrkan.se – Accessed December 1, 2010
http://www.svenskakyrkan.se/husby/ – Accessed November 21, 2011
http://www.thework.com/index.php – Accessed February 13, 2013
www.uniomystica.se – Accessed February 7, 2013
http://vedicart.com/ – Accessed February 11, 2013
www.visitdalarna.se – Accessed February 7, 2013
www.waldorf.se/index.php?option=com_content&view=article&id=13&I
    temid=16 – Accessed January 6, 2011
http://www.worldvaluessurvey.orgwvs.jsp – Accessed January 28, 2012

Emails

Beigi, Mehrdad – April 3 and April 5, 2012
Brandberg, Peter – September 22 and 26, 2011
Hamad, Hussein – October 15, 2011
Hasselmark, Folke – November 20, 2008
Holgersson, Markus – January 7, 2012
Högås, Åsa – January 7, 2012
Liljeström, Mikael – January 17. 2008
Lindman, Jan – May 8, 2011
Maria – March 6, 2012
Sharya – February 25, 2013
Tholvsen, Öyvind – September 22, 2011

Interviews

Beigi, Mehrdad – March 27, 2012
Bülent Çorak, Vedia – October 13, 2011
Hamad, Hussein – Spetember 27, 2011
Kurian, Raphael – September 27, 2011
Liljeström, Mikael – November 17, 2008
Lindholm, Olivia – November 22, 2011
Litborn, Anders – October 9, 2009
Markus, Alexander – January 23, 2010
Mases, Per – March 6, 2009
Norman, Elisabeth – October 11, 2010
Nyberg, Elisabeth, Call reception in Falun – March 28, 2012
Shanti Kristian – April 23, 2012

Sharya – April 23, 2012
Thimberg, Conny – September 28, 2009
respondent 1, Siljan UFO-group – September 28, 2009
respondent 2, representative Freemasons – January 10, 2012
respondent 3, representative Swedish Druid Order – January 10, 2012
respondent 4, Karl
respondent 5, Monica
respondent 6, Berit
respondent 7, Gunnar
respondent 8, representative Fridhem – January 23, 2009
respondent 9, representative TOKA – March 15, 2012
respondent 10, representative Gym Borlänge – April 10, 2012
respondent 11, representative Masesgården – March 28, 2012
respondent 12, Karin – September 26, 2011
respondent 13, Pernilla – June 6, 2011
respondent 14, Arne – January 16, 2010
respondent 15, representative Stiftsgården – April 25, 2012
respondent 16, Catholic nun at St Davidsgården – March 6, 2009
respondent 17, Susanne – November 20, 2011
respondent 18, promoter of Hälsogränden in Hedemora – November 11, 2009
respondent 19, shaman from Azerbaijan – March 20, 2010
respondent 20, medium from Älvdalen – November 22, 2011
respondent 21, representative Wat Dalarnavaranam – September 29, 2009
respondent 22, priest, Church of Sweden – February 4 and March 19, 2010
respondent 23, two missionaries, Church of Jesus Christ of Latter-Day Saints –
    November 23, 2011

Other Material

Survey Materials 2008. Survey funded by the newspaper *Dagen*. Results
    archived at Liselotte Frisk.
Record 12142, Dialect and Folklore Archives in Uppsala, March 30, 2012.

Index

www.ingramcontent.com/pod-product-compliance
Lightning Source LLC
Chambersburg PA
CBHW071122280326
41935CB00010B/1090